Dissident
Daughters

Dissident Daughters

Feminist Liturgies in Global Context

Edited by Teresa Berger

Westminster John Knox Press
LOUISVILLE • LONDON

Book design by Sharon Adams
Cover design by Jennifer Cox

First edition
Published by Westminster John Knox Press
Louisville, Kentucky

This book is printed on acid-free paper that meets the American National Standards Institute Z39.48 standard. ♾

PRINTED IN THE UNITED STATES OF AMERICA

01 02 03 04 05 06 07 08 09 10 — 10 9 8 7 6 5 4 3 2 1

Library of Congress Cataloging-in-Publication Data

Dissident daughters : feminist liturgies in global context / edited by Teresa Berger.—1st ed.
    p. cm.
    Includes bibliographical references.
    ISBN 0-664-22379-6 (alk. paper)
    1. Liturgics. 2. Feminist theology. I. Berger, Teresa.

  BV178 .D49 2001
  264'.0082—dc21

                       2001045486

Blessed are the dissident
the borderlands are theirs

and this book is for them

Contents

Preface

Dissident daughters are made, not born—this adaptation of Simone de Beauvoir's groundbreaking insight ("One is not born, but becomes, a woman") is one way to account for the time it has taken for this book to see the light of day. *Dissident Daughters* was, indeed, many years in the making, years in which it was not always clear which daughter would see the light of day and what dissidence she would embrace.

In a sense, this book has its roots in a route I first traveled in 1984. Having taken my interest in liturgical studies from central Europe to North America, I encountered what came to be called the "feminist liturgical movement." I became a participant observer in this historic process of women's activism in the church (initially by collecting all the feminist liturgical books I could find as a curiosity). *Dissident Daughters*, with its global vision, slowly emerged out of this initially North Atlantic engagement with the struggle for women's rites.

One of the delights but also one of the pains of the subject matter of *Dissident Daughters* is its breadth. The book intrudes, albeit with varying degrees of intensity, into fields as diverse as biblical interpretation, feminist theory, theological method, theories of globalization, liturgical studies, and feminist historiography, to name only the more prominent of its interdisciplinary conversation partners. This breadth of conversation partners has been nurtured by a host of wonderful women, first and foremost the contributors to this book. They have gracefully filled my life with their stories of struggle and strength. From my immediate circle of friends who have nurtured the breadth of *Dissident Daughters*, I name only two here, my colleagues Mary McClintock Fulkerson and M. Kathy Rudy. The faculty seminar on "Gender, Religion, and Culture" that the three of us cochaired during the academic year 2000–2001 at Duke University has profoundly enriched my work. I thank the other seminar participants, Bill Hart, Ken Surin, Susan Thorne, and Maurice Wallace, for making many Friday afternoons of that academic year truly exciting times. Finally, my yearlong fellowship in the John Hope Franklin Seminars for Interdisciplinary Studies in the Humanities at Duke University accompanied the last stages of producing this book. As the material-social practice that is academia goes, being a "franklinista" has been an extraordinarily stimulating experience, and the Franklin Seminar's yearlong work on "Race, Religion, and Globalization" has left its mark on this book in a variety of ways. To Tomeiko Ashford, Leo Ching, Rom Coles, Gregson Davis, Michael Ennis, Katherine Ewing, Jean Jonassaint, Bill Hart (again), Bruce Lawrence, Walter Mignolo, Kaifa Roland, and Nicole Waligora: tausend Dank! And to Mark Olson, the Associate Director of the John Hope Franklin Institute for Interdisciplinary Studies, my profound gratitude for the myriads of ways in which he made my stay at the Franklin Center a wonderfully creative time.

A book such as this, with its global focus, is produced in the midst of very "different temporalities of struggle" (Lata Mani). Some stories stand out for me: I was caught in one of the worst snowstorms recorded in the southeastern United States, unable even to leave my home, when I first made contact electronically with two African women, Pauline Muchina from Kenya and Musa Dube Shomanah from Botswana. My heart was strangely warmed in the midst of subzero temperatures. My heart was deeply troubled, on the other hand, when I received an Advent 2000 e-mail from Palestinian Christians in Bethlehem. One of the women in Bethlehem had earlier agreed to write a piece for *Dissident Daughters*. Now the e-mail described an Advent of exploding missiles and beams of helicopters, of bullet sounds and tank shells. Instead of a Palestinian women's liturgy marking Jubilee 2000, the e-mail told of a silent candle-march through the old city of Bethlehem, symbolically taking back streets that had been targeted almost nightly for shelling. Different temporalities of struggle, indeed, are inhabited by dissident daughters around the world. In the summer of 2001, as *Dissident Daughters* went to press, one of its authors had to preside over a feminist liturgy of Christian burial for the woman who designed the ritual "Air Moves Us": Hildegard Weiler died of breast cancer at age 56.

There were lighter moments in the making of *Dissident Daughters*, such as when I received my first-ever electronic greeting card for International Women's Day from one of the dissident daughters. The message read *"Juntas Venceremos,"* and the card imaged five colorful women of all ages, now happily dancing on my computer screen. Colorful women and one man also helped with many of the connections behind the book (and although advances in globalization and information technologies have been contradictory and, indeed, deeply problematic for many women, *Dissident Daughters* has benefited from these advances in numerous ways). Beyond the dissident daughters themselves, I am grateful to Denise Ackermann, Michael Battle, Glynthea Finger, Musimbi Kanyoro, Dorothea McEwan, Carola Meyer, Nyambura Njoroge, Mercy Amba Oduyoye, and Edna Orteza for making connections. I owe Elizabeth Storey thanks for her friendship, her wise feet-on-the-ground theologizing, and her poignant stories of women's strengths and struggles.

I have received much institutional support that indicated to me that seeing *Dissident Daughters* mature was worth the wait. For 1995–1996, I received a grant from the Josiah Trent Memorial Foundation, Inc., through Duke University's Center for International Studies, that allowed me to study in depth feminist voices from the (so-called) Third World. In 1998–1999, a grant for Planning New Research Initiatives in the International Field from the Vice Provost for Academic and International Affairs at Duke University enabled me to lay the actual groundwork for this book. In 2000–2001, a Fellowship at the John Hope Franklin Institute for Interdisciplinary Studies at Duke University and a concurrent sabbatical leave granted by the Divinity School of Duke University provided much appreciated time and space to bring the book to completion. Funding from the Provost's Common Fund for 2000–2001 enabled the above-mentioned seminar on "Gender, Religion, and Culture." Finally, an invitation by the Faculty of Theology of Uppsala University, Sweden, to give a series of lectures in the spring of 2001 enabled me to present some of the research gathered in this book and to meet in person the women behind the *Sofia-mässor*, and especially Ninna Edgardh Beckman. I am deeply grateful for these opportunities. To the Center for European Studies at Duke University I extend my thanks for its support of my lectures in Sweden.

I continue to be grateful to my graduate assistant, David McCarthy, especially for his skills at editing and perfecting the English of the texts brought together in this book. During the summer of 2000, I also benefited from the work of another research assistant, William Jarrod Brown. He deserves thanks especially for his translation from the Spanish of the chapter from the Chilean group *Con-spirando*. I am grateful to Sung Wook Oh for his help in teaching my computer Korean.

There were many institutions that opened their doors, archives, libraries, and contacts to me, among them MISSIO in Aachen, Germany; the Frauenmediaturm in Cologne, Germany; the Frauenstudien- und -bildungszentrum in Gelnhausen, Germany; and WATER in Washington, D.C. The latter was an invaluable source for contacts with feminist liturgical communities worldwide. The libraries and their staff at Duke University, especially the Associate Director of the Divinity School Library, Roberta Schaafsma, and the wonderful women at Interlibrary Loan, continue to provide the excellent support I have come to rely on and appreciate so deeply. Ladyslippers, a North Carolina nonprofit organization dedicated to heightening public awareness of the achievements of women musicians and to expanding the availability of recordings by women, enabled me to listen to some of the wonderful songs used in the liturgies of *Dissident Daughters*.

Working with Westminster John Knox Press, and especially with Carey Newman, has been a very positive experience throughout. I am grateful to Carey for his expert coaching in the laborious process of bringing *Dissident Daughters* into the world (at least the world of print). To Priscilla Pope-Levison and John R. Levison I extend my thanks for connecting me with an excellent editor.

Finally, one faith community in particular has sustained me throughout these years. This community has embraced me, let me be both dissident and daughter, and continues to break open the bread of life: Immaculate Conception Catholic Church here in Durham, North Carolina. It was in that church, during a festive All Saints' Day liturgy with its reading of the Beatitudes, that the epigraph for this book was born. For those who are church with me at this parish, and especially for Fr. David McBriar, O.F.M., *Deo gratias*. My life has been graced by your presence.

It might seem odd that the preface to *Dissident Daughters* concludes with this note about a regular parish, and a Roman Catholic one for that matter. But such are the lives of many women: as daughters of God we continue to find grace in the midst of ambivalence and struggle. *Dissident Daughters* is a collection of stories of women making room to encounter grace, that is, to discern, name, welcome, and celebrate the presence of the Holy One, in the crucible of our lives.

Teresa Berger

on International Women's Day,
which in the liturgical calendar
borders the feast days of three "international" women:
the North African Saints Perpetua and Felicitas
and Saint Frances of Rome

Acknowledgments

Grateful acknowledgment is made to the following for permission to print (copyrighted) material:

Con-spirando for "'Con-spirando juntas': hacia una red latinoamericana de ecofeminismo, espiritualidad y teología," *Con-spirando* 1 (1992): 2–5.

Jeanne Cotter and Mythic Rain Productions for "From My Mother's Womb," in *Bring the Feast: Songs From the Re-imagining Community* (Cleveland: Pilgrim Press, 1998), 15, copyright Mythic Rain Productions.

Margaret Donaldson for her prayer "We Come to You, O God, Our Mother and Our Father."

Wendy Esau for the text of her reflection on Hagar at the 1999 Ecumenical Seminar on African Women's Theologies, Kalahari Desert School of Theology, Kuruman, South Africa.

Walter Farquharson for "Stay with Us through the Night," in *Voices United: The Hymn and Worship Book of The United Church of Canada* (Etobicoke, Ont.: The United Church Publishing House, 1996), 182.

Diewerke Folkertsma and the publisher Narratio for Folkertsma's psalm "Song of the Exile." The Dutch original appeared in Diewerke Folkertsma, *Eva, poets je appel: tot ze glanst* (Gorinchem: Narratio, 1992), 27.

Colleen Fulmer, Martha Ann Kirk, and The Loretto Spirituality Network for "Dancing Sophia's Circle," in Colleen Fulmer, *Dancing Sophia's Circle* (Albany, Calif.: Loretto Spirituality Network, 1994), 16–17.

"In Your Presence," in Colleen Fulmer, *Dancing Sophia's Circle* (Albany, Calif.: The Loretto Spirituality Network, 1994), 22–24.

"'No' Song," in Colleen Fulmer (music) and Martha Ann Kirk (ritual and dance), *Her Wings Unfurled* (Albany Calif.: The Loretto Spirituality Network, 1990), 44.

"Spirit Movin' Where She Will," in Colleen Fulmer (music) and Martha Ann Kirk (ritual and dance), *Her Wings Unfurled* (Albany, Calif.: The Loretto Spirituality Network, 1994), 64.

Odd Granlid for the poem by Hans Granlid, in *Gyllene Stunder* (Stockholm: R&S, 1974).

Per Harling for Hymn 803, in *Psalmer i 90-talet* (Stockholm: Verbum, 1994).

Jane Parker Huber for "Called as Partners in Christ's Service," in Jane Parker Huber, *A Singing Faith* (Philadelphia: Westminster Press, 1987), 68.

Christina Lövestam for "We Break This Bread," Hymn 835, in *Psalmer i 90-talet* (Stockholm: Verbum, 1994).

Carolyn McDade and Surtsey Publishing for

"Sister, Carry On," by Carolyn McDade, from Carolyn McDade and Friends, *Sister, Carry On*, cassette and book (Orleans, Mass.: Surtsey Publishing, 1992).

"This Ancient Love," by Carolyn McDade, from her album *As We So Love* (Orleans, Mass.: Surtsey Publishing, 1996).

"This Tough Spun Web," by Carolyn McDade, from her album *This Tough Spun Web: Songs of Global Struggle and Solidarity* (Orleans, Mass.: Surtsey Publishing, 1984).

Diann Neu and WATER for "Blessed Be the New Year," in Hannah Ward et al. (eds.), *Celebrating Women*, new ed. (Harrisburg, Pa.: Morehouse Publishing, 1995), 127.

NewStart 2000 for its "Millennium Resolution."

Reclaiming for "Air Moves Us," recorded on *Chants: Ritual Music* from Reclaiming Community & Friends (Sebastopol, Calif.: Serpentine Music Productions, 1987).

Gillian Walters and Jacqui Mohlakoana for their intercessions, written for National Women's Day in South Africa.

Betty Wendelborn for "We Are a Wheel, a Circle of Life," in *Sing Green: Songs of the Mystics*, 2nd ed. (Auckland, N.Z.: Pyramid Press, 1999), 1.

Lala Winkley for her Jubilee prayer, copyright Lala Winkley, 2000.

Miriam Therese Winter and the Medical Mission Sisters for

"Sing Lo! Sing, O Sophia," in Miriam Therese Winter, *Songlines: Hymns, Songs, Rounds, and Refrains for Prayer and Praise* (New York: Crossroad, 1996), 74, copyright Medical Mission Sisters.

"A Psalm for Every Woman," in Miriam Therese Winter, *Woman World: A Feminist Lectionary and Psalter: Women of the New Testament* (New York: Crossroad, 1991), 266, copyright Medical Mission Sisters.

World Council of Churches for

"Come, O Holy Spirit, Come" ("Wa wa wa Emimimo"), Nigerian traditional chant, trans. I-to Loh, in *Bring the Feast: Songs from the Re-Imagining Community* (Cleveland: Pilgrim Press, 1998), copyright World Council of Churches and the Asian School of Music, Liturgy, and the Arts.

Ann M. Heidkamp, "A Litany of Women's Power," in Iben Gjerding and Katherine Kinnamon (eds.), *Women's Prayer Services*, 3rd ed. (Mystic, Conn.: Twenty-Third Publications, 1991), 25, copyright World Council of Churches, Church Women United.

Introduction

Mapping the Global Struggle
for Women's Rites

TERESA BERGER

The hand that rocks the cradle should also rock the boat.[1]

Over the last four decades, women-identified[2] liturgies have come to circulate the globe and are now celebrated in Peru and the United States, Australia and Iceland, Korea and Canada, Chile and Sweden, the Philippines, Germany, southern Africa, and many lands of the proverbial "and so forth." *Dissident Daughters* maps this globally circulating movement of women's rites, gives voice to the women activists in it, and features liturgies created and celebrated by fourteen communities of women in different parts of the world.[3] At its conclusion, the book identifies a theological challenge embodied in these women-identified communities and their celebrations. I will claim the vibrant growth of these communities and the knowledge inscribed in their liturgies as a defining site for theological reflection in our time, born in the crucible of women's rites.

Let me here provide a context for understanding both the emergence of women-identified rituals across the globe and the origin of this collection. The geographic breadth of the book is novel, since little or no attention has thus far been paid to women's liturgies beyond the (so-called) First World. Indeed, there has been little recognition that such liturgies exist outside of North America and Europe; to date, Western voices have defined the discourse of women's rites. These rites, although they have attracted considerable attention, have not yet been understood in their place in a global context. In contradistinction, this collection maps women-identified communities and their rituals in multiple sites around the world. The "globality" of *Dissident Daughters* is, however, based neither on facile assumptions of sameness nor on a cheap theological cosmopolitanism. Much recent theorizing both of women and of globalization makes such assumptions difficult to sustain. Rather, the globality *Dissident Daughters* claims focuses on local sites of struggle for women's rites. The distinctiveness of these local sites surfaces not least of all by the juxtaposition of these different sites in this book. In a sense, *Dissident Daughters* itself is the global contextualization it claims to make visible, by joining together between the covers of one book women-identified liturgical communities as far apart as 여성교회 in Korea, *Kvennakirkjan* in Iceland, and *Con-spirando* in Chile.

This may seem a quite restricted vision for the globalness of the struggle for women's rites. My reasons for embracing this limitation are threefold, at least. For one, I refrain from facile claims to globalness because of both the discursive explosion around notions of globalization, and the persistence of inadequate theoretical frameworks for the "global,"[4] including "global Christianity" and "the world church."[5] Many claims to globalness, especially in the religious realm, rest on theoretical sand in that they insufficiently account for the underpinnings of their notions of the global. And even the best theorizing of processes of globalization always lags behind these processes themselves,[6] one of whose characteristics is precisely their rapidity. Second, many dissident daughters themselves are intentionally local rather than self-consciously global in their vision. That is to say that, although joining the voices of dissident daughters between the covers of one book suggests them to be part of a grassroots globalizing movement, these groups, for the most part, are no transnational advocacy network.[7] I am moreover convinced that the claim that feminism is a worldwide theological flow[8] needs to be substantiated "from below," that is, by highlighting the distinctiveness of local sites of women-identified theological production. Thus, while I do assume that women-identified liturgical communities can only be understood in their place in a global context, my starting point is the multiplicity of distinct communities and the differing material realities that produce them.

Dissident Daughters sketches its map of the world of women at worship by giving voice to women at the center of diverse local communities who tell their own particular stories of struggle, growth, and inspiration. As will be readily evident, these communities live in "different temporalities of struggle."[9] Some communities are well established; they emerged out of second-wave feminist activism in the church and can look back on almost a quarter-century of celebrating women-identified liturgies. Other communities are just beginning with liturgies celebrated in the company of women; they emerge in dialogue with differentiated feminisms and major cultural shifts in women's lives. One or the other community has disbanded in the midst of specific situations of social upheaval. Together, the communities featured here stand for countless other groups not documented in *Dissident Daughters*. Among them are some communities that have been documented elsewhere.[10] Clearly, *Dissident Daughters* has many sisters and cousins, some of them with children of their own.

ROOTS AND ROUTES

All these women-identified communities have emerged in different local sites, each within its own distinct cultural, ecclesial, and geopolitical context. The particularities and differences are an important reason for seeing these narratives side by side. Born out of communities that emerged in the increasingly globalized world of the late twentieth century, however, these communities also participate in some common developments, even if their impact is felt differently in different contexts. Concretely, the global flow of women-identified liturgies can be seen as part of a larger confluence of circulating movements that significantly shaped Christian practices in the twentieth century. In order to understand the emergence of women-identified liturgies, a look at these movements is indispensable. In what follows, I highlight four such movements in particular: the renewal of worship life, the emergence of international networks of Christian women, the worldwide impact of the women's movement, and the rich array of feminist theologizing and activism in the church.

From "Man's Liturgy" to Women's Rites

Since the beginnings of the early twentieth-century liturgical renewal (and women's engagement with it), "women" and "worship" have shaped the ecclesial landscape in distinct ways. Both gained special momentum in the second half of the twentieth century due to particular cultural and ecclesial developments, among them especially the second wave of the women's movement, and the liturgical reforms sweeping through the churches. For the most part, official liturgical reforms were implemented just before churches found themselves confronted with sustained feminist critique. For many women, therefore, dissatisfaction with existing worship patterns grew despite all the liturgical reforms now put in motion. Indeed, worship became a focal site of women's protest within the churches. Many women responded by developing alternatives to existing worship practices. By 1974, the first *Sistercelebrations* were in print in North America,[11] and European materials followed within a year (actual worship services obviously preceded these publications by some time). These worship services were not limited geographically to the North Atlantic world. In other parts of the world, however, these women's rites often remained "undocumented." The earliest community in the postcolonial world featured in this collection, *Talitha Cumi* in Peru,—it originated in 1983—has not published any of its liturgies.

Initially, the changes brought about in women's rites vis-à-vis traditional (even if now reformed and reforming) liturgies concentrated on individual elements, and the new worship services tended to be designed as occasional "special events." These services thrived in diverse contexts: in women's groups in parishes, in adult education centers, in divinity schools, in independent feminist communities, and in a variety of other ecclesial and nonecclesial settings. In the early 1980s, an avalanche of publications of "Women's Prayer Services," "WomanWorship," "Feminist Liturgies," and "Women Church Celebrations" began. By the 1990s, there was a clearly established tradition of worship services by and for women, or, more precisely, a "feminist liturgical tradition."[12] At the turn of the new century, women-identified liturgies and rituals are celebrated across the globe, and the literature on "feminist accounts of self-consciously constructed ritual" continues to multiply.[13] There are now long-term committed liturgical communities of women all over the globe. There are also regular women's worship services in parishes, women-identified celebrations at large gatherings of women, and lively networking between many of these women at worship. *Dissident Daughters* documents this development.

These new liturgical traditions are supported by an unparalleled explosion of religious material by and for women. There are hundreds of new women-identified hymns and songs, meditations and creeds, and a host of new prayer books specifically for women. Leaving *The Ladies' Pocket Prayer Book* of her grandmother behind, a Roman Catholic woman might now turn to *The Woman's Prayer Companion*, which invites her to "pray life events" and "to celebrate women of inspiration," all this "in Breviary format featuring all-inclusive language."[14] The evangelical woman can seek inspiration from *When I'm on My Knees* with its "devotional thoughts on prayer for women."[15] A pentecostal or charismatic woman will reach for *Women of Prayer: Released to the Nations*, by the Women's Aglow Fellowship International.[16] And the non-charismatic woman committed to a global vision need no longer turn to "private and universal prayers for the women of America" that called her foresisters to save the rest of the world through a prayer crusade by American women, who are "free beyond all other women in the world."[17] Instead, the global-minded Christian today has available to her an anthology of "everyday prayers from women around the world."[18] Within this explosion of religious materials by and for women, *Dissident Daughters* renders visible a distinct cluster of women and their religious practices, namely, those women who experience themselves simultaneously as daughters of God and as dissident daughters in and of the church.

What precipitated the emergence of these dissident daughters and their distinct women-identified rites? The answer lies in the fact that, on the one hand, the official renewal of worship life largely bypassed the starkly gendered nature of worship practices in the church. On the other hand, this official renewal also remained mostly untouched by the profound cultural shifts in women's lives that, within just a few decades, allowed women to shape their own lives in ways unimaginable for their mothers and grandmothers. The official liturgical renewal thus left many women dissatisfied. The liturgy continued to be a "man's liturgy,"[19] albeit renewed. An early feminist publication described succinctly "How the New Woman Feels in the Old Worship Service": "There are two major aspects of the liturgy that need to be liberated—its language and its leadership."[20] Scrutiny of "man's liturgy" deepened as feminist tools of analysis grew sharper. While early critiques noted problems such as male leadership and exclusive language, nuanced criticism soon appeared as more complex examples of marginalization, of silence, and of misnaming surfaced. A growing feminist awareness brought the recognition of wide-ranging gender asymmetry for women at worship. As Miriam Therese Winter put it:

> I have sung songs that women have written,
> but seldom in church on Sunday.
> I have even prayed to my Mother God,
> but not in the sacred rites.[21]

Given such experiences, a liturgical exodus into a promised land of women-identified prayers, hymns, creeds, readings, and liturgies began. New communities emerged as a movement of "feminists in exodus within the church," as Rosemary Radford Ruether described them in her influential book *Women-Church: Theology and Practice of Feminist Liturgical Communities*.[22] A significant shift took place: from women praying "pre-prepared" liturgies, these feminists moved in a liturgical exodus—within the church—to a sacred space of women claiming their own rites. The voices of dissident daughters are all related to this movement in one way or another, although in very different forms of construing the relation of "exodus" to "within the church," in very different geographical and cultural locations, in very different ecclesial environments, and in the midst of different kinds of "women." The liturgies produced by women-identified communities by now have set in motion a reception history of their own, not only in the many collections of feminist liturgies themselves but also in wider liturgical collections that include, in increasing numbers, women-identified liturgies.[23]

There is, however, no simple linear progression from man's liturgy to women's rites, even if women-identified devotional materials have flourished, if women-identified liturgical communities continue to grow, and if their liturgical materials circulate globally and, in some cases, have been mainstreamed in the wider church. These developments are accompanied by a renewed insistence, in some parts of the church, on priestly (that is male) predominance and thereby on the renewed marginalization of women in liturgical life. The Vatican's proposed *General Instruction* for the forthcoming revised edition of the *Roman Missal*, for example, specifies that lay eucharistic ministers (many of whom are women) may not place consecrated hosts into sacred vessels themselves, must receive the sacred vessels from the priest rather than picking them up with their own hands, may not cleanse the sacred vessels after Mass, and may only consume remaining consecrated wine if the priest administers it to them. These ritual minutiae of a larger return to the *norma patrum*, the "norm of the Fathers," contrast sharply with the liturgical lives of many women eucharistic ministers in local parishes. These minutiae contrast in much more pronounced ways still with the ritual space dissident daughters have claimed for themselves. The asynchronicity between this return to the norm of the Fathers, on the one hand, and the liturgical richness present among dissident daughters, on the other hand, surely marks liturgy as a highly politicized site in our time.

So much for man's liturgy, the liturgical renewal, and the struggle over women's rites. An analogous development took place for another crucial movement in the churches of the twentieth century: the ecumenical movement. Here, too, women moved from seeking permission to be included to constructing their own vision of the movement. In the process, vibrant networks of Christian women worldwide emerged, many of them actively engaged in the production of new liturgical, spiritual, and artistic resources.

The Ecumenical Movement:
Connecting Christian Women

Christian communities, one might say, have had a globalizing impetus whenever they heeded the imperative to "go into all the world and proclaim the good news to the whole creation" (Mark 16:15). However, this globalizing impetus took on particular shape and force with the nineteenth-century missionary movement, and then again on the heels of rapid processes of globalization in the second half of the twentieth century. Christian women engaged these globalizing movements in a variety of ways, one of them being the creation of international networks of Christian women. These networks ranged from those of confessional families (for example, the World Federation of Methodist and Uniting Church Women), to issue-centered networks (for example, Women's Ordination Worldwide), to those of particular guilds and regions (for example, the Circle of Concerned African Women Theologians), to the informal networking between some of the women's communities portrayed in this book. In what follows, I highlight one network of particular importance for the emergence of women-identified liturgies, the network of Christian women engaged in the ecumenical movement. In at least two ways, *Dissident Daughters* is a living testimony to the strength of this network. For one, many communities featured here are profoundly influenced by the ecumenical movement, from inspiration drawn from the Women's World Day of Prayer to energies focused through the Ecumenical Decade of Churches in Solidarity with Women. Second, many of the vital contacts behind *Dissident Daughters* came through networks established through the ecumenical movement. I am thinking particularly of the role women like Mercy Amba Oduyoye, Musimbi Kanyoro, and Nyambura Njoroge (all of them in ecumenical leadership positions) played in my efforts to connect with women from Africa. What then about this international network of women which emerges with the ecumenical movement?

Women are no latecomers to ecumenism, even if many histories of the ecumenical movement suggest so. The story of the ecumenical movement can be told in such a way that women become visible as important "movers" from the beginning.[24] The ecumenical movement, after all, emerged at the same time as the first wave of the women's movement. The women's movement forced women-identified questions on the agenda of the North Atlantic world, including its churches. The ecumenical movement emerged out of nineteenth-century movements in which women had achieved a certain prominence. In the missionary movement in particular, women had developed a women-identified vision (*Woman's Work for Woman* was not only the title of a publication but also a recurring theme of women in the missionary movement) that championed work across national boundaries. One of the ways in which women shaped the early missionary movement was through practices of prayer. Methodist women, for example, called for "Prayer at Noontide Encircling the Earth," while others invited women to set aside time on Sunday afternoon for prayer for missions.[25] The best-known liturgical initiative of women in the missionary movement is undoubtedly the Women's World Day of Prayer—a (still healthy) foremother of the women-identified liturgies and rituals that now span the globe. This first ecumenical liturgical initiative of modern times goes back to Mary Allen James, an American Presbyterian, who was president of a women's home mission board. In 1887, James called on other women to join in a day of prayer for "home missions." This day of prayer became an annual event. Three years later, two North American Baptist women, Helen Barrett Montgomery and Lucy Peabody, called for a similar day of prayer for "foreign missions." The idea of women connecting in prayer

across denominational lines and around the globe spread rapidly. In 1919, the
two days of prayer were combined, and in 1927 this day of prayer officially
became the Women's World Day of Prayer. It is celebrated to this day by
Christian women (and some men) around the world on the first Friday of
March.[26]

The start of the ecumenical movement proper is usually dated to the 1910
World Missionary Conference in Edinburgh. Subsequent to this conference,
a little-known study on *The Place of Women in the Church on the Mission Field*
was published (1927), an indication that the "woman question" continued to
intervene in the ecumenical movement.[27] When the World Council of Churches
began to take shape in the 1930s, women initiated a worldwide questionnaire
on the place of women in the different churches. Based on the answers to this
questionnaire, Sarah Chakko (1905–1954), a Syrian Orthodox from India and
one of the early non-Western ecumenical leaders, presented a report to the
founding assembly of the World Council of Churches in Amsterdam. After
the 1948 Assembly, Kathleen Bliss (1905–1989), of the Church of England,
published a worldwide study, based on the preassembly questionnaire, entitled *The Service and Status of Women in the Churches* (1952). Meanwhile, the
World Council had created a Commission on the Life and Work of Women
in the Church, with Sarah Chakko as chair. At the 1954 Assembly in
Evanston, this commission became the Department on the Cooperation of
Men and Women in Church and Society. The emphasis on cooperation continued throughout the early 1960s. By the time of the fourth assembly at
Uppsala in 1968, however, fundamental cultural shifts in women's lives were
taking place, and the story of "women in the *oikoumene*" changed to a distinct
"*oikoumene* of women."[28] The fact that women gained sustained access to
theological education and to positions of leadership in many churches proved
particularly important for this change. Women now developed consciously
women-identified theological positions, suspicious of facile Band-Aid
approaches to the marginalization of women. Dialogue increased between
women of the First and Third Worlds, nurtured particularly by the South
African Brigalia Hlophe Bam, who headed the World Council's Women's
Desk. With the 1970s, the feminist ecumenical vision increasingly took
shape. The 1974 Berlin Consultation on "Sexism in the 1970s," the first ecumenical "women's only" consultation, proved to be a watershed event. Feminist voices became a conflictual presence in the ecumenical movement,[29]
ever strengthening in theological conviction and imaginative expertise but
also calling forth more sustained negative reaction and resistance. The 1991
Assembly of the World Council of Churches in Canberra saw a crucial
embodiment of this in the address of Korean feminist theologian Chung
Hyun Kyung. Chung's address rightly has been claimed as one of the most

dramatic, controversial, and widely discussed speeches of the ecumenical movement.[30]

The ten years from 1988–1998 were celebrated by many Christian women (and some men) around the world as the Ecumenical Decade of Churches in Solidarity with Women. The Decade's objectives centered on empowering women to challenge oppressive social and ecclesial structures, on affirming women's leadership and role in the church, on giving visibility to women-identified perspectives and practices, and on encouraging churches to stand in solidarity with women, against all structures of marginalization and exclusion.[31] The Decade was brought to a close with a Decade Festival in Harare in 1998, in conjunction with the eighth Assembly of the World Council of Churches in Zimbabwe. More than one thousand women from around the world joined in the festival, which included a liturgy centered on violence against women in the church. In North America, the Decade spurned one of the most controversial events in recent ecclesial memory, the Re-Imagining Conference in Minneapolis in 1993. The idea for this conference had originated as a way of marking support for the Ecumenical Decade at the half point through its ten years. In the uproar that followed the gathering of two thousand women (and some men) in Minneapolis, liturgical practices, especially the Milk and Honey Ritual, surfaced as one of the most contested features of the conference.[32] Liturgy, once again, was identified as a peculiarly marked site of struggle for women.

This sketch of the growth of global networks of Christian women has only scratched the surface of the development of an *oikoumene* of women.[33] I have, for one, only looked at the international level and at the World Council of Churches. Many more stories of women moving the *oikoumene* could be told on the local level and at the grassroots. Nevertheless, the thrust of the development is clear: women have always moved the churches, but in the last century, women's visions have developed in distinctly transnational and women-identified ways. Women force certain subjects on the churches' agenda, such as women's access to leadership positions, violence against women, ministerial sexual harassment, and women-friendly ways of worship. Women question the established ecclesial discourse; they engender a new ecumenical vocabulary ("round-table," "re-imagining," "mending of creation") and create new liturgical texts and practices. Women privilege new conversation partners, especially poor women, women from marginalized communities and regions, and women from other faith traditions. Frequently, liturgical and ecumenical concerns go hand in hand, as was the case with the Women's World Day of Prayer and now is true for *Dissident Daughters*. But before I turn to the dissident daughters themselves, a third movement needs to be added to the two sketched previously for a fuller picture of the influences shaping women-identified liturgical communities: the women's movement proper.

The Women's Movement:
"Now It's a Global Movement"

The two movements previously highlighted, the liturgical movement and the ecumenical movement, emerged in a world that had felt the impact of the women's movement. This movement developed in the second half of the nineteenth century, initially in the North Atlantic world. From the very beginning, women forged international links, their most prominent early embodiment being the International Council of Women (1888). The claim "Now It's a Global Movement"[34] thus applies to much of the history of the women's movement, but the meaning of "global" has changed profoundly over time.

Although recent works in feminist theory have problematized assertions of global sisterhood that are predicated on essentializing and/or liberal notions of "woman," many of the communities featured in *Dissident Daughters* emerged within the second-wave women's movement and continue to value its commitments. It is therefore important briefly to review the developments here.

Several women's organizations in the religious realm internationalized somewhat earlier than their nonreligious sister organizations. The Baptist laywoman Mary Webb, for example, established the Boston Female Society for Missionary Purposes in 1800. Women created the first international cross-denominational missionary agency, the World's Missionary Committee of Christian Women, in 1888.[35] The women's missionary movement (counting all female foreign missionary societies) was by far the largest organized women's movement in the United States.[36] And the Women's Christian Temperance Movement became the largest international women's organization of the nineteenth century, with many subsequent international women's groups modeling themselves on its organizational pattern.[37] Religious-based worldwide organizations of women thus preceded and paralleled other movements, such as abolitionism, suffrage, socialism, and various movements of moral reform that began to link women across geopolitical boundaries.

In the latter part of the nineteenth century and throughout the first half of the twentieth, the women's movement's internationalizing was quite clearly bourgeois and dominated by women of European origin.[38] Geopolitically, the movement centered around what could be called a feminist North Atlantic.[39] Embedded in this North Atlantic internationalist consciousness, however, was a commitment to the flourishing of all women everywhere. This commitment came to the forefront in the wake of the second wave of the women's movement in the 1960s. The decade marked a period of major cultural shifts in women's lives.[40] This was particularly the case for white middle-class women in Europe and North America who began to work outside of the home in large numbers. But there were other cultural shifts that soon affected women almost everywhere, such as the rise of new reproductive technologies, changing sexual practices, diversifying family patterns, and an increasing awareness of women's marginalization and, more starkly, of pervasive violence against women. The second-wave women's movement signaled both the demise of any one normative narrative of "woman" and the search for alternative narratives. This search was marked by popular slogans such as "Sisterhood is powerful" and "Until every woman is free, no woman is free" as well as the celebration of "global sisterhood."[41] There was a concomitant stress on the transnational nature of women's concerns, from literacy to reproductive health, from violence against women to trafficking in women, from women's work to women's rights. International Women's Day, celebrated around the world on March 8, or the United Nations' World Women's Conferences (Mexico, 1975; Copenhagen, 1980; Nairobi, 1985; Beijing, 1995) are expressions of this understanding of the global nature of women's concerns.

Essentializing presuppositions were questioned by women who contested the notion of "woman" or "women's experience" as a false universal, since these women did not belong to the white middle-class women who had defined the initial feminist discourse. Recent years have seen a "pluralization of feminisms,"[42] and a recognition of the extent to which women's struggles are locally situated and context-specific.[43]

The changes in the global political economy and the revolution in information technologies since the 1980s have had profound effects on the lives of women. These changes are both progressive and contradictory, both inclusionary and exclusionary.[44] Globalization has both undermined women-specific struggles and created new spaces for different types of organizing. Beyond claims to universal sisterhood, a strong insistence on distinct local sites of women's struggles has emerged.

Many of the communities featured in *Dissident Daughters* are deeply rooted in the women's movement and in its theoretical framework. Dissident daughters also participate in the broader cultural shifts that undergird the pluralization of feminisms, but this is more obvious in some communities than in others: where a group of dissident daughters happens to have a poststructuralist theologian in its midst, her feminist sensibilities will shape a liturgy in ways different from a community created and led by liberal feminist activists. Beyond these individual contingencies, however, there are features of the postmodern world that increasingly shape the majority of dissident daughters. For example, at the beginning of the twenty-first century "virtual sisterhood" and cyberfeminisms have emerged as new sites of globalizing for all strands of the women's movement.[45] The fact that most of the women-identified communities featured in this book use e-mail to communicate and that some of them have established their own Web sites and manage Web-based knowledge resources shows the impact of information technologies on dissident daughters. Participants from Namibia and Botswana in the Seminars on African Women's Theology, for example, had learned about the seminar through the Web. In telling contrast to how the Web facilitates the travel of information, some participants in that seminar had to travel fourteen hours by bus to actually attend. Still, the speed of the global circulation of women-identified liturgical materials has increased rapidly, and with it the possibility of exchange of such materials. Global circulation has become, quite literally, a matter of seconds.

Faith and Feminism: A Theological Vision of Diverse Women's Flourishing

The women's movement found a vibrant embodiment in the academy in the field of women's studies and in academic feminist work within traditional disciplines. Theology, as one of the (more) traditional disciplines, slowly opened to feminist tools of analysis on the one hand and women activists within and beyond the churches on the other. Feminist theologizing emerged from these developments and by now is a multivocal and self-critical convergence of voices "from the perspective of diverse women's flourishing."[46] The term feminist theology has come to have two distinct meanings. On the one hand, feminist theology can serve as an umbrella term for a wide range of theological work by women from all over the world who see themselves committed to women's flourishing. On the other hand, feminist theology refers more narrowly to theology done by relatively privileged white women living in the West. Women in the "rest" of the world have found other ways of naming their women-identified theological struggles, thereby differentiating themselves from white feminism. To ignore this is to risk the erasure of the distinct differences in theological visions of women's flourishing.[47] In the last two decades, especially, women's theological voices from the postcolonial world— including the Third World inside the First World—have emerged with increasing force. Despite all the differences, these theologies typically share a conflictual engagement with three other forms of theology: traditional (Western) theology, male-dominated liberation theologies, and, quite often, white-feminist theologies.[48] Beyond these shared concerns, however, the differences between these women-identified theologies stand out. Latin American women theologians develop their vision against the background of a strong class-conscious tradition of liberation theology done by Latin American male theologians. African women have inherited a particular interest in "culture" from African theology but see both "gospel" and "culture" more critically and more clearly gendered than their male counterparts.[49] Asian feminist theologians work in the context of Christianity as a tiny minority religion. One of their particular interests is thus the importance of non-Christian traditions, myths, and practices for Christian feminist discourse. And differently racialized women in the First World continue to develop theological reflection out of their own communities, be they mujerista, womanist, Asian American, or Native American.

At the intersection of academic feminism in theology and women's activism in the church, Christian feminists converged in the early 1980s under the vision of Women Church. Elisabeth Schüssler Fiorenza, one of the shapers of this vision, described such an "*ekklesia* of women" in the following way: "The *ekklesia* of women is part of the wider women's movement. . . . Its goal is not simply the 'full humanity' of women, since humanity as we know it is male defined, but women's religious self-affirmation, power, and liberation."[50] Particularly with the 1985 publication of Rosemary Radford Ruether's book *Women-Church: Theology and Practice of Feminist Liturgical Communities*, prayer, ritual, and liturgies became increasingly visible in this feminist process of ecclesial transformation. As Elisabeth Schüssler Fiorenza insisted, "Only by reclaiming our religious imagination and our ritual powers of naming can women-church dream new dreams and see new visions."[51] Not surprisingly, several of the communities featured in *Dissident Daughters* claim Women Church as their inspiration and their home, and two at least have adopted this name for themselves: 여성교회 in Korea, and *Kvennakirkjan* in Iceland. But there are also dissident daughters, such as in the Netherlands, who consciously opt for other ways of naming and defining themselves, foregoing Women Church as a common denominator for women-identified struggles across the globe.

READING RITE

In the confluence of the developments just described—the renewal of worship, the emergence of international networks of Christian women, the globalization of the women's movement, and the strengthening of feminist activism in the churches—women-identified liturgies and rituals emerged. With them, liturgy developed into a crucial site of women's activism in the church. Indeed, liturgy has become one of the most politicized of ecclesial sites in our time. For many women, the "right to ritual" is "the symbolic equivalent of the right to vote and receive equal pay," as Catherine Bell puts it.[52] The importance of liturgy as a site of struggle over symbolic resources that shape women's religious lives cannot be emphasized strongly enough. For the Christian tradition in which ritual authority was the prerogative of a male priesthood, or, more recently, a caste of liturgical experts, the fact that women themselves now actively claim ritual authority by constructing and interpreting their liturgical lives, is a primary mode of claiming power.[53] To put it differently, women have moved from liturgical consumption and reproduction to production, as they grasped liturgy as a crucial site for the negotiation of faith and feminism. Claiming women's rites has involved a recognition both of the regulatory power of the traditional liturgy and of worship as a potential site of alternative and oppositional liturgical practices. Ninna Edgardh Beckman, in her contribution to *Dissident Daughters*, points out the complicated ways in which feminist liturgies both protest against and, at the same time, depend on dominant liturgical patterns. She emphasizes how feminist liturgies both represent efforts to destabilize dominant patriarchal liturgical patterns by establishing an alternative built on feminist commitments and, at the same time, are dependent on the dominant discourse for their own alternative construction. To put it differently, one could say that the struggle for women's rites is always both transgressive on as well as parasitic of established liturgical practices. That liturgy has become a primary mode of claiming power and a distinct site for the negotiation of faith and feminism is evident throughout the narratives collected in this book. As strategic ways of such negotiation, the women-identified liturgies of *Dissident Daughters* provide rich examples of how rituals emerge and how social change, in this case especially changes in gender systems, affect ritualization (Christian women-identified liturgies are not alone here; there are analogous developments in other faith traditions, for example the long struggle of Jewish women to pray publicly at Jerusalem's Western Wall[54]).

Liturgical Field Notes

At heart, *Dissident Daughters* might be seen as a collection of liturgies. It would then be one among innumerable such collections. Many of these belong to particular confessional families, but there is also a growing body of ecumenical collections and, by now, a sizeable body of feminist liturgical materials. Typically, however, these collections simply reproduce liturgical texts. There is virtually no attention to social location, cultural context, and material realities, except for pointers in the liturgies themselves.[55] Collections of liturgical texts alone, however, invariably serve to decontextualize and dehistoricize, since by only reproducing the liturgical text, these collections occlude the particular material realities that produced the liturgies and determined their meaning in the first place. In contradistinction, *Dissident Daughters* focuses on the communities themselves that create and celebrate liturgies, that is, on local agency and production. Texts of actual liturgies are also provided, but these come at the end of what might be called liturgical field notes, narratives describing the communities that created and celebrated these liturgies. Both the stories and the liturgies are inextricably woven into material reality, that is, social, economic, cultural, and political relations.

Only Stories?

If the narratives of *Dissident Daughters* function as liturgical field notes, contextualizing the actual liturgical texts, these stories are also much more than preludes to liturgical texts. To understand the importance of these narratives for *Dissident Daughters*, a look at storytelling and narrative is helpful. Storytelling and narrative as important ways both of knowledge production and of social analysis came to the forefront in emancipatory movements in the 1960s, particularly in the women's movement. I honor this legacy with the peculiar practice of narrativity embodied in *Dissident Daughters*. At the same time I understand experiences as well as narratives to be theory specific, that is to say, I take them to configure events. Narratives, especially in literary form, thus cannot be positioned over and against abstract theory. Rather, narratives themselves are a form of reflection and reasoning; they are an interpretive discourse. The narrative protocol followed by *Dissident Daughters* is a clear indication of this reflexive structuring of the stories told. In fact, the stories included in *Dissident Daughters* were crafted in response to specific questions I raised in a questionnaire for the contributors, even if women then chose quite different ways of telling their stories. The topics of the questionnaire ranged broadly, from the history and the markers of identity of the community itself; to its geopolitical, social, and ecclesial locations; to liturgical materials and practices and their roots; to reasons for the choice of the particular liturgy included with the narrative. But reflexivity is by no means an element imposed on *Dissident Daughters* by sheer editorial power. Contrary to the popular assumption that ritual is a precritical activity,[56] reflexivity is a prominent element in many of the new women's liturgies themselves: a phase of reflecting on the liturgy is common for many women-identified communities and in some cases is built into the ritualizing process itself.

Given that I appreciate narratives as a form of both knowledge production and social analysis, the narratives of *Dissident Daughters* also can be read as a form of history making. The stories told here stand as witnesses to a historic process, namely the "irruption" of women in the world of ritual in the second half of the twentieth century. These narratives thus create a historic memory; they are part of the production of the history of women activists within the church. This history making is no easy task but a labor-intensive process, as became obvious again and again in the writing and editing of the narratives. I was struck by the intensity with which some of the authors wrote and rewrote their own histories until these finally took a form that satisfied the writers. It was precisely the more historical parts of the narratives that women rewrote more frequently than any other part.

Dissident Daughters is a process of writing women-church history. In light of the occlusion of women's lives in liturgical historiography, *Dissident Daughters* safeguards histories of women's engagement with the world of ritual in our own time. As a piece of history writing, *Dissident Daughters* participates in the "precarious" nature of such an enterprise, and it is well to underline this at the outset. Dutch feminist biblical scholar Lieve Troch has put it well in a self-critical look at her own construction of feminist activism in the churches in the Netherlands: "Writing a small piece of history—especially of a rapidly developing movement—is precarious. We must always keep in mind certain critical questions: What becomes visible and why? In whose interests? What is hidden, intentionally or unintentionally?"[57]

Privileging the Particular

While the struggle for women's rites may be ubiquitous, it almost always takes place locally and does not necessarily lay claim to universal significance.[58] Consequently, the narratives of *Dissident Daughters* do not thrive primarily on the "global" or the "international" as theoretical frameworks but instead invite attention to the ways in which meaning is constructed in specific contexts. Who the "daughters" are and what "dissidence" might mean depend on a multitude of factors, especially varying and changing gender systems. Gender takes different forms as it is inflected by ecclesial and geopolitical location, ethnicity, sexual preference, class, and other markers of difference. Rituals consciously gendered from and to the social location of women correspondingly take different forms, even when and where a shared style seems to emerge. To put this by way of an example from *Dissident Daughters*: naming a community Women Church "means" differently in North America, in Korea, in Iceland, and in Germany, as in each context gender as well as church take different forms. In order to underline these differences, I have chosen to retain local names and characters where possible. This retention seemed especially important in light of the fact that *Dissident Daughters* is published in U.S. English—the dominant language of the globally homogenizing world.[59]

The "Glocality" of Women's Rites

The insistence on the distinctiveness and particularity of the different sites featured in *Dissident Daughters* does not, however, imply that any of these women-identified liturgical communities are strictly local and indigenous productions. Roland Robertson has introduced the term "glocalization," adopted initially from the business world, to overcome the binary of the global and the local.[60] The communities represented in *Dissident Daughters* are particularly vivid examples of the inadequacy of this binary. In a growingly migratory, hybrid, and cyberspatial world, these women-identified communities are shaped by a variety of transcultural linkages (primarily of the ecclesial and/or feminist kind) all the while focusing on their own local context. In fact, recent theories of globalization have insisted that globalization and localization are complementary processes and that there is a "constitutive relationality" between globalization and localization.[61] Let me illustrate this constitutive relationality, this glocality, of *Dissident Daughters* with a few examples. The transcultural linkages of these communities are evident, for example, in the migration of peoples written into the very fabric of *Dissident Daughters*. Thus, at the roots of the Peruvian community *Talitha Cumi* stand two North American women, whose missionary vocation had brought them to Peru. These two women were influenced in the 1960s and 1970s by the growing feminist activism in their North American home church that they received and adapted to their Peruvian context. The distinct migration of missionary work thus produced the linkage between North American and Peruvian churchwomen activisms. Other communities of *Dissident Daughters* are similarly shaped by the migration of peoples: the associate pastor of 여성교회 in Korea is a missionary from the United Church of Canada. One of the founding members of *Con-spirando* in Chile was born in Germany; the solidarity movement there with progressive social movements in Latin America brought her to Nicaragua and eventually to Chile. An international speaking engagement of a North American feminist theologian influenced the formation of the British Catholic Women's Network, and three women from the Network were in turn deeply shaped by their pilgrimage to the Dutch motherhouse of the International Grail Movement. There are other migrations that shape dissident daughters, especially those related to coloniality (by which I mean colonialism, as well as postcolonial and neocolonial realities). *Vrouw-en-Geloof Beweging* in the Netherlands, in particular, struggles with truthful relations between white women and women of color, many of whom live in the Netherlands as a result of Dutch colonial history in Asia and Africa.

There are also transcultural linkages inscribed in the geopolitical and social location of different communities: WATER in Washington, D.C., is located in a vibrantly multicultural metropolitan area; its liturgies, not surprisingly, almost always include multilingual texts. 여성교회 in Seoul is particularly committed to the Filipina migrant workers in the city; its worship services with and for these migrant workers are consequently held in English. *Kvennakirkjan* in Iceland confronts the international sex trafficking in women by protesting Reykjavík's striptease establishments. Transcultural links are also visible in the materials used in the liturgies of *Dissident Daughters*. Several communities mention the drawing of inspiration from worship resources provided by the Women's World Day of Prayer, the World Council of Churches, or feminist liturgies produced in other contexts. Many of the actual liturgies and rituals of *Dissident Daughters* witness to the fact that women-identified materials circulate globally. Transnational meetings, networks of women, and, last but not least, cyberspace are particularly fertile ground for this global circulation, which for some groups—such as Women Church in South Africa—has been vital for their survival. These transcultural links are multidirectional and, at times, surprising. There is the obvious borrowing of materials from North America, from spirituals to feminist prayers to creeds and women's songs. But a resource book by and for Christian women in the Philippines can also draw on insights from Central American feminist scholar Elsa Tamez.[62] *Kvennakirkjan* in Iceland can include a Spanish song in its liturgy, and German and Chilean women-identified rituals meet in their common attraction to an ecofeminist spirituality (which for the German women finds a focus in the spirituality of the medieval mystic Hildegard of Bingen, and for the Chilean women grounds them in the spirituality of the native peoples of their land).

These transnational linkages of *Dissident Daughters*, however, coexist with strong antiglobal and localizing strategies. Some of the communities featured here clearly choose resistance strategies to dominant processes of globalization and dominant forms of the flow of global capital. *Con-spirando* in Chile has turned to the native summer time and to colonial carnivalesque practices to bring meaning to the celebration of Christmas in the Southern Hemisphere. *Talitha Cumi* in Peru has taken public action protesting the commercialization and sentimentality of Mother's Day, challenging people to discern the real and pressing needs of Peruvian women. One of the key ritual events for the Canadian women's group The Circle is their "Ritual of Re-Membering," a response to the Montreal Massacre in which fourteen women engineering students were murdered in 1989 by a male student who, he claimed, hated feminists. The Filipinas gathering to celebrate the Year of Jubilee 2000 protest globalization and its adverse effects on women and the environment. *Kvennakirkjan* fights the global trafficking in women.

Many women-identified liturgies also draw consciously on local and indigenous traditions, thereby validating the regional and the particular. 여성교회, for example, uses traditional Korean forms of ritual drama and rice cakes and chilled ginger tea as part of its liturgies.[63] In Central America, a women's group uses indigenous Mayan symbols for God, and a creation liturgy includes a prayer from the *Popul Vuh*, the Mayan Book of the Dawn of Life.[64] *Talitha*

Cumi incorporates into a liturgy offerings to *pachamama*, the indigenous earth mother and uses the leaves of the indigenous coca plant in a ritual. One of the services of the group Women and Worship in Melbourne, Australia, includes a litany, "Hannah's Heirs," that begins with a list of biblical women but then focuses on Australians as heirs of the biblical women's hope and courage. Filipinas draw on indigenous instruments, foods, cloth, flowers, music, dances, and a native creation story in their celebration.

All the examples given here of transcultural as well as antiglobal and localizing elements in *Dissident Daughters* are ultimately pointers to the glocalization deeply embedded in women's rites. These rites, and the communities that produce them, are sites simultaneously of exchange, resistance, compromise, and transformation. To assume that, as women-identified rituals, they are by necessity "countercultural"[65] is too simple a description of the complex interplay of resistance, ambivalence, complicity, borrowing, and adaptation in women's rites. Such an assumption is also predicated on too facile and unified a notion of "culture" as the backdrop to these rites. A telling example of the complexity of feminist "countercultural" ritualizing appears in the *Pista-Lakbayan* celebrated by Filipina women: the liturgy contains strong antiglobalization messages and at the same time makes use of a song from an American blockbuster movie without the women experiencing this juxtaposition as a contradiction.

Which Dissident Daughter? Whose Story?

From the insistence on the distinctiveness of local sites and the recognition of the glocality inherent in these sites, it is time to move to a closer look at the dissident daughters joined in this book. In all their distinctiveness, many of these women-identified liturgical communities can be said to share certain features, although the meaning of these features clearly differs as they are inflected by various markers of difference. First, most of the communities of *Dissident Daughters* were created by Christian women in some form of leadership position, be it that of a missionary, an ordained minister, or a person with academic theological training. Several women at the heart of the communities featured here hold advanced degrees or doctorates in theology, and the majority trained, at least in part, in the North Atlantic world. Overwhelmingly then, these dissident daughters are no subaltern subjects, even if they do find themselves marginalized in their ecclesial communities and particularly in the site they claim for themselves, the liturgy. From what I have witnessed, heard, and read, I am convinced that there are groups of women closer to being subaltern subjects who create and celebrate women-specific rituals. I am equally convinced that we need to find other ways of documenting these women's rites beyond a book such as *Dissident Daughters*.

Second, and related to their educational and ministerial positions, many dissident daughters explicitly embrace forms of feminist theologizing, sometimes having worked with or currently working with the first introduction of feminist theology in a given ecclesial and geopolitical location. One dissident daughter was the first woman to be ordained in her church, and many others were among the first. Third, in terms of geopolitical location, it is notable how many dissident daughters find themselves in capital cities or metropolitan areas. These women's groups have thus arisen in or close to geopolitical centers of power. Some theorists of the globalization of the women's movement have argued that there is a correlation between urbanization and industrialization and the spread of the women's movement. Many communities of dissident daughters seem to support this theory, if only for the particular kind of women's movement associated with second-wave feminism as it originated in the North Atlantic world. Another shared feature of dissident daughters is the commitment many of these groups have to progressive social movements, especially to local women's movements. But there are other social movements that dissident daughters engage. The German *Frauenstudien- und -bildungszentrum* has roots in the student revolts of the 1960s, the founding mothers of WATER in the civil rights movement in the United States. Women Church in South Africa is related to the antiapartheid struggle. *Con-spirando* traces its origins to the awakening of women to gender issues in the antidictatorial struggle in Chile. And many dissident daughters continue to align themselves with local political struggles, be it support for the reunification of North and South Korea or for the recognition of the women drafted for military sexual slavery as is the case for 여성교회 in Seoul; or support for land rights for aboriginal people as is the case for the women's group at Fitzroy Uniting Church in Melbourne, Australia; or support of striking workers at a Shoemart factory in the Philippines.

Ecclesial Borderlands

Dissident daughters also share telling institutional characteristics (or lack thereof). Most groups with Protestant roots have structural links with the "mother" church, and, in several cases, these groups are funded or otherwise supported by the church. At minimum, they are tolerated within the institution. Groups of Catholic origin, on the other hand, are less likely to have any ecclesial affiliation, although one group of dissident daughters with Catholic roots is linked institutionally with a religious community of women. Working within the ecclesial institution and being dependent on its good will, or at least its tolerance, has on the whole proved difficult for women-identified liturgical communities of Catholic origin. Obviously, the dissident daughters featured in this book range broadly as regards group formation, from a dozen women gathering regularly in private homes to large national gatherings of women once every four years. This range of group formations shows well the different levels at which women organize and ritualize. Dissident daughters are not confined to any one level of being church.

For almost all communities of dissident daughters, though, whether Catholic in origin or not, whether small or large, the boundaries of ecclesial identity have become distinctly blurred. The oxymoronic wording is intentional here: while traditional ecclesiologies must find such blurring of ecclesial boundaries problematic, theological reflection attentive to postmodern theories of culture will, from the outset, assume Christian identity to be hybrid, unstable, composite, and relational with wider cultural materials. "Church" or "denominations" become not fixed categories but shifting, unstable, flexible bodies, multiply positioned across coordinates such as geography, gender, class, and ethnicity. Many dissident daughters clearly invite this kind of destabilizing of traditional ecclesiological categories. Theological reflection open to such destabilization presents new ecclesiological possibilities. Such theological reflection, for example, will not be forced to assume that the journey of some dissident daughters "from Christian Tradition to the Sacred Feminine"[66] can lead nowhere but outside of the Christian faith. Several communities of dissident daughters, after all, no longer recognize a sharp boundary between, on the one side, Christian and, on the other side, broader movements of feminist spirituality and ritualizing. *Dissident Daughters* thus renders visible a space described only inadequately as "in and on the edge of the churches"[67]—inadequate because the grammatical connector "and" still suggests the existence of two distinct spheres. Granted that many dissident daughters have left behind the struggle "to fit into" traditional church structures, at least as a primary concern, they also refuse to be defined as "outside," *extra ecclesiam*, or to validate the binarism underlying such definitions. Rather, these women-identified communities defy traditional ecclesiological demarcation and claim a space of their own at the very border of traditional ecclesiology. In this borderland, dissident daughters exist with all the complicated richness that such a space offers.[68] Precisely their ritualizing can be seen as an ecclesial form of border politics—the transgression and thereby subversion of ecclesial borders and their exclusionary powers—both in discourse and in ritual practice.

A Shared Style

Finally, there is the question of shared characteristics among women-identified liturgies in global context. Ever since feminist liturgies first emerged, there have been attempts to describe their distinctive features and commonalities. Several such descriptions are available and do not need to be repeated here— although they do need to be reread in light of the global context provided for women-identified liturgies by *Dissident Daughters*.[69] I propose instead to see women-identified liturgies as sharing a peculiar liturgical style[70] that emerges out of the struggle of women claiming their rites. Notice that there is no attempt here to define overarching theological themes in advance of the narratives or to hold the narratives accountable to a fixed set of theological topoi. Rather, *Dissident Daughters* begins with the women-identified liturgical communities themselves, how they construct the stories of their own growth and struggle, how they understand and shape worship, how they name the Living God, the Holy One in their midst. What emerges with the stories of these communities and their ritualizing is remarkably close to the characteristics of what has been called theologies of the people.[71] These theologies, as Kathryn Tanner has described them, are eminently practical and hospitably inclusive ("syncretistic"), exhibiting a certain isolating selectivity and attention to form over content, and possessing an open-ended flexibility that responds easily and quickly to change. The communities of *Dissident Daughters* and their ritualizing match this description quite well. Issues that surface in these communities and their liturgies cluster around certain recurring themes but are addressed very differently in different contexts. That is to say, diversity surrounds an apparently common set of themes. A concrete example might be the different forms the engagement with sex tourism and trafficking in women takes in the Philippines, on the one hand, and in Iceland, on the other. Similar diversity surrounds recurring themes such as the re-reading of Scriptures, the reconfiguring of tradition, the appreciation of indigenous and local materials, the sacrality of nature, and coalition-building among different women and their struggles. These themes are all relevant for the women-identified liturgical communities of *Dissident Daughters* but are engaged quite differently in each community.

The Representation That Is *Dissident Daughters*

Let me return to the questions raised previously: Which dissident daughter? Whose story? My own conceptual and editorial decisions ("power") have obviously shaped which dissident daughter and whose story is included in this book. More than that, I accept the fact that in generating a representation— in this case an image of women-identified liturgical communities in global context—I am also endowing this representation with performative force. Representation is never simply a question of "what is happening out there."[72] Let me, then, spell out some of the factors that have influenced the representation that is *Dissident Daughters*. Rather than hiding its interpretive strategies, feminist knowledge production endeavors to render visible its own processes of production in order to facilitate active and critical engagement with any representation it proposes.[73]

To begin with, I chose to limit the representation that is *Dissident Daughters* geopolitically in a particular way, namely, that no more than one community from any given country would be included. Obviously, this is no problem-free heuristic tool for describing cultural processes, even if one does not mistake "country" for a stable configuration.[74] The limitation by country creates a particular kind of representation and some painful lacunae (other heuristic choices would create their own problems of representation and exclusion). To begin with, outside of this book, for the one community in Iceland, there are a thousand in the United States; for the several smaller countries in Europe represented here, an equally dense spread of women-identified groups could be found in Canada. Second, for several geopolitical regions, other communities than the fourteen represented in *Dissident Daughters* could have been chosen, and some will contest whether or how representative each community featured here is for its own context. Third, communities of differently racialized women in one region could not be rendered visible within this roster of representation. There are, therefore, no separate womanist or mujerista communities among these dissident daughters.[75] In order to offset the most glaring problems of this representation, I have attended to continental representation (even if fully aware of *The Myth of Continents*[76]) and privileged chronology rather than geography for the basic outline of the book (knowing that such form of history writing has its own problems[77]).

Which dissident daughter and whose story is included between the covers of this book also depended on who responded positively to my invitation and who ultimately submitted a narrative. In the best of all women-identified worlds, the book would have featured stories also from Brazil, the Pacific Islands, Eastern Europe, the Caribbean, and Central America; more stories from Africa; and one from the Middle East, Italy, India, and Japan.

Rethinking Representation:
A Note on the Daughters of Africa

Africa, from the very beginning of this project of mapping the struggle for women's rites, held images of ritual riches but also particular challenges. Foregrounding these challenges will make clear why the representation that is *Dissident Daughters* was born out of and remains a struggle as far as African women are concerned. To begin with, my initial strategies of connecting with women's groups all over the world yielded close to no response from Africa. For quite a while, as dissident daughters came together from all over the world, African sisters of these dissident daughters remained elusive. Understanding this elusiveness and its implications for the present book became a pressing problem. I found possibilities of a resolution through several conversations with Mercy Amba Oduyoye. This will not surprise anyone who has followed the flourishing of African women's theological discourse; Mercy Amba Oduyoye is at the heart of this flourishing. In our conversations, she was clear that, to her knowledge, there were no established women-identified liturgical communities in Africa, that is women's groups that ritualize regularly, with stories of growth, struggle, and evolving liturgical patterns with a feminist orientation.[78] In the conversation in which Mercy Amba Oduyoye made that point most forcefully, however, she also described in loving detail a closing liturgy that had been part of a Jubilee 2000 celebration by African women theologians in Ghana. The liturgy had included a ritual pouring of water as a symbol of the tears of women; during this ritual, it had begun to rain. The gathered women experienced the rain as God weeping with them over the sufferings of women. When I asked who had created the liturgy and whether there had been a text for it (that I might include in *Dissident Daughters*), Mercy Amba Oduyoye simply laughed: "We just made it up. At the end we all said, 'This was wonderful.' Then we forgot about it."

Through this conversation, several things became clear. First, of course African Christian women do ritualize and celebrate in women-identified ways, especially when they come together for workshops, consultations, and conferences. As Mercy Amba Oduyoye has put it in one of her writings on African Christian women: "Not all read or write, but all talk, pray, and sing."[79] These celebrations of African women bear characteristics of what *Dissident Daughters* names "women-identified liturgies," that is, celebrations gendered from and to the social location of women. The liturgy that Mercy Amba Oduyoye described, for example, was a response to a streak of murderous violence against women in Ghana in the months preceding the Jubilee 2000 conference. Over twenty women had been murdered and the perpetrators never found. The pouring of water was a ritual weeping of African women over the deaths of their sisters—a women-identified liturgy par excellence. Second, African women are surrounded by and live in multiple contexts of rich ritualization, from African indigenous traditions[80] to the rituals of African-instituted churches[81] and those of other Christian communities.[82] These processes of ritualization, however, particularly as they relate to women, remain largely invisible in theological literature and thus have not shaped the representations of African theology. Third, there is a host of women-identified liturgical materials generated by African women. In ecumenical collections, African women's poems, reflections, prayers, and songs abound. For the most part, however, these liturgical materials are not captured under the rubric "women-identified liturgies." Musa W. Dube Shomanah, a Botswanan biblical scholar[83] who is also the author of several poems and songs, captured this division succinctly when she responded to my invitation to contribute to *Dissident Daughters* by noting, "But I am not into liturgy."[84] When I therefore sought out liturgies and communities of women that produce these liturgies, I naturally drew a blank.

Fourth, as Nyambura Njoroge pointed out, "liturgy" is yet to be a subject of inquiry by African women theologians themselves.[85] Worship simply has not surfaced as a priority among women theologians in Africa, at least not as a scholarly endeavor. Fifth, the celebrations in women's groups, and the songs, poems, and prayers generated by women in Africa are for the most part not linked to established women-identified liturgical communities in the sense that this collection features them.[86] However, all the elements of such women-identified liturgical communities are there in Africa—minus the institutional form they have taken in other parts of the world (this fact might present a question mark for the forms of institutionalization lived by other dissident daughters). Given the absence of established women-identified liturgical communities in Africa, I have opted to adapt the format of the present book in order to include the rich ritualizing of Africa women in *Dissident Daughters*. Jana Meyer and Pauline Muchina tell the story of workshops on African women's theologies in southern Africa in which liturgical celebrations were integral to the gathering—even if the claiming of women's rites was not the central concern. Wilma Jakobsen shares the struggles of a fledgling women-church movement in South Africa and some of its liturgical materials.

LETTING DISSIDENT DAUGHTERS
SPEAK FOR THEMSELVES: YES AND NO

The time has come to turn to the individual narratives of the communities featured in this book and to let dissident daughters speak for themselves. However, short of merely describing the outline of the book, the claim that what follows simply are the voices of dissident daughters is neither as easy nor as innocent as the words suggest. Beyond the structuring of the narratives provided by my questionnaire, I would love to assert that the following stories are those of the women activists themselves, that these women speak with their own voices, bearing witness to how they came into being, how they nurtured themselves, and how they worship the Holy One in their midst. This claim, with all its naivete, however, is hard to sustain, since it veils my (at times strong) editorial hand in this project. It is more accurate to say that I have shaped these narratives not only by providing a narrative protocol but also by editing in depth the narratives I received. This might involve, on the simplest level, looking for English translations of texts by Hildegard of Bingen as they are read in one of the liturgies. My editorial interventions, however, went well beyond these minor details. Editing routinely meant either shortening narratives, reorganizing individual parts, or asking for more materials. At some points, it involved adding information about specific local contexts and geographies—which the writers themselves took for granted but which readers in other parts of the world would not know. In some cases, the authors themselves engaged in an intense process of rewriting and redesigning their own narratives. And in one case, the beginnings of the narrative lie in an interview I did with the author about the particular community in question.

A particular struggle faced by anyone editing texts from a variety of different language backgrounds is the (non-)translatability between different linguistic worlds. Although most authors chose to write in English, this language for many was not their mother tongue.[87] What kind of English would lend voice to *Dissident Daughters* proved a long and drawn-out struggle (not helped by the fact that English is not the editor's mother tongue, either). In the process of editing the English in one narrative, for example, its author instructed me not to make too many "improvements." She wanted to make sure that "the women back home" would still recognize themselves in this text. There are other than linguistic, although no less inevitable, complexities of editing cross-cultural narratives in English. In the case of the Korean narrative, my editorial work involved struggling to teach my computer Korean; for the Icelandic story, my computer had to master Icelandic fonts. And making the intricacies of U.S. copyright laws seem relevant to how liturgies are created in other parts of the world continued to be a problem. All this goes to say that the narratives of *Dissident Daughters* are mediated stories, sites of the negotiation of differing languages, of collaborative struggles, of coproduction, of activist and academic linkages. How can it be otherwise in such a project?

A word remains to be said about the structure of the book. After this introductory chapter, the remainder of *Dissident Daughters* is given to narratives of fourteen different women-identified liturgical communities. These narratives are arranged in chronological order with the oldest community being featured first. I have chosen chronology as the organizing principle rather than, say, geography, so as to bring to the forefront the historical emergence of these communities. The concluding chapter, in the form of a postscript, reflects on the theological importance of women-identified liturgical traditioning witnessed in the preceding chapters.

1

Come, Sophia-Spirit

WATER in Washington, D.C., U.S.A.

DIANN L. NEU

IN THE BEGINNING

WATER, the Women's Alliance for Theology, Ethics, and Ritual, is an international feminist educational center, a network of justice-seeking people that began in 1983.[1] Mary E. Hunt, a Catholic feminist-liberation theologian and ethicist, and I, a Catholic feminist liturgist and psychotherapist, cofounded WATER in response to the need for serious theological, ethical, and liturgical development for and by women. Mary was the one who first heard women calling for a place of our own to "do" feminist theology and spirituality. She wrote a short proposal, and we gathered a dozen women from diverse ecumenical backgrounds to discuss this need. The women empowered both of us to answer the call. We responded by starting WATER. Situated in Silver Spring, Maryland, one block from Washington, D.C., capital of the United States, and one block from the well for which Silver Spring is named, WATER plays an important role in the success of the women's spirituality movement and in the renewal of church and society. We work locally, nationally, and internationally doing liturgies and programs, projects and publications, counseling and collaboration work. We help people to actualize feminist religious values and bring about social change. We work in an increasingly interreligious context, examining the roots of our respective traditions and building on their strengths to provide a value-based future for our children and ourselves.

WATER is unique in that it is the only organization in the United States, perhaps in the world, that attempts to develop a broad-based, diverse, and international Alliance of feminists in religion. Beyond academically connected groups or denominationally related caucuses, WATER seeks to welcome and empower feminists of faith who are activists, academics, and ministers—in short, all who seek to work in coalition on projects that will foster egalitarian and democratic ways of being religious in the pursuit of a just society. The Alliance is a network of groups and colleagues around the world motivated by feminist faith commitments. The network grows through common projects, regular communications, and information sharing. Our name, WATER, created by Mary Hunt, and our logo, which I designed, best express our identity as a feminist spirituality center.

CLAIMING OUR RITES

Three decades ago hundreds of thousands of feminist theologians, clergy-women, and laywomen started the women's spirituality movement in the United States that brought modern feminism into churches, synagogues, mosques, and ashrams. I was one of these women. We challenged women and men to rethink the basis of religious practice: interpretation of sacred texts, liturgical language and symbols, styles of leadership and relationships, and decision-making processes. We created spaces for women to do feminist work. Feminist liturgy developed gradually from the confluence of historical, political, secular, and religious awareness. It emerged in the United States from the struggles of the twentieth-century movements on behalf of oppressed peoples—civil rights, anti-Vietnam war, the women's movement, women's ordination, gay and lesbian rights, human rights, reproductive choice. The feminist liturgical movement, countering historic male co-optation, asserts that women must shape liturgical traditions to remember their own stories as well as those of other marginalized people. Otherwise, values and shared meaning will be lost.

WATER is known for the feminist liturgies we create and celebrate. The WATER community gathers periodically for feminist liturgy. WATER liturgies are also used as models by many feminist and justice communities worldwide.[2] In the Washington area, women-church communities and women's spirituality groups[3] pray monthly with worship models and themes focused on seasonal changes, women's life cycles, justice issues, wise foremothers, solidarity work, and community building. WATER in turn invites these Washington-area feminist communities to gather quarterly to worship and network. For larger gatherings we rent space from a sister center. Recent liturgies were celebrated for International Women's Day with "Women Crossing Worlds: In Solidarity and Friendship"; Pentecost with "Come, Sophia-Spirit"; summer solstice with "Praise the Sun"; harvest with "A Women's Harvest Festival"; and the winter solstice with "From the Womb of Night."[4]

WATER programs at home and abroad include liturgy as an integral component. When we gather for a day or weekend workshop, we open and close with liturgy. We weave song, dance, and symbol throughout our time together. Our ongoing groups begin each session with a few moments of silence and close with a short ritual using a symbol that focuses on the topic. For example, when WATER's feminist spirituality group discussed women's friendships, I, as facilitator, placed a large bowl of water and floating candles on a low table in the center of the group. At the end of the session I asked each woman to name a friend, speak words about the friend's shared wisdom, and float a candle in the water to honor her. Friends could reconnect in the ripples of water and the warmth of candlelight.

We are called on nationally and internationally to create liturgies for conferences and workshops and to teach others the process. People phone and e-mail WATER for help with innovative liturgies for marriages and commitments, naming ceremonies and house blessings, funerals and cronings, World AIDS Day and reproductive choices, healing from abuse and celebrating anniversaries. Our prayers, liturgies, and articles are reprinted internationally in many languages. Participants find WATER a place where they can be feminist and religious, where they can pay attention to their spirituality and politics, and where they can participate in a community without compromising their spirituality or explaining their presuppositions.

When WATER liturgies are celebrated with people from English-speaking countries or at conferences where English is primary, we frequently include Spanish, German, French, and other tongues to bring global realities to bear. In other settings our liturgies are adapted and translated into the language(s) of the communities celebrating them. *WATERwheel*, WATER's quarterly newsletter, features in each issue a feminist liturgy that can be adapted for use by various groups worldwide. WATERworks Press, WATER's publication arm, produces liturgical resources for feminist and justice communities. The *Women-Church Source Book, Women-Church Celebrations: Feminist Liturgies for the Lenten Season, Women of Fire: A Pentecost Event*, and a series of feminist *haggadoth* for inclusive seders offer models for groups to adapt for their own use.[5] The *WATER Spirit* series is forthcoming. In three volumes this series will document and disseminate the liturgical texts that have been created by and for the WATER community over the past eighteen years.

WATER liturgies keep alive the memory and imagination of the community of women believers and those children and men who identify with them. These liturgies bring feminist religious wisdom to public expression. They empower feminists and various communities for social transformation. Inspiration for these texts comes from retrieving the inclusive aspects of diverse religious traditions, listening to women's music, reading feminist writings, participating in and paying attention to liberation struggles worldwide, reading the morning paper, listening to nature, and being with women in other cultures. WATER has a bookcase (a "sacristy") in the office that is filled with liturgical materials from around the world: cloths, statues, bowls, rocks, shells, candles, bells, percussion instruments, various symbols, books, and music (especially by women).

SHARING A RITE

The following liturgy was celebrated with feminist liturgical communities in the Washington, D.C., area who gathered together on Pentecost, the major Christian feast day that celebrates the birth of the church and the renewal of ministry and community. Representatives from thirteen base communities joined one another to call on the Holy Spirit, Sophia-Spirit, Divine Woman Wisdom, who appears as God's own being, to continue her call for the liberation of all from patriarchy and kyriarchy.[6] This Pentecost time together provided an opportunity for many feminist liturgical groups that meet regularly in small communities to feel the energy and power when people from many communities, prayer circles, and women-church groups join together for liturgy and fellowship. Periodically we all need to be with a crowd, with those who are birthing a feminist church and society.

The WATER staff worked on the script for this liturgy: Diann Neu wrote the text; Mary Hunt edited for theological content; Cindy Lapp chose the music; Carol Scinto did the copyediting. We invited a cross-section of women and girls representing each of the communities to take leadership roles in proclaiming the script. These dancers, readers, musicians, and blessers ranged in age from eight months old to seventy-four years. They spoke English, Spanish, German, and French; they were African American, Mexican American, and European-American; Catholic, Mennonite, Presbyterian, Women-Church, Episcopalian, Methodist, and Jewish.

We gathered outside in the garden of the Center for Educational Design, a sister center in Washington, D.C., run by the Religious of the Sacred Heart. Rosemary Luckett, a local artist, designed the eight Sophia trees that circled the perimeter to mark the space. The dancers hung colored cloths and ribbons from the tree branches. We sat on chairs inside the circle of trees and on cloths inside the circle of chairs. Luckily the weather cooperated. Three low-platform altars with red woven cloths formed the center. One altar held three baskets filled with three different home-baked breads, six goblets of juice and wine, and six red napkins; another held an oil lamp; and the third had chimes, pinwheels, and bubbles for the children. Each participant was given a pink paper with the music for the songs. Red and pink were the colors for the day. At the close of the liturgy, participants were invited to share refreshments.

This feminist celebration of the ancient feast of Pentecost was designed to reclaim the Pentecost story and to evoke new meaning for the participants, and beyond. On the one hand, one never knows the impact of such a gathering; Sophia-Spirit moves where She wills. On the other hand, some impact is measurable. Sixty women, children, and a few men from thirteen local communities and justice organizations responded to the invitation to celebrate this Pentecost liturgy in the ancient tradition of coming to a central place, perhaps a cathedral, to be church together. When WATER staff invited representatives from these communities to participate, each person we contacted expressed delight in being asked to share her gifts and wanted to be asked again. These women and girls shared leadership for different parts of the liturgy. The choir, dancers, readers, and blessers practiced together before the liturgy. One choir member said that using inclusive language for Sophia-Spirit in the songs, prayers, and texts was a new and empowering experience for her. Cindy Lapp, mother of three-year-old Cecilia Lapp Stoltzfus, reported that Cecilia often asks, "When can we go back to church outside?" Cecilia enjoyed running around the large yard, being part of setting up, and taking the ribbons out of the trees, and she often requests, "Sing the Sophia songs with me again, Mom." Giving young children options to participate in an informal setting offers parent and child an opportunity to share spirituality. One mother, noting the child inclusiveness of this liturgy, looks forward to bringing her children to the next gathering. We anticipate the participation will grow.

The WATER staff itself was so pleased with the response to this liturgy that we plan to host another Pentecost celebration the coming year and are designing other quarterly liturgies to continue bringing together local communities. We value and enjoy the collaborative planning process that called forth the creative skills of the WATER community. The Women-Church Convergence, a coalition of thirty-four women's groups throughout the United States whose roots are in Catholicism, has used the liturgical text for "Come, Sophia-Spirit" on several occasions. This text will become known to other women's base communities and will be used as a model for future feminist liturgies, perhaps even help traditional church communities to include Sophia-Spirit in their celebrations. Being included among *Dissident Daughters* also brings this liturgy and liturgical experience to a wider audience.

A FEMINIST LITURGICAL VISION

In this Pentecost liturgy, "Come, Sophia-Spirit," we keep alive the memory and imagination of the community of Sophia-Spirit. We are a feminist church. We rekindle a feminist liturgical vision. I image a future when we are so filled with Sophia-Spirit that we go forth hand in hand from our feminist liturgies and sweep away all violence and oppression. I dream of a new dawn when women and those marginalized will be respected, freed, and filled with power to actualize our liturgical gifts. I hope for a time when our eucharistic tables overflow with food and drink to feed all the homeless and the hungry of the world. I long for the day when all the wounded and abused will receive the love, healing, and nourishment of Spirit-Sophia. I envision a year when we make quilts from altar cloths and vestments and with them warm our children and homeless friends. I yearn for a millennium when all creation returns blessings for the many gifts each has received and all have enough simply to enjoy life. I see a new creation that includes all in the breaking of the bread, the raising of the cup, and the doing of justice. In the meantime, let us empower one another and our various communities through feminist liturgies for spiritual nourishment and social change. Then we will all have additional energy to do justice. Let those who have ears to hear, hear. Let those who have eyes to see, see. Let those who have hearts to feel, feel.

COME, SOPHIA-SPIRIT: A PENTECOST LITURGY

The liturgy includes as many presiders as you choose, dancers, a choir, a narrator and four disciples (readers), three blessers, and two members to lead responses. The liturgy begins with a dancer walking to the center of the circle, and the choir leading the Nigerian chant, "Come, Sophia Spirit, Come." During the chanting, the dancer blesses the space with an Indonesian dance and invokes Sophia-Spirit from the four directions of the world.

ALL	"COME, SOPHIA-SPIRIT, COME"[7]
(chanting)	Come, Sophia-Spirit, come.
	Come, Sophia-Spirit, come.
	Come, come, come.

Call to Gather

Today is Pentecost, the birthday of the church. This is the day we commemorate when the Holy Spirit comes to her people. We know this Holy Spirit is She. *Sophia* is her Greek name, Wisdom her English name, *Chokmah* her Hebrew name, *Sapientia* her Latin name. Who is Sophia? Why do we speak about Sophia-Spirit today?

Wisdom theology talks about God as Sophia, Divine Woman Wisdom, who appears as God's own being. In the writings of the early Christian community, Sophia seems to disappear, yet a deeper reading shows that Sophia assumes the functions of the Spirit. Spirit-Sophia's presence is God's Spirit. Early Jesus traditions called Jesus Sophia's prophet and Christ-Sophia. Divine Woman Wisdom, Sophia-Spirit, God with us, continues her call for the liberation of all women, children, and men from patriarchy and kyriarchy. Today we celebrate the power and presence of Sophia-Spirit with us. Please echo after me:

ALL
(echoing)

May Sophia-Spirit rise inside me like a rushing wind.
May Sophia-Spirit leap within us like a revolutionary fire.
May Sophia-Spirit flow through the world like a life-giving breath.
Let us share and receive her Spirit.

CHOIR
(inviting all
to chant)

Come, Sophia-Spirit, come.
Come, all loving Spirit, come.
Come, come, come.

Introduction

Why is WATER gathering communities together on the day of Pentecost? Many of us meet regularly in our small communities. Sometimes we need to feel the energy when people from base communities, women's prayer circles, and women-church liturgy groups join together. This is that time. We come from a variety of communities today. Let us hear the names of the communities represented here. Someone call out the name of your group, and then we will all add, "Sophia-Spirit is here."

The different groups call out their names, and the community responds to each name with

Sophia-Spirit is here.

Look around. Notice the faces among us. Turn to those around you and introduce yourself by saying, "Hi! I'm _____ (name). Sophia-Spirit is here."

Individuals introduce themselves to each other by name.

Song   "SING LO! SING, O SOPHIA"[8]
(led by the   **Sing lo! Sing, O Sophia! Wisdom come to widen**
choir)   **my heart.**
                       Sing lo! Sing, O Sophia! Wisdom, come abide in my
                           heart.

I looked to my neighbor, now what did I see?
Wisdom come to widen my heart.
A sweet, sweet Spirit beckoning to me.
Wisdom, come abide in my heart.

I looked deep within me. Oh, how can this be?
Wisdom come to widen my heart.
I saw Sophia looking back at me.
Wisdom, come abide in my heart.

I looked to Sophia for setting me free.
Wisdom come to widen my heart.
A deep, dark Presence liberating me.
Wisdom, come abide in my heart.

The following prayer is spoken while two dancers invoke Sophia-Spirit, using red cloths in conjunction with their movements.

Prayer for Justice

Come, Sophia-Spirit, embrace us and free us.
Come, Sophia-Spirit, enter into the depths of our longing.
Come, Sophia-Spirit, renew our passion for justice and beauty.
Come, Sophia-Spirit, breathe vitality into our struggles for change.
When we are fearful, challenge us.
When we are lonely, give us community.
When we are hurting, heal us.
When we are weary, open us to new dreams.
Open our closed minds
So that we may listen to those who are different from us.
Unclench our hands so that we may reach out to others.
Open our closed eyes so that we may see the needs of the world.
Unclog our ears to hear the agony of war and violence.
Open our closed hearts so that we may love the elders.
Come, Sophia-Spirit. We ask this in your name.
Amen. Blessed Be. Let It Be So.

The choir leads the chanting of "Veni, Sancte Spiritus" in four parts. Four disciples (readers) and the two dancers kneel together in the center of the circle, praying aloud quietly, "Sophia-Spirit, come." The singers chant, "Veni, Sancte Spiritus." The narrator stands and proclaims the Pentecost story, Acts 2:1–21[9]:

Reading

> When the day of Pentecost came, they were all gathered in the same place. They came from many different communities and regions: young and older; speaking many languages of different professions, religious people who practiced their faith in various ways. They came from all corners of the land: Washington, D.C.; Silver Spring, Md.; Alexandria, Va.; Takoma Park, Md.; McLean, Va.; Germantown, Md. . . . Suddenly they heard the sound of a rushing wind shaking the house where they were. Something that looked like tongues of fire hovered above each one of them.

The Spirit-dancers start to whirl toward the disciples, trailing red cloths. On reaching the disciples, the dancers swirl the cloths over the heads of the four, who then stand. In what follows, the dancers swirl cloths around all participants.

> Suddenly, all of them, women, men, and children, realized that they were filled with the power of Sophia-Spirit. They began to speak in different languages in the power of the Spirit.

The choir leads the chanting of "Veni, Sancte Spiritus" singing the verse, "Come, Sophia-Spirit, from heaven move forth with your glorious dance."[10] The dancers move spontaneously. The four disciples face the congregation from the four corners, the four directions, and alternate the following texts.

> Hearing this sound, a crowd assembled, devout people from every continent known on earth: Africa, Asia, Europe, South America, North America, Antarctica, Australia. All were amazed and astonished, for all of them heard the words preached in their own language.

> Why, I hear these people speaking Chinese. How could they learn Chinese?

> They speak Serbian! It's a miracle—as though there had never been a Tower of Babel.

I hear them speaking Swahili. How can this be?

Sie sprechen Deutsch.

Se hablan español!

On parle français.

Whether the pilgrims were from large cities or country villages, they heard the disciples proclaiming in their own language the wonderful works of the Spirit.

These words of the prophet have come to pass: "In the days to come, it is God who speaks, 'I will pour out my Spirit on all humanity. Your daughters and sons shall prophesy. The young shall see visions. The old shall dream dreams. I will pour out my spirit and they shall prophesy.'"

The choir leads the chanting of "Veni, Sancte Spiritus" with the verse, "Come from the four winds, Sophia, Come, breath of God. Come blow your power through us. Renew and strengthen your people."

Sophia-Spirit was given not only to the early community, but to us as well.

To each person the Spirit gives gifts.

There are many gifts, but the same spirit;

Many works, but the same Holy One.

Through Sophia-Spirit someone receives intelligence, another holiness.

Someone else the gift of distinction, and yet another subtlety.

Assurance is given to some,

To others, steadfastness,

And to still others is given the gift of clarity.

There are those who are irresistible, free from anxiety and humane.

The gifts of the Spirit are without number.

But all gifts are from the same Spirit, who distributes them as She pleases.

For all of us belong to the one body, the body of Sophia-Christ.

Whether Jew or Greek, female or male, black, brown, yellow, red, white,

Gay or straight, differently abled or able bodied, poor or rich,

We have all been baptized into one body by the same Spirit.

And that Spirit calls us to proclaim the good news to all people.

Whether in known or unknown languages,

Whether in the language of the child or the adult, of the haves or have-nots

Until justice comes,

We are all called to proclaim that Sophia-Spirit is rising in all creation.

To her be all glory forever and ever.

ALL   Amen. Blessed be. Let it be so.

The choir leads the chanting of "Veni, Sancte Spiritus," adding the verse, "Kindle in our hearts the flame of your love, that it may spark and bring new life. May it glow and reach to all forever."

Two members lead the congregational response, alternating.

A Congregational Pentecost Response

Filled with the gifts and power of Sophia,
We honor and act on the power of justice.

We honor and act on the power of justice.

We honor and act on the power of forgiveness.

We honor and act on the power of forgiveness.

We honor and act on the power of hospitality.

We honor and act on the power of hospitality.

We honor and act on the power of . . . Tears . . . Integrity . . . Affection . . . Sexuality . . . Work . . . Struggle . . . Friendship . . . Truth . . . Prayer . . . Peace

Invitation to Shared Reflection

Sophia-Spirit shares her gifts with each of us and with our communities. What Sophia-Spirit gifts do you bring and what Sophia-Spirit gifts do you see in your community? What does it mean to see ourselves as part of something far bigger than we are? How will you use your gifts to build this global movement? Let us share with three or four people around us.

Children, girls and boys, come around the altar. These chimes, pinwheels, and bubbles are symbols of Sophia-Spirit. Sophia-Spirit is another name for God. She is our friend. Have fun now playing with these gifts of Sophia-Spirit. Singing will bring us back to the whole group.

The choir leads the chanting of "Veni, Sancte Spiritus."

Collection

We have shared gifts Sophia-Spirit has given to us and to our communities. We know that to keep this movement going we need money. Let us now be generous people and share our financial offering with this community. Come, put your money in the basket.

Song   "GUIDE OUR FEET"[11]

Prayers of the Gathered

Let us pray together. Our response is "Sophia-Spirit, flow through your people."

We pray for the people fleeing war-torn lands, especially for the women who have been raped and the families who have lost their loved ones.

Sophia-Spirit, flow through your people.

We pray for the end to violence, for an end to gun use and the fear that inspires it, for an end to domestic abuse and the unsafe homes it creates.

Sophia-Spirit, flow through your people.

We pray for economic justice in this millennium, for the equitable sharing of this earth's abundance.

Sophia-Spirit, flow through your people.

We pray for our children, that they may be safe and well, lively and loving, heirs to our faith and shapers of their own.

Sophia-Spirit, flow through your people.

What other prayers do we offer? Tell us and we will respond.

The choir leads the singing of "Guide Our Feet," singing the verse, "Flow through us while we run this race, for we don't want to run this race alone." Three blessers then come forward to three different places in the center, face the gathered, and pray in turn:

Eucharistic Prayer[12]

Lift up your hearts.

We lift them up to Sophia-Spirit.

Let us give thanks to our gracious Mother God, Divine Woman Wisdom, Sophia-Spirit.

It is right to give her thanks and praise.

Blessed are you, Loving and Challenging Friend, Sophia-
Spirit.
With joy we give you thanks and praise for creating a diverse
world
And for creating women in your image.
You call us to share your story,
So we join all creation in singing your praises:

The choir leads the singing of the refrain "In Your Presence."[13]

O Wisdom Sophia, Wisdom Sophia,
The power and presence of God.

Blessed are you, Womb of All Creation, Sophia-Spirit.
You create women, men, and children in your image.
From age to age you form us from your womb;
You breathe your breath of life into us.
And you call us to share your story,
So we join all creation in singing your praises:

O Wisdom Sophia, Wisdom Sophia,
The power and presence of God.

Blessed are you, God of Our Mothers, Sophia-Spirit.
You call diverse women to participate in salvation history:
Eve, Lilith, Sarah, Hagar, Miriam, Naomi and Ruth,
Mary, Mary Magdalene, Tecla, Phoebe, Hildegard of
Bingen,
Sor Juana Inés de la Cruz, Sojourner Truth, Joan of Arc,
Maura, Ita, Dorothy, Jean, and countless others,

And you call us to share our stories,
So we join all creation in singing your praises:

**O Wisdom Sophia, Wisdom Sophia,
The power and presence of God.**

Blessed are you, Creator of all seasons and all peoples,
  Sophia-Spirit.
You call us each by name
To be prophets, teachers, house-church leaders, saints,
And to image your loving and challenging presence.
You call us to share their stories,
So we join all creation in singing your praises:

**O Wisdom Sophia, Wisdom Sophia,
The power and presence of God.**

Blessed are you, Companion on the Journey, Sophia-Spirit.
You have built yourself a house,
You have hewn seven pillars,
You have prepared a rich banquet for us.
And you call us to share your story,
So we join all creation in singing your praises:

**O Wisdom Sophia, Wisdom Sophia,
The power and presence of God.**

*Each blesser puts her script on the table, picks up a cup of drink and a basket of bread
(that also has a small paper with the following words). The three blessers pray together:*

Extend your hands over the bread.
Blessed are you, Holy Bakerwoman, Sophia-Spirit.
In your abundant love you welcome all to come and dine.
You proclaim from the rooftops,
"Come and eat my bread, drink the wine that I have drawn."
And you call us to share your story,
So we join all creation in singing your praises:

**O Wisdom Sophia, Wisdom Sophia,
The power and presence of God.**

The blessers put the bread and drink back on the table and face into the circle, praying:

> Come, O Holy Sister, Sophia-Spirit, upon this bread, wine,
>   and juice.
> Come as the breath and breathe your life anew into our
>   aching bones.
> Come as the wind and refresh our weary souls.
> Come as the fire and purge us and our church of sexism, het-
>   erosexism, racism, class exploitation, colonialism, ageism,
>   and all evils.
> You call us to share your story,
> So we join all creation in singing your praises:
>
> **O Wisdom Sophia, Wisdom Sophia,**
> **The power and presence of God.**
>
> Come, Soul Sister, Sophia-Spirit,
> And bring the new creation:
> The breaking of bread,
> The raising of the cup,
> The doing of justice.
> You call us to share your story,
> So we join all creation in singing your praises:
>
> **O Wisdom Sophia, Wisdom Sophia,**
> **The power and presence of God.**
>
> Eat, drink, and partake of the banquet of life.
> Receive the love, healing, and nourishment of Sophia-Spirit
> As we pass the bread and goblets around the group.

The choir leads the singing of the Communion song.

Song   "SPIRIT MOVIN' WHERE SHE WILL"[14]
             We're seein' how a mighty wind sweeps the surgin' waters,
             Spirit movin' where she will, birthin' the light from darkness.
             O Spirit movin', O Spirit movin',
             O Spirit movin', movin' within your daughters.

We're seein' how creation breathes, woven by this artist,
Tapestries of pain and grace, fire, flesh, and stardust.

We're seein' how our sister pain makes us strong in wisdom;
Broken bread that feeds our world, claimin' our faith and vision.

We're seein' how that leaven grows, long silent voices speakin',
Tellin' a story never told, the nations to justice leadin'.

We're seein' a compassion born, the circle's growin' stronger;
Lettin' our children live in peace, copin' with wars no longer.

Sending Forth

(by the three blessers) Friends of Sophia, let us go forth with courage,
For Sophia-Spirit is with us.

For Sophia-Spirit is with us.

Let us go forth to liberate all women, children, and men from war and violence,
For Sophia-Spirit is with us.

For Sophia-Spirit is with us.

Let us go forth to recognize the face of Sophia in all creation,
For Sophia-Spirit is with us.

For Sophia-Spirit is with us.

May Sophia-Spirit rise inside me like a rushing wind.

May Sophia-Spirit rise inside me like a rushing wind.

May Sophia-Spirit leap within us like a revolutionary fire.

May Sophia-Spirit leap within us like a revolutionary fire.

May Sophia-Spirit flow through the world like a life-giving breath.

May Sophia-Spirit flow through the world like a life-giving breath.

Greeting of Peace

Let us share and receive Sophia-Spirit by offering one another Pentecost peace. Blow into your hands. Feel Sophia-Spirit's breath within you. Blow this greeting to the earth and to the world. Using hands that are now filled with the power of Sophia-Spirit, let us offer one another a Pentecost greeting of peace.

The choir leads the singing of "Dancing Sophia's Circle"[15] as the dancers gather all into a spiral dance.

Closing Song
and Dance

"DANCING SOPHIA'S CIRCLE"
Ring us round, O ancient circle, Sophia dancing free,
Beauty, strength and Holy Wisdom,
    blessing you and blessing me.

2

Women Rise Up, Close Ranks!

Talitha Cumi in Lima, Peru

ROSANNA PANIZO

IN THE BEGINNING

Talitha Cumi came into being as a direct result of the Second Latin American and Caribbean Feminist Meeting held in Lima, Peru, in July of 1983. This gathering of feminists from all over Latin America and the Caribbean gave us the impetus to create *Talitha Cumi*: a group of women with both feminist and Christian commitments, a *Círculo de Feministas Cristianas*.[1] Several of the founders of *Talitha Cumi* attended the Second Latin American and Caribbean Feminist Meeting and participated in its workshops. These workshops dealt with a broad range of subjects, from reproductive rights, the family, and sexuality; to older women, peasant women, and racism. One of the workshops centered on "Church and Patriarchy." Gathering in this workshop, we realized that there were several of us feminists from all over the continent who recognized ourselves as coming from a Christian tradition or background (it is important to remember that the "evangelization" of our continent had its violent beginnings five hundred years earlier in the arrival of the Iberian conquistadors).

After the Second Latin American and Caribbean Feminist Meeting, some of us Peruvian women decided to continue our conversations about the role of the Christian tradition in our lives and in the lives of the women we worked with. All of us were on a journey of discovering the meaning of being both a Christian and a feminist in Peru. I myself did not, at that time, realize that such a double commitment was possible; it seemed a contradiction in terms. *Talitha Cumi* was born out of this journey of Christian women within the larger women's movement, a movement that itself was part of a broad progressive movement of social transformation throughout the continent. One part of this progressive movement of social transformation was liberation theology, which had emerged in the 1960s and grown substantially in the 1970s. Some of us who formed *Talitha Cumi* in the early 1980s came from a liberation-theological perspective. At the same time we were critical of the lack of attention to women's issues within liberation theology. This, in fact, was one of the issues addressed in the above-mentioned workshop on "Church and Patriarchy." The final statement produced by that workshop included the following sentence: ". . . we feel that theologians who are attempting to contribute to the search for a more just Latin American society are not making a real contribution to Latin American Liberation unless they include women's issues."[2] At the same time we were also critical of the then-emerging Peruvian feminist movement since this movement paid very little attention to religious issues. The key analytical tool at the time was "patriarchy," but using that category without engaging in depth one of the most patriarchal structures in our culture was a blind spot, to say the least. There were, of course, feminist voices of criticism and denunciation of the power of the church as it related to structures of oppression and exploitation, but in the early stages of the feminist movement in Peru, the engagement with religious traditions stopped there.

TALITHA CUMI!

Our name, *Talitha Cumi*, speaks of our Christian background. Nowadays, there is also a well-known hard rock group with that name, but we were the first to name ourselves *Talitha Cumi*. Claiming a name is crucial for claiming identity, and the choice of *Talitha Cumi* as our name highlighted our distinctiveness within the feminist movement. When the first Peruvian feminist groups emerged in the 1970s, several adopted names of Peruvian women, such as Flora Tristán, Manuela Ramos, or Aurora Vivar. Trying to find a name for our group, we initially considered a Spanish name, or a word that would link us to the Andes, the highlands of Peru, with their strong indigenous traditions. But in the end we chose biblical words, words Jesus had spoken (a dominical command, in a sense, and one handed down in Aramaic, no less): "*Talitha cumi*, . . . young woman, rise up" (Mark 5:41).

We women in *Talitha Cumi* came from diverse and international backgrounds. Some of us were Peruvians. Others came from the United States, Australia, New Zealand, Canada, and Ireland (many of the international women were in Peru because of missionary work). We were elderly and young, Roman Catholic and Protestant, lay women and religious, homemakers, social workers, students, married and single. In the early years of *Talitha Cumi*, I myself was still in seminary, training for ordained ministry in the Peruvian Methodist Church. Several of the religious sisters in our group lived in communities in poor neighborhoods. Most *Talithas*, however, came from the middle class. But our root commitment was to poor women, the elderly, prostitutes, students, and our own neighbors. Around this commitment gathered Christian feminists, women from leftist social movements, and those from liberation theology.

Although we came from diverse backgrounds, the sense of community in *Talitha Cumi* was much stronger than the sense of difference. We did talk a lot about our differences, including very sensitive issues such as abortion (about which we had quite divergent opinions), but we learned that our differences were a part of us, and we learned to live with them. There was also a powerful sense of community beyond the local level, since we realized early on that we were part of a global community of women. The Second Latin American and Caribbean Feminist Meeting, which was the midwife of *Talitha Cumi*, had given us a strong sense of an international network of women activists. Today, *Talitha Cumi* is linked with a number of other groups of religious feminists in the Americas: in Chile, the United States, Brazil, and Canada. Communication and interaction are fluid, and each group maintains its uniqueness, yet we share common concerns. Some *Talithas* are members of women's religious communities who have their own links with women's communities worldwide. We also maintain links with other Peruvian Christian women who have formed groups outside of institutional churches, such as CACTUS, a group of young pentecostal women, and KAIROS, an ecumenical women's group linked to seminaries that focuses on research on women and religious issues. We join efforts with these groups, for example, when feminist theologians such as Elsa Tamez (Costa Rica), Mary John Mananzan (Philippines), Rosemary Radford Ruether (U.S.A.), and Ivone Gebara (Brazil) visit our country.

OUR CONTEXT: DOUBLE MILITANCY

I still find it incredible that feminism emerged in Latin America during one of the most difficult times in our history. During the 1960s and 1970s, military regimes and nominal democracies caused thousands of people to disappear and violently repressed progressive social movements in the name of "National Security." One of the first things Latin American feminists challenged was the militaristic, phallocentric, and patriarchal paradigm of the state. Feminists joined forces with other groups and organizations of resistance, denouncing social, economic, and political oppression and exploitation. The realities of state repression and of class struggle thus profoundly shaped the praxis of the feminist movement in Latin America. Peru's particular crises must be seen in this context. In the 1950s, the state attempted to develop institutional policies for women in Peru, largely within a conservative framework. In the 1960s, women activists raised their voices within the labor movement and joined the struggle of their brothers, fathers, and husbands. Women were present among the peasants laying claim to land and emerged as activists in the first shantytowns growing around the larger cities. These women, however, did not raise gender-specific claims. In the 1970s, Peru had a military regime with a populist flavor. The administration of President Velasco initiated economic, educational, and institutional reforms, but these spurned an economic crisis that in turn produced a massive protest movement against the state. Numerous grassroots organizations emerged: of high school and of university students; of school teachers and of university professors; of construction workers, phone company employees, state civil employees, journalists, indigenous peoples, miners, peasants, retirees, and women. This period also witnessed the two largest general strikes in Peruvian history.

It was in this context of social upheaval that women's groups began to emerge. Their vision was fueled by three different approaches to "women's reality." The first approach was institution based and conservative; its main bearers were Roman Catholic parishes. The focus was on providing training and assistance, especially to grassroots women. A second approach was that of leftist politics. This approach promoted the participation of women in the social struggle and focused on the political conscientization of women. A third approach was the feminist one with its clear agenda of women's rights. ALIMUPER (*Acción para la Liberación de la Mujer Peruana*, Action for the Liberation of the Peruvian Woman), created in 1973, was the first such explicitly feminist group. One of ALIMUPER's earliest public demonstrations, at the occasion of a Miss Perú contest, centered on women's rights in relation to our bodies. ALIMUPER and other groups made visible how sexual oppression was linked with other realities of oppression, especially the economic oppression of capitalism. Feminists pointed out, for example, how women's health was not simply a question of controlling one's body by showing the role international organizations played in state policies in Peru. Institutionalized violence in society came to be linked to daily domestic violence; the dynamics of power in the configuration of the state were paralleled with the dynamics of power within the household.

In the early 1980s, working-class women in Peru were in the vanguard of grassroots survival struggles that increasingly challenged the social and economic policies of the conservative Belaúnde Terry and the populist Alan García administrations. Within these grassroots women's organizations flourished mother's associations, people's kitchens, the "glass of milk" initiative for children, and networks of health and legal promoters. The first two initiatives were mainly supported by the state, the Roman Catholic Church, and various nongovernmental organizations (NGOs); the third initiative was mainly supported by the United Left, and the fourth mainly by feminist NGOs. During the 1980s, the grassroots leadership of these initiatives was constantly threatened by the *Sendero Luminoso*, a Maoist armed group. The *Sendero* killed several grassroots activists, among them María Elena Moyano, who had lead a protest march against the *Sendero's* violence. Moyano was killed by dynamite by a *Sendero* woman dressed as a peasant.

As a result of the diversity of approaches, the Peruvian women's movement continues to present diverse political practices. First, there are those groups that organize their actions around women's traditional roles in reproduction, in the struggle for survival, and in the welfare of the family. Then there are groups that organize their agendas around political parties, workers' unions, and women's associations. Last, there are groups that attend to gender divisions from a feminist perspective. These three different perspectives have been present within the women's movement ever since its beginning. Although different, these perspectives are not mutually exclusive, and women activists in Peru have been able to strategize and articulate their actions together.

What about the role of the churches? Here, too, we find different practices. The first practice is that of the institutional church that helped to organize and that supported those (more traditional) groups that focused on women's reproductive roles. A second practice is identified with what liberation theologians have called the "church of the poor." This ecclesial practice evolved as a distinctly class-conscious practice of priests, lay missionaries, and men and women who formed base ecclesial communities that empowered people in their struggle for survival. In many cases, these two practices overlapped, and both of them were critical, although for very different reasons, of a third practice that emerged, namely, the feminist one. The traditional institutional part of the church quickly denounced feminism as a threat to the traditional values of society, the Christian faith, and the family. The progressive "church of the poor" in the 1970s adopted the discourse of the Peruvian left, critiquing feminism as an imperialist import, a movement of middle-class women who promoted issues irrelevant for the majority of poor women. A movement for women's liberation was deemed unnecessary since liberation could be achieved only through a wider revolutionary movement that at some future point would then eliminate the oppression of women. Both of these church-based perspectives saw feminism as divisive and disruptive.

We *Talithas* were critical of both perspectives since each ultimately represented an institutional and patriarchal understanding of women's lives. We agreed that our country needed revolutionary change, but history had taught us that revolutions did not per se change the reality of women's lives for the better. We were convinced that neither capitalism nor socialism alone could eliminate women's oppression (we did follow closely events in Central America, especially in Nicaragua and El Salvador, and the involvement of women in progressive social movements there). In those years many feminists talked about *doble militancia*, double militancy. These women took part both in leftist political parties and in feminist groups. But several of us in *Talitha Cumi* embraced a different kind of double militancy: one side of our militancy was directed not so much at political parties but at our churches. As feminists, we were simultaneously clergy in various denominations or members of religious communities, of base ecclesial communities, of parishes identified with the poor; we lived in poor neighborhoods or worked as professors of theology from a prophetic perspective. All of us were identified with poor women, and we brought their concerns to the religious institutions within which we worked.

A good example of our Christian feminist *doble militancia* came with the two visits to Peru of Pope John Paul II in 1984 and in 1987. The Pope's visits were widely seen as attempts to rally the Peruvian Catholic bishops behind a condemnation of liberation theology and behind strictures on the ecumenical space that had been created in Peru. For the Pope's second visit, *Talitha Cumi* signed an open letter to our "brother John Paul II" that highlighted the extreme poverty and violence and the ecclesial indifference to and oppressive church teachings on issues of sexuality, abortion, and reproductive rights that shape many Peruvian women's lives. This letter was signed by women from thirteen different feminist groups that had formed a feminist collective, *El Colectivo del Movimiento Feminista*. *Talitha Cumi* had a delegate in this collective. As Rivkah Vaage, a member of our group says, *Talithas*, with their religious roots, were considered the "conscience of the feminist movement in Perú."[3]

One of the continuing dilemmas we wrestled with was our position vis-à-vis popular religiosity, that is, the wide range of popular religious practices embraced particularly by poorer women but alienating to many of us. Initially, we simply committed ourselves to being there, in the world of the poor, including its devotions, processions, and other expressions of popular religiosity. With the years and with deepened feminist scholarship, we discovered better ways to interpret these cultural expressions, their dynamics, and how people understand and negotiate their own religious practices. This was easier for those *Talithas* who came from a Roman Catholic background than for those of us who were Protestants, since as Protestants we came with different experiences of popular religious practices.

CLAIMING OUR RITES

Our group emerged out of a broad range of concerns at the intersection of feminist and ecclesial commitments. Liturgy was but one of these concerns. As a part of our struggle with our faith and our experiences in the different churches, we searched for different ways to celebrate our faith, our commitments, and our dilemmas and beliefs. We began to meet every other Wednesday night at the center *Creatividad y Cambio* in downtown Lima; *Talitha Cumi* still meets there to this day. The center belongs to an NGO headed by two Maryknoll sisters who were founding members of *Talitha Cumi*. There, we began to create our own sacred space and to articulate a new liturgical language: new meaning for old words, new words for old and new realities. The liturgical space felt like an oasis, a place and space that I longed for: no orthodoxy, no right formulas or words, times of silence, times of no words if we did not find any. We had to trust in each other to be able to share our experiences and our innermost feelings about being a woman, in a church, in Peru. It was a time of searching, of looking for inspiration.

Looking back I can see that this searching was part of a larger liturgy, a celebration of encountering each other. From the beginning, we also invited women from the wider feminist movement to our liturgies. Several women followed our invitation, especially during holidays such as Easter and Christmas, but also for our *Jornadas*, reflection days that ended with an open liturgy. *Talitha Cumi* provided a ritual space for the wider feminist community, and our feminist friends appreciated this. We celebrated our liturgies in private homes, retreat centers of religious communities, parishes, and meeting places of other feminist groups. Given that we were in Peru, our gatherings were always contingent on larger Peruvian realities: if there was a general strike, or a major power outage, or a car bomb explosion in downtown Lima, women might not be able to get to our gathering, and it would be cancelled.

As for the world of symbols in our liturgies, we were soon involved in a process of discovering indigenous traditions, especially those of the Andean highlands where the majority of Peru's indigenous population lives. *Talithas* who worked in the highlands facilitated this process. We were, after all, not only Christians but also Peruvians, and we wanted to connect with the indigenous traditions of our country. We learned, for example, to honor *Pachamama*, the indigenous earth mother, as an expression of our ecofeminist commitments. We grew to appreciate the corncob as an ancient symbol of unity; *chicha*, a popular refreshment made from corn that has ritual connotations; and the coca leaves that are used in Andean rituals. These indigenous symbols came to stand side by side with the biblical symbols of light, darkness, salt, or food in our celebrations.

Music is another fundamental part of our liturgies, and we learned to draw on a wealth of different sources: songs from women's religious communities in other parts of the world; services and materials from ecumenical gatherings, such as the World Council of Churches; Latin American songs; and songs of the women's movement. We also adapted hymns and changed lyrics at ease. Our music thus is a collage of different experiences, commitments, and resources. Most songs are in Spanish, but there may also be the occasional song in English or catchphrases in one of the indigenous languages.

Early on we wrestled for several weeks with how to name God in our lives and in our liturgies. We acknowledged and claimed our freedom to name God in different ways at different times: Father, Mother, Sister, Friend. We named Jesus our friend, our brother, our *compañero*. The early years with all their searching were very intense, and it seemed that we could not wait to get together again, since *Talitha Cumi* was the only space we had in which to explore the intersections of our faith and our feminism.

Our meetings soon developed a pattern. We usually begin with a time of gathering and sharing what is going on in our own lives and in our society— the violence, the corruption, unemployment, all the factors that concretely shape our lives and the lives of Peruvian women. After this time of gathering, we share a meal together. Then we do our work: we discuss a reading; we plan a project; we organize and strategize; we read letters from other groups around the continent and from *Talithas* abroad. The gathering ends with a ritual. Our rituals celebrate different things: the birthday of a *Talitha* member, my ordination as a United Methodist minister, Mother's Day, International Women's Day, the Christmas holiday season, or International Day of Nonviolence Against Women. Sometimes we take a symbol as the central focus of a liturgy, such as water, or an apple. We also take time to remember: our great grandmothers, grandmothers, mothers, our childhood, women who marked our lives, women in Peruvian history, known and unknown. We invoke the presence of all these women in our midst by claiming their presence with us, in our liturgies and in our lives: *presente*!

The liturgy below was celebrated in January of 1986, at the end of a reflection day that looked back to the old year and forward to the new. Since *Talitha Cumi* was formed in 1983, we have been celebrating liturgy in the company of women for almost twenty years now. The liturgy below is fairly typical of our celebrations as they evolved in the early years.[4]

SHARING A RITE

A Time of Silent Meditation

Song   "GRACIAS A LA VIDA"
*We begin our celebration with a famous song by Chilean folk singer Violeta Parra,
"Thanks to Life." The song celebrates life, in all its fragility and ambiguity (Violeta
Para committed suicide soon after writing this song).*[5]

A Time to Remember
One of the women invites us to remember important recent events in our lives as
Talithas:

> Let us remember!
> We remember, sisters, with what dedication we prepared the
> document for the Pope's visit . . . how we shared our
> outrage!
> We remember, sisters, Mother's Day . . . how we struggled
> with the widespread veneration of this image of women as
> mothers!
> We remember our reflection day last June . . . how the
> thought and work of Rosemary Radford Ruether enriched
> our faith and our commitment!
> Finally, we remember the reflection day in September . . .
> how we attacked patriarchy in our own lives!

Moments of Reflection
All share their memories of the past year.

Scripture   THE RESURRECTION OF DORCAS (ACTS 9:36–42)
Reading   Now in Joppa there was a disciple whose name was
                Tabitha, which in Greek is Dorcas. She was devoted to
                good works and acts of charity. At that time she became ill
                and died. When they had washed her, they laid her in a
                room upstairs. Since Lydda was near Joppa, the disciples,
                who heard that Peter was there, sent two men to him with
                the request "Please come to us without delay." So Peter got
                up and went with them; and when he arrived, they took
                him to the room upstairs. All the widows stood beside him,
                weeping and showing tunics and other clothing that Dorcas

had made while she was with them. Peter put all of them outside, and then he knelt down and prayed. He turned to the body and said, "Tabitha, get up." Then she opened her eyes, and seeing Peter, she sat up. He gave her his hand and helped her up. Then calling the saints and widows, he showed her to be alive. This became known throughout Joppa, and many believed in the Lord.

Communal Reflection

Together, we reflect on this reading from the New Testament.

Song   "MUJER NUEVA"

This is one of our feminist adaptations of well-known hymns and songs. We took a popular song by Juan A. Espinoza, "Hombres Nuevos," which celebrates, from a liberation theological perspective "man's" struggle for freedom and hope. We turned the male-dominated text into a feminist song by substituting "woman" for "man": "Mujer Nueva, New Woman."

Moments of Inspiration

Each participant brings to the circle a symbol of power (such as a stole, a book, or a pen) and explains to the group why she has chosen this particular symbol to signify power for her. After each participant has shared her choice of a symbol, the symbols are exchanged with the neighbors on the right and then given back to their original owners with the following words: "I give you back your symbol of power that you may be strong, and may be inspired today and always." We close the circle by embracing each other.

Song   "CIERREN FILAS LAS MUJERES"

The concluding song comes from the early feminist movement in Peru and expresses well some of its militancy: "Close Ranks, Women." The song denounces everything from machismo, violence, rape, and torture to the use of women's bodies in advertising, and it calls on women to close ranks, to break the silence, and to organize for change.

Dissident Daughters Celebrate

Women and Worship at Fitzroy Uniting Church, Melbourne, Australia

CORALIE LING

IN THE BEGINNING

We are an open circle of people who want to continue to widen our circle. We meet in an old bluestone church in Fitzroy, an inner-city suburb of Melbourne, Australia. Our church building is dwarfed by high-rise flats built by the government as subsidized housing for people on low incomes. Many of the residents are refugees from Vietnam and the horn of Africa. Our building looks very traditional, but when people come inside for the first time, they are surprised to see the floor carpeted in blue and a circle of chairs with a central round table. There is no pulpit or sanctuary. In the early days of this building, Fitzroy was a middle-class suburb, in fact, the first suburb of Melbourne, but it became a depressed area from the beginning of the twentieth century onward. Today property values are very high, and many homes have been renovated, but there is still great poverty, drug dealing, and homelessness in Fitzroy. The worshiping community in the nineteenth century was made up of middle-class Presbyterians. By the turn of the century, the community had become a mission church supported by the central Melbourne church that provided kindergarten for children, training programs for youth, and welfare for the poor. Now, at the beginning of the twenty-first century, our church continues to provide a strong multicultural kindergarten and child-care program. Many of the children come from Muslim and Buddhist families, so the major festivals of all the faiths represented are celebrated in the children's center. We also host a number of human rights groups concerned with land rights for aboriginal people, justice and development in East Timor, and a new start for psychiatrically disabled people.

The Fitzroy worshiping community today is made up of people who are attracted to the feminist, inclusive, lively, and justice-oriented nature of our liturgies and life together. Our mission statement emphasizes respect for racial and cultural differences, room for different voices, and diversity in worship. However, the worshiping community is predominantly European in racial background. Many members of the community are lesbian, gay, or bisexual. Some members have transferred from traditional churches where they experienced disenchantment, harassment, or abuse, and some have no previous religious experience and have come seeking a spiritual path for their lives. The age range is from twenty to eighty, and occasionally children come with adult friends, parents, or grandparents. Many of the community work in caring professions as chaplains, ministers, teachers, nurses, social workers, and human rights workers. Some people are students, some are unemployed, and some are on various kinds of pensions, such as a disability or a supporting mother's pension.

THE UNITING CHURCH IN AUSTRALIA

The worshiping community is a congregation of the Uniting Church in Australia. The Uniting Church, formed in 1977, brought together people from the Congregational, Presbyterian, and Methodist traditions. The Uniting Church has a strong ecumenical vision and, after the Catholic and Anglican traditions, is the next largest Christian denomination in Australia. In the last few years the Uniting Church has been engaged in a debate on sexuality that has centered on the ordination of openly homosexual people. Fitzroy Uniting Church has strongly supported the inclusion of homosexual people in its life and ministry and actively sought support for this attitude in the whole church. In the wider Uniting Church, Fitzroy is seen as different because of its feminist and pro-gay stance. I have been the minister of Fitzroy Uniting Church since 1991. The congregation called me as someone who was committed to a feminist theological approach to ministry and shared leadership. It has been a rare challenge to develop a feminist spirituality with the congregation and one I have enjoyed immensely.

CLAIMING OUR RITES

There are two worshiping groups associated with Fitzroy Uniting Church. The first one is the group that meets every Sunday morning and on other special occasions during the Christian year, such as Ash Wednesday, Good Friday, and Christmas Eve. Fifty or more people comprise this group of both women and men though the proportion is usually about two-thirds women and one-third men. The worship on Sunday morning follows the themes of the *Revised Common Lectionary*, authorized for optional use in the Uniting Church. A monthly pattern usually has the first Sunday for Eucharist, the second Sunday for a biblical study within the liturgy, and the third Sunday for a more reflective service. On the fourth Sunday a cutting-edge theme concerning justice in the workplace or the community generally is explored by a member of the congregation or a visiting speaker. The worship on most occasions is planned by one person but with many opportunities for the congregation to contribute. Members light candles; do readings; offer comments, questions, and stories to enlarge the prepared sermon; share joys and concerns; engage in intercessory prayers with candles and silence or with words; serve each other bread and wine; and participate in drama, dancing, and singing.

A good example of the liturgy of the Sunday morning worship at Fitzroy Uniting Church is the 1999 Easter Day Eucharist. The central round table was covered with a gold and white cloth on which stood a tall Christ candle surrounded by yellow flowers, grapes, wheat, and four round white candles. A loaf of crusty bread and chalices of wine also stood on the table. The congregation sat around the table. On the walls in the background hung Easter banners: a Tree of Life reminiscent of the Australian wattle; a bird in feminist colors of purple, green, and white, flying free of a cracked open egg; and a butterfly. The liturgy began with a lighting of the Christ candle, an Easter greeting, and an alleluia chant accompanied by the whole congregation using percussion "eggz" (a plastic egg shape containing seeds). As more candles were lit, the alleluia chant and percussion broke out again. The chant was followed by a contemporary Easter hymn sung to a traditional Easter tune. The opening prayers acknowledged signs of Easter life and hope in our Southern Hemisphere autumn. An Easter children's story focused on the bilby, a native animal with long ears, something like a rabbit but in danger of extinction.[1] The bilbies enlist the help of a mythical Australian bush creature, the bunyip, to paint and deliver eggs. This is a transforming experience for the grumpy bunyip. The children in the congregation were encouraged to think of ways to give life to the bilbies and to go on a hunt around the church for some hidden chocolate bilbies. Following another contemporary Easter song to an old Easter tune, the Easter story in John 20 was read. The sermon drew on two Easter symbols: stones (both in how they prevented women's ministry and therefore had to be rolled away, and in how in the empty tomb they formed a space for exploration and meeting Sophia Christ ahead); and the image of Mary Magdalene, a woman whose story has been one of death and resurrection through the centuries, from apostle to the apostles, to prostitute and sinner, to the prophet and preacher again ahead of us. People in the congregation added their comments about Mary Magdalene and resurrection stories from their own lives.

A contemporary song to the tune "Go Down Moses" urged Mary Magdalene and her heirs to stand up as priests and prophets.[2] As the offering was received, the people shared their joys and concerns. This practice is a part of every morning service, and we move from this sharing to prayers of intercession as candles are passed around the circle and people offer silent or spoken prayers. Another song then led into a eucharistic prayer celebrating liberation and resurrection. Often our address to the divine includes Sophia as we acknowledge the wisdom of God that has a feminine face. We seek to use inclusive language for the divine as well as for people. In the Eucharist, the minister breaks the bread and raises the cup and all the people in the circle share the bread and wine with each other. The Easter service concluded with a new Easter song and a strong Easter blessing.

Although this is the Easter service, it is also an example of the usual form of Sunday worship of the Fitzroy congregation, a group of women and men from the Reformed tradition of the Uniting Church in Australia. The Fitzroy congregation differs from many congregations in the Uniting Church because of its emphases on active congregational participation and circular seating, its appreciation of a range of feminist theologies and biblical scholarship, and its use of feminist and inclusive language.

WOMEN AND WORSHIP

Fitzroy Uniting Church sponsors a second worshiping group called Women and Worship. This group is for women only and meets on the fourth Sunday of the month at 6:00 p.m. From the late 1960s and into the '70s the Fitzroy church developed a strong social justice focus as part of its mission. Much of this focus centered on analyzing the causes of poverty and planning development for the inner city. In the 1980s, the justice focus centered more strongly on sexuality and gender issues, and this has continued through to the present. Women from the congregation realized that they needed a worshiping space apart from men where they could reflect on their own experience and develop their own voice and spirituality. Some of the women had experienced violence and abuse at the hands of men and only felt safe in a women's space. Women and Worship was begun in 1987 and has continued on a regular basis since then. It is the only regular women's worship in Melbourne and probably all of Australia that is actually sponsored by a church congregation as part of its mission.[3] Over the years since 1987 many women have come to Women and Worship from all over Melbourne, from country areas and other states. Some women have drawn on the Fitzroy experience to start their own independent women's worship or spirituality group, but so far no other church congregation has sponsored a Women and Worship program. One of the reasons that this program has been ongoing for almost fifteen years has been the strong support from the Fitzroy Uniting Church community.

Some of the women who currently attend Women and Worship are Uniting Church clergy who find much of the usual Uniting Church worship frustrating and oppressive because it is nonparticipatory and uses noninclusive language. At Women and Worship, these clergywomen can be themselves and develop further a feminist spirituality. Some women travel from outer suburbs or from the country so that they can be part of an inclusive feminist worship. Many women who come from a great distance have a church heritage that forbids the ordination of women (such as Catholic or Anglican women from the Ballarat Diocese in the country), and our space offers them an alternative to a patriarchal church. Some of the women have been deeply hurt in traditional churches because of clergy abuse or because of rejection when they were honest about their own sexuality or supportive of family and friends who were gay. Women and Worship offers them a safe meeting place to test new paths on the spiritual journey. Some of the women have realized that a feminist analysis in their studies or workplace is essential but have nowhere else to go when they look at their faith from a feminist perspective. While Australia has been at the forefront in establishing equal opportunity legislation that forbids discrimination on the grounds of gender, the churches are exempt from this legislation.

Women and Worship is an introduction to feminist theology and liturgy for women who want to bring feminism and faith together. The women in the worshiping group come from a wide range of backgrounds. Some have degrees in theology; some are theological students; some work as teachers, nurses, social workers, ministers, or religious sisters; some have no paid employment; some are retired; some are married; some are single; some are lesbian or bisexual; some are heterosexual. Most have a European heritage, though some have an Asian heritage. Most speak English as a first language. Mothers and daughters, sisters, partners, and friends often come together. The ages range from the twenties to the seventies.

Usually somewhere between fifteen and thirty women form the worshiping group. A team of women meets to work out the themes of the worship services for a six-month period. When the themes are decided, different women volunteer to help with a theme that particularly attracts them. The themes are related to women's history, lives, concerns, and spiritual journeys. In 1999, we used alliterative themes such as Aberrant Artists, Boisterous Bodies, Conspiring Companions, Dissident Daughters, Energetic Eves, Feisty Friends, Gifted Goddesses, and Hannah's Heirs. For the year 2000, we adopted themes addressing feminism and the future. The worship, of course, is intentionally feminist. Inclusive language, feminine images for the divine, shared leadership, stories of women, the work of feminist theologians, and women's creativity are always in evidence in these services. When the planning group first meets, the women bring resources for the theme—music, poetry, graphics, a feminist piece of writing, an idea for action involving the group, an idea for the worship space in Fitzroy Uniting Church, an idea for something the women may take home to reflect on, such as an herb, a bookmark, or something to eat. One of the ideas for action on the theme of Aberrant Artists was to use a long ribbon of paper spread across the circular worship space. After the women had heard the story of an aberrant painter, they did some aberrant artwork themselves. Likewise, after hearing the story of an aberrant writer they wrote some aberrant words around the artwork. The paper strip was then made into two long hanging posters.

The particularly Australian aspects of the worship emerge in the stories the women tell of their own lives and in the poetry, songs, and other Australian resources we use. The aberrant artist mentioned above whose story we told was Clarice Beckett, who in the 1920s painted muted, misty scenes of Melbourne and its suburbs. She was dismissed as an aberrant un-Australian artist because the renowned male artists of the time were painting bold sunlit scenes of the Australian landscape, not cities. Because Australia has so many migrant traditions and is very multicultural, it could be said that it is an Australian characteristic to appreciate many cultural traditions. In the Women and Worship services, we draw on a wide range of cultural resources and also try to honor and affirm Australian women. In the Advent service of Women and Worship entitled "Hannah's Heirs," we recalled that Hannah's heirs include Australians. Here is an excerpt from our litany:

> We praise Hannah's heirs,
> **Whose lives give us hope and courage.**
>
> Shiphrah and Puah
> midwives of Israel
> whose defiance of Pharaoh's orders
> saved many Hebrew children in the time of Moses:
> **For their gift of hope and courage we give thanks.**
>
> Kahlah, Noah, Hoglah, Milcah, and Tirzah
> daughters of Zelophehad
> descendants of Asenath and Joseph,
> who convinced Moses

to allow women
to receive an inheritance:

For their gift of hope and courage we give thanks.

Syrophoenecian woman
whose approach to Jesus
on behalf of her sick child
helped him to see
a new aspect of his ministry:

For her gift of hope and courage we give thanks.

Hildegard of Bingen
twelfth-century mystic,
one of the great minds
of Medieval Europe,
abbess, scientist, scholar,
composer, visionary, poet:

For her gift of hope and courage we give thanks.

Caroline Chisholm
emigrant's friend,
tireless worker for young women migrants
in Australia of the early 1800s:

For her gift of hope and courage we give thanks.

Truganini
aboriginal Tasmanian,
worker for her people's survival,
refusing to be passive victim
of British colonization:

For her gift of hope and courage we give thanks.

Daisy Bates, C.B.E.[4]
journalist,
advocate on behalf of aboriginal people,
first woman to be appointed
Honorary Protector of Aborigines:

For her gift of hope and courage we give thanks.

Edith Cowan, O.B.E.
pioneer for women's and children's rights,
first woman elected to an Australian parliament:

For her gift of hope and courage we give thanks.

Dame Enid Lyons
widowed mother of twelve,
first woman to be elected
to the House of Representatives:

For her gift of hope and courage we give thanks.

Mary McKillop
teacher of the poor,
founder of Sisters of St. Joseph,
excommunicated
then beatified by the church:

For her gift of hope and courage we give thanks.

Dr. Faith Bandler
daughter of a South Sea Islander slave,
campaigner for rights for
aborigines,
Torres Strait Islanders,
and South Sea Islanders:

For her gift of hope and courage we give thanks.

Dawn Fraser, Evonne Goolagong Cawley, Cathy Freeman,
    Shane Gould, Betty Cuthbert
just a few of the women athletes
who struggle for recognition
in a world where male athletes
gain all the attention:

For their gift of hope and courage we give thanks.

Mary Gilmour and Oodgeroo Noonuccal (Kath Walker)
poets whose love for their country
shone in their poems:

For their gift of hope and courage we give thanks.

Jenny Kee
artist, survivor of the Granville train crash,
pioneer of Australian fashion design
using vibrant colors and designs
of the Australian bush:

For her gift of hope and courage we give thanks.

Once the planning group has spent some time sharing resources and ideas—and many things arise spontaneously during those conversations—the flow and shape of the liturgy are discussed. The involvement of all participants in the liturgy is always an important consideration, as are ways of introducing what the theme will be, what the women will take away from the liturgy, how women's experiences will be shared, and how women will be empowered to continue the journey along the feminist liberation spiral. While the pattern of the liturgy varies considerably from month to month, there is always some form of introduction to the theme in drama, words, music, or a meditation; some form of prayer; and some form of elaborating the theme perhaps through reflections on a biblical text, storytelling, interview, dance, or meditation on a feminist theologian's work. The liturgy usually includes a time for the sharing of women's news, issues, and networking, and often concludes with a strong feminist song and a blessing.

SHARING A RITE

The worship service of Women and Worship on Pentecost Sunday 1999 follows. The theme of the service was "Dissident Daughters." As this Women and Worship service fell on Pentecost Sunday, we chose to use the colors of red, representing the Spirit, and purple, representing the dignity of women, for the central round table. The table was covered with a purple and red cloth, and purple and red runners divided the table into four. In each corner stood a purple or red candle and in the center sat a vase of purple and red flowers. Around the walls hung various red Pentecost banners and brought into the circle was a red banner of a dove flying through a flaming sun around which were the words "Your daughters shall prophesy."

Twenty-five women sat in a circle around the central table. The service began with the chant "From My Mother's Womb," which enabled us to acknowledge we were a gathering together of daughters. The following introduction made a connection between being daughters who prophesy and envisage a different world and being dissident daughters who say "No" to every kind of oppression. The prayers recalled biblical women who had been prophetic and dissident. These prayers provided an opportunity for the worshipers to name historical and contemporary dissident daughters. The three readings allowed for strong dissent to the text of terror (Isa. 3:16–26) and for inspiration in the biblical text of liberation (Luke 13:10–17) and Mary Daly's *Wickedary* definitions. Three women had prepared short reflections on these themes. A song and dance followed the readings and reflections. The song, an adaptation of the well-known spiritual "Jacob's Ladder," has become a tradition in Christian feminist gatherings. The song "We Are Dancing Sarah's and Hagar's Circle" rejects the patriarchal ladder in favor of circles and now includes women of different races, Sarah and Hagar. The words were slightly altered to include daughters. The women worshipers did their own steps as they sang and danced around the circle.

A younger woman, a librarian who had experienced harassment in her workplace, and an older woman, an Anglican nun, had come prepared to tell the story of their own lives as dissident daughters. Their stories were followed by the story of the prodigal daughter, a retelling from a daughter's perspective of what it meant not to take responsibility for herself and leave home. As the story was told, one woman mimed with great expression what was happening in the story. Another humorous story was told of a daughter whose first name was "Silence." She was a vocal woman whom her church really wanted to keep, so they kept "Silence" in their church. Some other women in the circle then shared their own stories of being dissident daughters. A song celebrating the gifts and stories of women was followed by an offering. A basket was passed around the circle as various women announced events and concerns that the gathering might support. The service closed with a prayer for strength to continue acting dissidently and resisting patriarchy, a dissident song and dance, and a blessing for the ongoing journey.

The women who attend this worship find support and strength to continue their lives in Australian society, where a spirituality of resistance to patriarchal values is needed. The theme of this particular Women and Worship was a strong affirmation of feminist women who are a minority in the institutional churches. In this worship these women have the opportunity to hear feminist voices and develop a feminist liberation spirituality. Some of the women who come to this worship will continue in their own institutional church with a spirituality of resistance. Others will be part of the wider Fitzroy Uniting Church community. Others will only come to this particular women's worship but will, in many ways in their lives, continue the dance of the dissident daughters.

DISSIDENT DAUGHTERS: A PENTECOST LITURGY

Chant   "FROM MY MOTHER'S WOMB"[5]
                   From my mother's womb and grandmother's tongue,
                   I have heard my name, been given my song.
                   With their blood and their beauty I have grown strong.
                   With the fire of love and rage I will sing on!

The leader introduces and reads the following three texts:

Introduction

"Your Daughters Shall Prophecy" (Joel 2:28)—a Pentecost theme for Dissident Daughters.

"Let your word be 'Yes, Yes' or 'No, No,' anything more than this comes from the evil one." (Matt. 5:37)

Whatever we do,
Wherever we go,
Yes means Yes
And No means No.[6]

Song

"'NO' SONG"[7]
There is a piece of wisdom that all the world must know;
The same Spirit who bids us to say yes also bids us to say no!
So I say:
No! No! A thousand times I'll say no!
Read my lips, it's so clear, just open your ears, I'm sayin' No!
No! No! No!
No, no, no, no! No, no, no, no, no! No, no, no, no!

Prayer

Sophia, Creator, you made us in your image. We are women who say "yes" to every kind of generativity and creativity. We are women who say "no" to every kind of threat and oppression.
Thanks be to you, Sophia Creator, for every woman who has said "no."

We especially remember these daughters who prophesied.
Miriam who led the women in a dance from bondage to liberation.
Huldah who set in motion a reformation of Hebrew religion.
Anna who discerned the coming of God amongst us.
Thanks be to you, Sophia Creator, for every woman who has said "No."

We especially remember the dissident daughters of the Bible.
Miriam who said "No" to the male voice representing God.

Huldah who said "No" to the male voice representing biblical authority.

Anna who said "No" to the male voice speaking liberation.

Thanks be to you, Sophia Creator, for every woman who has said "No."

At this point, the community is invited to freely name more women who have said "No." The response to each naming is: Thanks be to you, Sophia Creator, for every woman who has said "No."

Three Readings

A TEXT OF TERROR (ISA. 3:16–26)

The LORD said:

Because the daughters of Zion are haughty
    and walk with outstretched necks,
    glancing wantonly with their eyes,
mincing along as they go,
    tinkling with their feet;
the Lord will afflict with scabs
    the heads of the daughters of Zion,
    and the LORD will lay bare their secret parts.

In that day the Lord will take away the finery of the ankles, the headbands, and the crescents; the pendants, the bracelets, and the scarves; the headdresses, the armlets, the sashes, the perfume boxes, and the amulets; the signet rings and nose rings; the festal robes, the mantles, the cloaks, and the handbags; the garments of gauze, the linen garments, the turbans, and the veils.

Instead of perfume, there will be a stench;
    and instead of a sash, a rope;
and instead of well-set hair, baldness;
    and instead of a rich robe, a binding of sackcloth;
    instead of beauty, shame.

Your men shall fall by the sword
    and your warriors in battle.

And her gates shall lament and mourn;
    ravaged, she shall sit upon the ground.

A reflection follows on how this is a text of terror for daughters.

A TEXT OF LIBERATION (LUKE 13:10–17)

Now [Jesus] was teaching in one of the synagogues on the

sabbath. And just then there appeared a woman with a spirit that had crippled her for eighteen years. She was bent over and was quite unable to stand up straight. When Jesus saw her, he called her over and said, "Woman, you are set free from your ailment." When he laid his hands on her, immediately she stood up straight and began praising God. But the leader of the synagogue, indignant because Jesus had cured on the sabbath, kept saying to the crowd, "There are six days on which work ought to be done; come on those days and be cured, and not on the sabbath day." But the Lord answered him and said, "You hypocrites! Does not each of you on the sabbath untie his ox or his donkey from the manger, and lead it away to give it water? And ought not this woman, a daughter of Abraham whom Satan bound for eighteen long years, be set free from this bondage on the sabbath day?" When he said this, all his opponents were put to shame; and the entire crowd was rejoicing at all the wonderful things that he was doing.

A reflection follows on how this is a text of liberation for daughters.

The texts "Daughter-Right" and "Daughter-Blight" from Websters' First New Intergalactic Wickedary of the English Language[8] *are read.*

Song   "WE ARE DANCING SARAH AND HAGAR'S CIRCLE"[9]
and Dance
(free stepping)

Some Daughters Speak

Ruth, a young woman of our community, speaks of her dissident acts. Mary Ann, an older woman, speaks of her dissident acts. Saralyn tells and Wendy mimes the story of the prodigal daughter (a retelling of Luke 15:11–32). Clare tells the story of a daughter named "Silence" (this daughter speaks out, and her church says "Silence" must be kept in our community). Other women in the circle tell of their experiences of being dissident.

Song   "COME, CELEBRATE THE WOMEN"[10]

Offering and Sharing of Women's News

Prayers of Dissident Daughters

> With Miriam we pray
>
> **Strengthen your voice, Sophia, in each of us**
>
> With Huldah we pray
>
> **Strengthen our resolve to prophesy**
>
> With Anna we pray
>
> **Strengthen our actions for liberation**
>
> With dissident daughters of every age we pray
>
> **Strengthen our resistance to patriarchy and its evils of war, exploitation, and silencing**

Song and Dance   "WE ARE DANCING DISSIDENTLY, DAUGHTERS ONE AND ALL"

Blessing

> The blessing of the God who creates dissident daughters,
> Of Sophia Christ who raises up bowed down daughters,
> And of Sophia Spirit who empowers daughters to prophesy,
> Be with us now and with our ongoing journey.

4

Celebrating Women's Power

Oecumenische Vrouwensynoden in the Netherlands

DENISE J.J. DIJK

At the end of the historic *Oecumenische Vrouwensynode*—the first ever women's synod in Christian history—well over three hundred Christian feminists from different churches all over the Netherlands gathered for a special worship service. It was the summer of 1987. We were meeting at *Kerk en Wereld*, an adult education center in Driebergen; our closing worship service was broadcast on IKON-Radio, the Interdenominational Broadcasting Company in the Netherlands. The theme of the worship service was "Celebrating Women's Power." Many of us experienced the synod as a whole and its closing liturgy in particular as a "coming out" of the Dutch Christian feminist movement *Vrouw-en-Geloof Beweging* (Woman-and-Faith Movement). In hindsight, this historic *Oecumenische Vrouwensynode* was only the first of other women's synods to come. Anna Karin Hammar, from the Women's Desk of the World Council of Churches, had first suggested the idea of a women's synod in 1985. After the first *Vrouwensynode* in the Netherlands, women's synods were held in several European countries, and in 1996, the first European-wide Women's Synod took place in Gmunden, Austria. Dutch women from *Vrouw-en-Geloof Beweging* were coinitiators of this European Women's Synod.

IN THE BEGINNING

Vrouw-en-Geloof Beweging had emerged in the mid-1970s when Dutch women in different denominations—laywomen, women in church employment (pastoral workers, clergy, church officials), and feminist theologians—began to share their experiences of discomfort in the churches. Theologians such as Catharina

Halkes,[1] Maria de Groot, Fokkelien van Dijk-Hemmes, and Sienie Strikwerda-van Klinken stood at the cradle of this grassroots women's movement in the churches. In this movement, Christian feminists began to articulate their experiences in church and society in ways that signaled, "This is not it." The experiences of discomfort were not limited to traditional patterns of worship. The discomfort also surfaced as pain, anger, and even rage, for example, at the exclusion of women from sacramental ministry in the Roman Catholic Church. In the early stages of feminist activism in the churches, this discomfort revolved around the perceived "androcentrism" of the faith, liturgy, pastoral care, adult education, and parish work. Soon, however, small groups of women all over the Netherlands made it their business to reshape the church's ministry themselves, from pastoral care, exegesis, and liturgy to adult education. Women, for example, formed feminist pastoral care groups where people were trained to counsel survivors of sexual violence and to attend to their specific needs (such as offering support for speaking not only about the abuse itself but also about the violation of religious trust in and through the abuse). Survivors and counselors realized that "home" as well as worship was an unsafe place for many women.[2]

Feminist activism in the church also gained some institutional ground. In Protestant churches and in several Roman Catholic dioceses, women's commissions were established and granted (limited) powers by church officials. In several provinces, autonomous feminist Christian centers sprang up offering women space to become persons in their own right. Local *Vrouw-en-Geloof* groups—often closely related to traditional Catholic and Protestant women's organizations—engaged in a process of feminist Bible study. Exegesis was facilitated by the skills of Dutch feminist biblical scholars such as the late Fokkelien van Dijk-Hemmes (her death at age fifty in 1994 was untimely in many respects), Jonneke Bekkenkamp, and Magda Misset-van de Weg. Through the consciousness-raising process of connecting women's own readings of biblical texts with their particular life experiences, new life stories and a new liturgical practice emerged.[3] Feminist theologians and students organized themselves nationally in the Interuniversity Working Group for Feminist Theology. The Working Group connects women students and feminist theologians in various disciplines. University professors and doctoral students meet yearly for five days to exchange research. Two of us specialize in the field of feminist liturgy. Students also organize meetings on themes relating specifically to their needs as women students.

CLAIMING OUR RITES

In the late seventies, women in *Vrouw-en-Geloof Beweging* began to claim their own rites,[4] and some groups and individuals within the movement have continued to focus on liturgical matters. There are several forms this focus can take. Some groups meet, either for a shorter period of time or as a long-term commitment, to develop their own forms of Christian worship in an autonomous setting or in a local church prepared to give room to women claiming their own ritual authority. Other groups develop liturgies in their local parish or congregation. Women might thus conduct a series of parish-based worship services related to feminist concerns raised by *Vrouw-en-Geloof Beweging*. Finally, women's rituals emerge in local groups and at regional and national gatherings out of particular themes these groups are working on. This process of ritualizing is stronger where Roman Catholic women take the lead in ecumenical groups. In the period before 1987, women-specific liturgical elements were rare in the national gatherings of *Vrouw-en-Geloof Beweging*. The more educational and reflexive the nature of the meeting, the less liturgical the gathering seems to have been.

On the national level, several church-related adult education centers also warrant special mention in connection with the emergence of feminist liturgies in the Netherlands. *De Haaf, Contact der Continenten, De Tiltenberg*, and *Kerk en Wereld* each developed special programs related to feminist activism in the churches. *De Tiltenberg*, the motherhouse of the International Grail Movement for women, is the one place in the Netherlands where women-church liturgies have been celebrated regularly since 1985. The monthly, women-only celebrations are inspired in part by the liturgical principles developed by feminist liturgist Diann Neu from WATER in the United States. Moreover, task forces on women in church and society are in place within the National Council of Churches and the Catholic Council for Church and Society. These task forces explicitly cover developments in feminist liturgy and promote women-identified celebrations. Communication between all these groups happens through two feminist theological magazines and through yearly conferences. In the magazine *Vrouw en Woord*, women regularly publish new songs and liturgical texts and thus make them available for reception and feedback. The women's songs published there have been gathered in two volumes entitled *Eva's Lied* (Eve's Song).

OUR CONTEXT

The origins of this movement of women claiming their own rites are related to broader cultural developments, especially to second-wave feminism. Second-wave feminism in the Netherlands was influenced by two European intellectual traditions: the Enlightenment and democratic utopian socialism. Religious feminism shares this influence and like the women's movement as a whole, was facilitated by broader cultural shifts. In the 1960s, for example, young women were for the first time explicitly and "en masse" encouraged to pursue higher education and professional careers. Abortion came to be legalized. Changes to the social security system weakened the traditional link between the "right to work" and the role of the family breadwinner. Until the late 1960s this breadwinner had been assumed to be male; hence when a female civil servant married, she lost her job. In the '60s, this family ideology began to crumble. Changes in theology, liturgy, and church life echoed these cultural shifts. Among these, the following were especially significant: women entering Roman Catholic theological education; the opening of ordained ministries to women by the Dutch Reformed Church and the Reformed Churches in the Netherlands (the Lutheran Church in the Netherlands, the Mennonite Churches, and the Remonstrant Brotherhood [Arminian Church] had already opened all ordained ministries to women at the beginning of the twentieth century); the growth of ecumenical relationships; the emphasis on democratization within liturgical practice; the anthropological turn in theology; and the birth of feminist theology.

For much of Dutch history, Christianity dominated both the religious and social landscape of the Netherlands. In recent years, however, the influence of Christianity on our society has weakened significantly. Today, fewer than forty-five percent of the population consider themselves Christian. The vast majority of these belong to the Roman Catholic, Dutch Reformed, and the Reformed Churches in the Netherlands. Church members increasingly find themselves living alongside agnostics, Muslims (mostly originating from Turkey and Morocco), Jews, Hindus, and Buddhists. Christians in the Netherlands are predominantly white, middle-class, and heterosexual. Only a small number of women and men of color are Christians. Their roots lie in the "rich" colonial history of the Netherlands in the Moluccan Islands, Surinam, and several African countries, such as Ghana.

Silently and almost imperceptibly the feminist movement *Vrouw-en-Geloof Beweging* emerged in the churches in the Netherlands. Many of us, participating in one or two of the groups mentioned previously, somehow knew that we were part of a movement that had a name. By the middle of the 1980s approximately one thousand women's groups existed. They usually consisted of ten to thirty women, who struggled with themes like unemployment, heterosexism, the division of paid and unpaid labor, an analysis of unequal power relationships between men and women in church and society, the formation of a critical feminist spirituality,[5] the discovery of her-story between the lines of history, and the transformation of Christian liturgy into feminist Christian celebration. For the most part, the groups worked in isolation from each other, and attempts to give the movement more structure encountered strong resistance. The emphasis on local autonomy and opposition to hierarchical structures meant that the majority of these women's groups lacked ties with local or national institutions. Until 1987, there was no umbrella organization for the women's movement within the churches. Even *Vrouw-en-Geloof Beweging* was only a loosely knit movement, without a national board. It was only with the *Oecumenische Vrouwensynode* that the women's movement in the churches took on explicit forms of governmentality. Thus, at the beginning of the 1990s, women for the first time were chosen to be members on the board of the Ecumenical Women's Synod Foundation. From then on a specific group took responsibility for forms of continuity in *Vrouw-en-Geloof Beweging*.

THE FIRST *OECUMENISCHE VROUWENSYNODE* (1987)

In 1986, a group of women working with a task force of *Kerk en Wereld*, an adult education center related to the Dutch Reformed Church, drew up plans for the celebration of the tenth anniversary of the women's work of this center. The women wanted to make visible, for one another and for the churches, the ecumenical network of women that had formed. They wanted to highlight the "face," the power, and the skills of the many groups within the feminist movement in the churches. The women planned a gathering that would bring diverse women's groups together. They envisioned a set of recommendations as the outcome of this gathering, recommendations for women-specific policies to the churches, the National Council of Churches, and theological faculties and divinity schools. In August of 1987, well over two hundred Christian feminists gathered for a five-day symposium entitled "Woman and Power— Women's Power." Divided into ten workshops, the women discussed policies and recommendations of importance to the different women's groups. During the first four days, liturgical events or moments of meditation were conspicuously absent from the gathering as well as its workshops and discussions. As previously mentioned, celebration had not been the custom in the national gatherings of *Vrouw-en-Geloof Beweging*. The workshop on liturgy at the 1987 gathering was a notable exception. The preparation of and leadership in the closing worship fell to the participants in this workshop who thus had a double responsibility: we discussed the concept recommendations relating to our field, and we prepared and led the closing liturgy. Fortunately, most of the topics discussed were "embodied" in ourselves. This was indispensable in the process of preparing the liturgy. Fokkelien van Dijk-Hemmes facilitated our discussions and acted as our scholarly resource person.

On the fifth day, the participants discussed forty-two recommendations in a special "coming together" (*syn hodos*) of women. This gathering was the actual *Oecumenische Vrouwensynode.*[6] Seventy women, representing different parts of the feminist movement in the churches, had been chosen to vote on the recommendations. These recommendations, which focused on urgent problems in the lives of the churches and women's lives, were then sent to the National Council of Churches and to individual judicatories. Through this first *Oecumenische Vrouwensynode*, the feminist movement became visible in the churches and presented and defined itself as the equal discussion partner of the churches in the Netherlands. The choice of the term "synod" was intentional. Christian feminists defined their gathering as a "church-assembly" of women and named themselves "church" (not "women church," although opinions on that subject were divided). This synod also was significant as an ecclesial political event: for the first time, the churches found themselves confronted by an official set of recommendations from women. Prior to 1987, the general public had identified *Vrouw-en-Geloof Beweging* with concerns over liturgical and theological language. In 1987, the *Oecumenische Vrouwensynode* made clear to the churches—and to the movement itself—a much greater depth of concerns. National groups began to speak out, such as the "Working Group Religion and Incest," the "Dyke-Theology Group," the "Working Group Eve and Impoverishment," and the "Group of Black Women." All these groups had emerged in a movement that was predominantly heterosexual, white, and middle-class.

During the preparation of the closing liturgy, women belonging to minority groups in *Vrouw-en-Geloof Beweging* had also begun to voice their concerns. We confronted each other in wholesome ways. Women on welfare pointed out to white middle-class women that the liturgy being put together only reflected the latter's life experiences and excluded the experiences of women made poor in our society. Shocked by this insight, the group confronted the possibility that we unintentionally were excluding other voices. One of the results of this learning process was an invitation to women participating in the other workshops to formulate prayer concerns during the closing liturgy.

THE SECOND *OECUMENISCHE VROUWENSYNODE* (1992)

The dialogue between women begun at this first synod, including its harsh clashes, and the challenge of discerning what community spirit meant amidst unequal power relations were two of the motives behind the second *Oecumenische Vrouwensynode*. The Christian feminist movement confronted differences between women in the movement itself that had surfaced during the first synod and found expression in its closing liturgy. The first synod was evaluated at several follow-up meetings. A group of fifty women suggested that a second synod should be held, and a network of focus groups formed for communication and strategizing. Within this network, a new focus group called "Celebrations" came into being. [7] The founding of this group marked considerable developments in feminist liturgy. In 1985, a once-only national event on women and liturgy had taken place. Three hundred women had gathered for a conference organized by the Roman Catholic campus ministry at the University of Nijmegen. In 1991, women active in women's celebrations and (semi)professionals in feminist liturgy met for the first time in an ecumenical setting. Within the network developed through the first *Oecumenische Vrouwensynode*, these women continued to meet regularly in the focus group "Celebration." The activities of this focus group in the bosom of the ecumenical network rendered women's liturgies and dialogue with the churches on women's liturgial concerns more visible to the feminist movement in the churches. Possibly, the existence of this focus group also accounts for the visible increase of liturgical activities at the second *Oecumenische Vrouwensynode* where several women from this group played important roles.

The motto of the second synod, "Journey Towards a Space, Open as Well as Bound," well reflects the aims of this gathering. During the second synod, women tried hard to make visible the many differences among themselves. They did so in a space that bound them together, namely in the common struggle for liberation of women that binds *Vrouw-en-Geloof Beweging*. Compared to the first synod, the second turned inward, in that it sought to create a five-year plan of action for itself. Before the synod, individual women and groups had been invited through the synod's newsletter—distributed free of charge—to describe their contribution to the synod. Women were also challenged to commit themselves to specifics in the plan of action of *Vrouw-en-Geloof Beweging*. Thirty workshops were held in the four days of the synod. The number of workshops showed that women had much to offer and that many of us had become (semi)professionals in our respective fields. Many of the themes were identical with those discussed at the first synod, but the perspective was different. The focus at the second synod was on the movement itself, its participants, and their possibilities now and in the future.

Compared to the first synod, liturgical activities increased remarkably; they now were daily events. The opening session set the tone by including songs from a rich variety of sources. We sang songs from the secular women's movement, especially from the democratic socialist feminist tradition. We sang songs used in local and regional celebrations of *Vrouw-en-Geloof Beweging* and songs from the Christian lesbian and gay movement in the Netherlands. At the opening session Diewerke Folkertsma presented her newly published book containing adapted psalms and life stories of the struggles of women on welfare: *Eva, poets je appel: tot ze ganst* (Eve, polish your apple: till it shines).

During the synod, some of us offered liturgical workshops on consciousness-raising related to inclusive language; strategies to change the liturgy of the churches we belong to; contextual theological reading of stories and songs of women (such as songs of *Vrouw-en-Geloof Beweging*, songs of black women servants in South Africa and stories of Muslim women in the Netherlands); celebrating with our bodies; and a "multicolored service" in which white women and women of color washed each other's feet. Other women, rather than offering a workshop, chose to facilitate a "Center of Silence" during the synod.

Women of color in the focus group "Womanist Theologians" offered a four-day workshop for black women only, facilitated by Doreen Hazel. The year of the second women's synod, 1992, was also a year of mourning, a year to remember five hundred years of colonialism and neocolonialism. In the liturgy of the group that spanned the four-day workshop (and that I know only through written reports, since I am white), the women fasted and mourned on the first day in remembrance of people who resisted racism.[8] On a mourning band, each woman bore the names of people to be remembered. Together, the women then enacted a public mourning ritual in which they marched, in silence, with chains around their feet. In another ritual they expressed their anger by creating a mourning cloth. The next day saw the celebration of their transition from death to life, of singing songs of resistance and struggle. The women burnt the mourning cloth and broke their fast. They created their own symbols of life and together produced a cloth of life, expressing their commitment and their contribution to the plan of action of *Vrouw-en-Geloof Beweging*. The women then dressed themselves in beautiful clothes and went to greet their white sisters. The decision of women of color to hold a separate focus group as well as a public silent march—held while other women were sitting outside enjoying their lunch—deeply affected this women's synod and the movement as a whole. From then on, racism was part of the agenda of our synods and gatherings.

On the fifth day of the synod, a global plan of action was presented to the six hundred women and the few men in attendance. This time, everyone voted. The plan centered on eight "scandals" affecting our lives as women: the violation of the bodies of white women and of women of color; the predominance of white culture; the worldwide exploitation of women; the denigration of lesbian relationships; ideological and economic exploitation; the oppression of black and white women in the churches; the absence of interfaith dialogue; and oppression by means of language. This list of scandals was not only directed at the movement itself. At a press conference, the plan of action was also presented to the chair of the National Council of Churches in the Netherlands (who cochaired the Dutch committee of the Ecumenical Decade of Churches in Solidarity with Women). After the presentation we gathered for the closing liturgy that a group of five women had prepared (Fokkelien van Dijk-Hemmes had served as the scholarly resource once again). The theme of the celebration was "Moving in the Tracks of Mirjam: Symbols become Cymbals." The life stages of the prophetess Mirjam provided the thematic and liturgical focus. After the liturgy, all were invited to visit the "Market of Possibilities," where different individuals and focus groups shared their work and sought collaboration.

THE THIRD *OECUMENISCHE VROUWENSYNODE* (1997)

After this second synod, there was no doubt that another synod would be held. The *Oecumenische Vrouwensynode* had become a tradition. The same is true for the process of evaluation and preparation taking place between the synods. Typically, the board of the *Oecumenische Vrouwensynode* organizes a one-day national gathering between synods to discuss a specific topic and to give the opportunity to meet each other. In between the second and the third *Oecumenische Vrouwensynode*, two developments stood out as of particular importance for the continuity of the movement: the synod acquired a staff and an information bulletin. Two women, Annelies Knoppers and Joke Koehler, worked for the *Oecumenische Vrouwensynode* as staff at *Kerk en Wereld*. Their positions were subsidized by the churches (until 1998 when their work was terminated due to financial restrictions). The bulletin of *Oecumenische Vrouwensynode* is important as a news medium that informs women about developments, decisions, and activities to come. The bulletin also tracks the activities of individuals and groups committed to the working plan of the second synod in the provinces, the regions, and the cities.

As far as liturgical developments are concerned, the bulletin is silent on the struggle for inclusive language in the churches, an important issue at the second synod. Other sources, however, indicate that individual women (Coby van Breukelen, Denise Dijk, Marian Geurtsen, and Joanne Seldenrath) continue to work on this issue. The Interuniversity Working Group for Feminist Theology, for example, organized a conference at *Kerk en Wereld* jointly with the board of *Mara*, the Dutch journal of feminism and theology, to celebrate the tenth anniversary of the journal. The theme of the conference was ritual and feminist celebration, and the conference appropriately ended with a closing ritual. To my knowledge this is the first time that this particular group in *Vrouw-en-Geloof Beweging* included a ritual in its scholarly gatherings. Furthermore, Annelies Knoppers's work on the activities of *Vrouw-en-Geloof Beweging* after the second synod shows that women in local communities and groups focus primarily on two issues: language and liturgy and the impoverishment of women. In the eyes of women at the grassroots, language and liturgy are thus top priorities and gaining momentum in the local church.

By the time of the third *Oecumenische Vrouwensynode*, held at *Kerk en Wereld* in 1997, recommendations of the first synod regarding worship and pastoral care had found their way into the churches. The Arminian Brotherhood was the first church explicitly to expand liturgical language in its book of worship (one of the authors of this worship book, the Reverend Lideke In 't Veld, chaired the first and second *Oecumenische Vrouwensynode*). In 1999, the synods of three Protestant churches named sexual abuse as sin: as an evil in the eyes of God and an injustice towards a fellow human being. The synods stressed that the church clearly has to take the side of the victim of sexual abuse. Two working groups of women volunteers, the Foundation of Sexual Abuse/Violence in Pastoral Relationships (SMPR) and the National Working Group Religion and Incest, are now institutionalized and funded by the churches.

On the way to the third synod, women sensed that the problems they faced were identical to those of five or ten years ago. Women expressed the need for new approaches to these problems, for new energy, and for new visions to stir up society. The metaphor of "arousing all the city" (Acts 21:30) became the central focus for the third *Oecumenische Vrouwensynode*. Our question was, What would a city look like that women wanted to live in? The question echoed a famous song by the late Joke Smit, one of the pioneers of second-wave feminism in the Netherlands: "There is a land women want to live in." At the third synod, "city" stood for the public and political sphere, including such elements as communication, culture, city economy, and structure. Every day, the two hundred participants focused on a particular topic, and at the end of each day, two letters, written on large posters, were prepared on the day's discussion. These letters were hung on the walls for all to read and comment on. One significant additional letter was written during the synod, namely, on the ordination of women. The letter was a response to the apostolic letter of Pope John Paul II, *Ordinatio Sacerdotalis*, on the nonordination of women in the Roman Catholic Church. On the closing day, a final "Document of the City," which included the most poignant pieces of the letters written during the synod, was presented to the four hundred gathered women. The letter on the ordination of women was included in its entirety. This letter was also sent to the pope, the bishops, and the World Council of Churches.

Liturgically, the third synod continued in the tracks of the second. At the opening session, a newly published book with women-identified liturgical texts and songs was presented to the participants.[9] During the synod, members of a women's liturgy group from Groningen, *De Martini-kapel*, that has existed since 1981(!) offered a workshop out of which grew the closing liturgy. Each day of the synod began with two morning prayer services, organized by various groups, such as the "Working Group of Women in a Pluriform Society."

After the third synod, two national gatherings took place in February of 1999 and August 2000, and the fourth *Oecumenische Vrouwensynode* is scheduled for August 2002. In what follows, I share with you the closing liturgy of the first *Oecumenische Vrouwensynode* in 1987.

CELEBRATING WOMEN'S POWER

Introduction
(by one of the organizers)

This celebration has been prepared jointly by fourteen women.[10] The service marks the end of a symposium on "Woman and Power—Women's Power." We manifested ourselves as *ecclesia*, a church of women. *Vrouwenkerk* ["church of women"] does not mean a new institution. Rather, it is a movement of women inside and outside the existing churches, women who—inspired by the biblical vision of justice, freedom, and redemption—keep up the struggle against the structural sin of sexism. We have experienced that *Vrouwenkerk* does not consist of preprepared harmonious unity. There are differences in position and in interests: between black and white women, between Jewish and Christian women, between women on payroll and women on welfare, between lesbian and heterosexual women. Sisterhood and solidarity require guts: the guts to face reality through the eyes of women with a different perspective and the guts to draw consequences.

The workshop that discussed anti-Judaism during this symposium gave us the following midrash for our celebration, an adaptation of a midrash by Rabbi Moshe Leib of Sassow. This midrash inimitably makes clear what it means to look at reality through the eyes of your woman friend. I conclude with this midrash, a gift to all of us:

Tell me, my woman friend, do you love me?
I love you very, very much.
Do you know what is hurting me?
How can I know what is hurting you?

If you do not know what is hurting me, how can you say that
    you truly love me?
Loving, dearly loving someone, is knowing what hurts the
    other.

Greeting
(by one of
the organizers)

We greet each other
in the name of
I Will Be, our strength,
Our strength
once caught in a web
covered because we were invisible
buried, mutilated by names
that are not yours or mine
now that we become visible
our strength emerges
through our struggle and our yearning named
this our strength has changed:
no longer merely in service of others
but also, especially, in service to ourselves,
and our greeting blows wherever the Spirit wills.
She blows to everyone who is connected with us.

Song
of Support

"WHO HAS BORNE ME ON EAGLE'S WINGS"[11]

Prayer for Presence

Thou who art life
and calleth forth life
Thou who bringeth about separation
between darkness and light
and also bringeth us this morning:
a new day

We lay down in our midst
in your hands
that which keeps us restless and closemouthed,
that which terrifies us
that which puts us down and degrades us
that which infuriates us

that which gives us sorrow.
Have mercy on us.

Come, Spirit, strength of fire and wind,
blow through our lives.
Open us, that we will go
in the power of the Spirit.

Scripture   EXODUS 1:8–22
Reading

This reading is a translation of Fokkelien van Dijk-Hemmes.

Meditative Music

Song   "I CANNOT BUT RAISE MY VOICE"[12]
of Protest

Scripture Reading

This reading is an adaptation of Psalm 137 with the title "The Song of the Exiles," by Diewerke Folkertsma.[13]

In the land of the eater of humans
    our right to exist has been snapped off.
Our protest rings
    louder and louder;
for
those who oppress us
    demand submission from us;
those who deprive us of our rights
    want gratefulness!
How could I forget
    my remote origins?
I shall expose the mutilated story
    about my appearance,
I will lift it up again as a song of praise
    like crown jewels it will shine!

Voters and members of government
both will have to give account of their treachery,
    money-grubbers
    will be red-faced with shame.

At that time mountains of prejudice
   will be leveled and
heaps of stumbling blocks
   will be dug off.

Lamentation   "SAVE ME, O GOD, THE WATER RISES, AND RISES."[14]
All sing the first verse of Psalm 69.

Reflection   "THOU SHALT LET EVERY DAUGHTER LIVE."
This is a reflection by Fokkelien van Dijk-Hemmes on Exodus 1:22b.

Song of Hope   "THE DESERT SHALL BLOOM"[15]

Intercessions
The intercessions are interspersed with a sung refrain: "Therefore We Sing: Because Thou Art Thou . . ."[16]

Where are you?
Where can we find you?
In the whisper of lovers?
In the heart of the storm?

How are you to be recognized?
In our victory? In our fear?
In poverty, in wealth?
In black, in white?
What shall we name you?
Woman friend, my ally?
Eternal One, Lost One?

Who are you?
Mother, father,
My dearest, consuming fire?
Do you conceal your face from us?
Are you to be found in our pain, our sorrow?
Flame at the heart of our yearning for liberation?

Who are you?
Who belongs to you?
Shiphrah and Puah?
Crying Rachel, a dying Jesus?

We cannot find you in heaven,
on earth you sometimes are far away.
Can we look for you in our history?
Why seek the living among the dead?
Where are you?
In the Houses of Parliament? In the court house?
In the offices of local social services?
Behind the kitchen stove?
In our work?
In love, in treachery?
In those moments when we are lost for words?

Who are you?
Storm in our lives.
Whispered memory.
Justice dared.
Bread of our life, broken and shared.

Therefore we sing: because thou art thou . . .

We have shared our despair with each other,
we were able to encourage each other.
We want to discover people
who share despair and hope
in order to work for peace
and for justice together.

We pray for women of color and white women who
together on our way to alliance
have to face several stumbling blocks.
Give us the courage, the wisdom, and the will
to enter into this confrontation.

Therefore we sing: because thou art thou . . .

The following is spoken by a lesbian woman:

You, who are our potter [*pottenbakster*][17]
give all lesbian women in the churches
lust, love, fun, guts
to come out as dykes
to connect with one another.

The following is spoken by a survivor of incest:

> We do not ask you for liberation or for redemption
> on behalf of victims of incest,
> we rather ask you to stand by her side
> and throw in your lot with hers.
>
> **Therefore we sing: because thou art thou . . .**
>
> We pray for all women
> who feel powerless
> but are not power-less.
> Help us to do everything
> to do every possible thing within our strength
> to make life possible for each other.
>
> We pray for courage and perseverance
> for women within and outside the church
> we pray for administrators
> in the church and for policy makers,
> that their eyes, their ears, and their hearts
> will be open for women's interests.
>
> **Therefore we sing: because thou art thou . . .**
>
> Who are you?
> Where are you to be found?
> Voice that calls us to freedom?
>
> Be found here
> in us
> through us
> with us.

Song   "SONG TO COME ALONG"[18]

Sending Forth

> We have gathered here from many parts of the country
> to celebrate together ten years of *Vrouw-en-Geloof Beweging*
> we did not come empty-handed:
> one brought courage, the other brought pain
> one of us brought joy of living, the other brought struggle
> one brings us her flying into rage
> the other brings her jest.

We brought each other crown jewels and
heaps of stumbling blocks.
We also brought along Shiphrah and Puah,
we brought the guts of lesbian women,
we brought the tears of abused women,
we brought the strength of women of color.
Together we are the church of women.
Hereto the Spirit of the Name has called us
She exposes and makes us free
She empowers us to live for each other
She empowers us to set off for the struggle of liberation
of women and other human beings.
We give each other bread for the journey
for
we are on the verge of returning
to the part of the country we came from,
To heal, to liberate and feed
our own people, women,
in the place where we live.
And do not forget:
peace and justice will kiss one another.

Song "MAY WE BE FILLED WITH THE BREATH OF LIFE"[19]

Every participant receives a piece of bread (in a paper bag) to carry home with her.

5

We Are the Daughters of God

여성교회 in Seoul, Korea

SOOK JA CHUNG

IN THE BEGINNING

여성교회, our Korean women-church community, formally came into being in 1989,[1] when Korean feminist theologians and activists established a community along the lines suggested some years earlier by Western feminist theologians such as Letty M. Russell, Rosemary Radford Ruether, and Elisabeth Schüssler Fiorenza. Korean feminist theologians and activists dreamed of women themselves creating, leading, and celebrating feminist liturgies. Women theologians, especially, longed to put their feminist theologies into practice in a Christian community. Under the influence of Minjung theology, Korea's indigenous liberation theology, many pastors had started Minjung churches in the 1980s. Feminist theologies in Korea emerged from this grassroots movement, and a distinct women-church movement began that gave birth to our 여성교회 community in Seoul. Korean feminist theologies are rooted in understanding the Bible from the perspective of the oppressed and the marginalized and seek to stand by the side of those in need of liberation from the oppressive conditions under Korean political, social, cultural, and religious structures.[2]

In 1989, 여성교회 celebrated its first feminist liturgy at the Korean Centennial Building, built by the Presbyterian Church in 1985 to commemorate the centenary of Protestant missions in Korea. This is the same site where the tenth anniversary of 여성교회 was held in 1999. In the first year and a half, many Christian women came to our liturgies in search of liberation from established Korean Christian traditions. These women attended our worship services in the afternoon, after they attended the traditional Sunday morning worship in their own churches. They thus carried double responsibilities and dedicated themselves, physically and economically, to two distinct faith communities. Being members of two churches was difficult, but these women also did not feel comfortable leaving their original churches behind. As a result of this tension, the numbers of members of 여성교회 decreased even though more than two hundred women attended services at one time or another. A year and a half after the initial creation of 여성교회, the number of core members steadied at twenty or so. However, even throughout this time of "decreasing," roughly one hundred people attended regularly as visitors without becoming full members. Most of these regular visitors were theological students who had to leave for their own denominational ministries after graduating from seminary.

At its tenth anniversary in 1999, 여성교회 gave thanks for four women who had continuously attended its liturgies from the beginning. A book, 여성교회: *Stories of the First Ten Years*, was published for that occasion.[3] One of the four women declared that she could not leave 여성교회 because she had to hold up the poles of this church so that it would not crash down. It was these core members who invited me to be the pastor of 여성교회 in 1992, and I joined in the work of strengthening the poles of this church (I am a member of the Seoul Presbytery of the Presbyterian Church in the Republic of Korea, which officially sent me to 여성교회 as its pastor, but without any financial or spiritual support). Because these women, although few in number, had a special drive and passion to continue 여성교회, it has flourished with the power of their faith, expanding more and more in its own unique way in Korea.[4]

In 1997, 여성교회 started the Women's Center for Migrant Workers, 이주노동자여성센터, in an effort to live out its faith and commitment to those who are the most oppressed in Korea at this point in time. 여성교회 is located in the center of Seoul, the capital of Korea, with its twelve million inhabitants. 이주노동자여성센터 is located in a small city on the northeastern edge of Seoul, but its ministry is still an urban one. There are currently more than 140,000 undocumented migrant workers in Korea. 여성교회 stands not only with these migrant workers but on the side of all the oppressed, such as the Korean "comfort women" and the "prostitutes" around the military bases. We take part, for example, in the demonstrations in front of the Japanese embassy in Seoul for the rights of the survivor "comfort women." Issues such as the rights of these women rouse us as Koreans to assert independence from past Japanese colonialism (Korea was under Japanese occupation as a colony from 1910–1945) and to resist today's economic and cultural invasions as well as the sexual violence that has accompanied and continues to accompany war. Korea is still divided into North and South through a four-kilometer wide demilitarized zone at the thirty-eighth parallel, a legacy of the Korean War of

1950–1953. The two countries have only recently seen the beginnings of a thaw in their relationship, and 여성교회 supports efforts to seek the unification of Korea.

WE ARE CHURCH

여성교회 currently has sixteen core members and about ten occasional participants. Nine of the core members are theologically trained; the others are conversant with feminist theology. There are two Quakers, two Methodists, one Anglican, one Catholic, one Holiness member, one United Church of Canada member, and eight Presbyterians. All of us are Koreans, except for the member from the United Church of Canada. 여성교회 supports gay and lesbian lifestyles and groups, in part because of the deeply problematic character of marriages in Korea. There is much domestic violence, incest, and an increasing number of divorces. We in 여성교회 seek alternative models of family, based on equal partnership, both between the sexes and between those of the same sex.

Language is a very important issue in 여성교회. In 1994, for example, we turned our attention to the language of hymns. We studied the ecumenical Korean Hymn Book and began to rewrite some of its hymns from the perspective of feminist theology. We also collected hymns that use traditional Korean music and rhythms and changed the old traditional language transported from Chinese letters into popular Korean people's expressions. We gathered recent labor and student movement songs, as well as reunification and jubilee songs, and added them to the book. We created some women songs, too, including the "Song of 여성교회" (see the liturgy that follows). All these hymns we compiled together and published in *Our Hymns*, the hymn book we use in our liturgies.[5] *Our Hymns* also contains songs based on our reinterpretation of hymns in the Korean Hymn Book. Rather than drastically altering these hymns, we tried to be attentive to the original writers' intentions. First, we changed patriarchal and hierarchical exclusive expressions into inclusive ones. Ways of naming God such as "father," "Lord," and "head of the church" were changed simply to "God" and "Jesus." We also altered language that is authoritarian and militarized; for example "triumphant" and "victorious Lord" was replaced by "love" and "peace." Images that deny this world and focus on a future world in heaven were refocused onto a reign or community of God that can be actualized in this world. The language that stressed personal blessings was changed to a language of sharing in community. The traditional understanding of "salvation," focused on the blood of Jesus, was shifted to a new understanding of salvation as the actual living community of oneness through reconciliation and the practice of love and justice.

여성교회 has an executive committee for its main decision-making body. Almost all the core members are committee members who rotate their roles every year. They also attend various groups within 여성교회 that create the liturgies and participate in different styles of worship. There is, for example, the music group that creates services focusing on music as the main medium, or the "English" group that gives members an opportunity to worship in a second language. Most prominent is the drama group that gathers every Friday evening to create drama worship services. These worship services grow out of Bible study sessions on particular themes. All the drama worship services of 여성교회, including the one that follows, are created in this group.

OUR WORLD

Korea, with its location in Northeast Asia, historically has been considered as part of the (so-called) Third World and as a "developing" country. In the last few decades, however, the country has undergone a phase of rapid industrialization and urbanization. Since 1997, this growth has faltered due to economic problems, and Korea has experienced the tightened control of the International Monetary Fund. At this point, it is not easy to specify whether Korea is a Third World country or not, since the economic growth so evident on the surface appears to be a First World characteristic. Internally, however, the country is suffering tremendously from foreign debts.

With the exception of Shamanism, all Korean religious traditions have been imported to Korea from various other parts of the world. Buddhism and Confucianism for the most part came from China. Together, the three traditions of Buddhism, Confucianism, and Shamanism have strongly influenced Korean people's lives. For example, many Koreans think that lighting candles and using a gong are Buddhist practices, and some therefore are critical of 여성교회 for using a gong to begin worship and for lighting candles during the service.

CLAIMING OUR RITES

여성교회 has two regular worship services every Sunday. One of these services has been celebrated for over ten years by Korean Christian women every Sunday at 3:00 p.m. in the 여성교회 office. The other worship service is held at the Women's Center for Migrant Workers, 이주노동자여성센터, and meets every Sunday morning at 11:00 a.m., followed by a communal meal. 여성교회

services are held in Korean; the services at 이주노동자여성센터 are in English since the worshipers are almost all Filipina migrant workers. The English liturgies are prepared by the associate pastor of 여성교회, who is a missionary from the United Church of Canada to the Presbyterian Church in the Republic of Korea.

Worship is held every Sunday and follows the Korean church calendar. The pastor (myself) and the copastor each preach once a month. Other Sundays are devoted to creative worship services prepared by various groups in the congregation, such as the drama and music groups. The remaining worship services are given to guest speakers, some special occasions such as picnics, and creative liturgies such as body action worship, painting and artistic appreciation liturgies, storytelling liturgies, and combined worship services with the Women's Center for Migrant Workers, 이주노동자여성센터. The materials used in all these worship services, including messages and liturgies, are gathered together and published once a year.[6]

As far as liturgical space is concerned, the church office doubles as worship space. The Women's Center for Migrant Workers, 이주노동자여성센터, has its own space that is used both for worship services and as a shelter for migrant workers without jobs or housing. 여성교회 uses chairs in a circle; the Women's Center uses cushions for all to sit on the floor in a circle. Our liturgies reflect the present reality of Korean society because 여성교회 and 이주노동자여성센터 are located in the midst of people's lives. The cycle of our liturgies is created out of a combination of the Christian calendar, the Korean secular calendar with its national memorial days and festivals, and the calendar of 여성교회 with its anniversaries and retreats and picnics. The liturgies are freely created by group members and by the two pastors using drama, body language, action music, drawing, singing, and dancing. Our liturgies thus do not follow an established liturgical order but rather break free from traditional patterns.

The liturgies of 여성교회 are deeply rooted in the Korean social context. The lives of the weak and the poor and the women and children who suffer discrimination and oppression are valued and strengthened in our church. 여성교회 shares the life of Jesus Christ with the suffering Korean people, especially oppressed women, for their liberation and healing. 여성교회 believes and confesses that God has created human beings in the image of God; that Jesus Christ has achieved his mission of liberation of all people, especially women; and that the Holy Spirit is working with the oppressed, the weak, and women to strengthen them in overcoming their sufferings and in conscientizing themselves.

The most important element of any feminist liturgy should be the call to share one's life spiritually and materially. In Korean churches, however, there is no concept of "spiritual sharing" by church members or of "material sharing" by the pastors. In other words, pastors are expected to be the spiritual givers; the people respond and "thank the pastor" with material gifts. Also, if one person gives material help to the have-nots, or if a person gives spiritual help to the weak, this is a kind of sympathetic aid to the poor because the giver is richer, stronger, and wiser. It is not a true and equal sharing but rather a "one-way giving" to those "below." With this thinking, we can never hope to change the patriarchal and hierarchical structure of the church or of society. This is the weak point of male-centered ministry. There are, then, sexist and classist forms of discrimination and oppression rooted in the very structure of our churches, of the Scriptures, and of the lives of pastors (who often become the idols of Korean church women). In contradistinction, Korean feminist theologians seek to break down, metaphorically and in reality, the high altars of the huge churches and to reenvision church architecture so that altars and pulpits are on the same level as the pews.

Another problem in Korean churches, related to this elevation of the pastor to a seat next to God, is that people equate worshiping God with worshiping the pastor. This phenomenon of "worshiping the pastor" is rooted in an ideology that rejects God's partnership with human beings and created nature. "God who abides in us" became "the absolute other," and people became "absolute sinners." Being created in the image of God was a man's privilege; women were excluded from this imaging and seen as inferior. In order to remedy these distortions, women's ministry must be rooted in a vision of a God who cares for all people as a mother hen embracing her chicks. Women must embrace the image of a God who lives in and sustains all human beings, women and men. Women's ministry is thus built on the understanding that Jesus lived to practice God's will of equality. As the church was founded as a witness to the life of Jesus, the church, too, must be a community of equality. 여성교회 liturgies are based on these theological convictions and seek to embody them in worship.

여성교회 strives to be a democratic and equal community by denying authoritarian traditional religious practices and by opposing patriarchal and hierarchical church structures. The liturgies and Bible studies of 여성교회 are communal in nature, and the administration of the church is structured to enable the involvement of all members in all of the church's work. The liturgical center or altar, for example, is created on an office table set in the midst of the circle of worshipers. Central to our liturgical life are the drama worship services created by the drama group. This group meets weekly for Bible study in which the Scriptures are read from the perspective of Korean feminist theology and enveloped in a drama workshop. This process of Bible study and drama workshop can be seen as the heart of 여성교회 worship, especially when it is taken together with the Sunday worship service. Guests are invited for these drama worship services, and the understanding of the nature of 여성교회 is thus spread to the larger community. In 1994, for example, we took "Jesus" as the theme for our drama worship services, as we examined his humanity, social context, and ethnicity.[7] When, as part of this, we created the drama "Korean Woman Jesus," we were celebrating the fifth anniversary of 여성교회. In this drama worship service, 여성교회 was identified as a "female Jesus" struggling to be born.[8] Against a background of asking for economic and physical blessings from God in traditional Korean churches, we proclaimed in this drama that, on the contrary, a Korean Woman Jesus would clean up the churches and start a new community of equal participation and partnership. Instead of waiting for God to bestow blessings from above, we discover blessings within the community, living and learning together. We hope that such an image of Jesus can engender new models of being church.

As far as language is concerned, we oppose the exclusive language reigning in our traditional churches. We try to use more gender-neutral expressions for God such as Creator God, God of Justice, God of Peace, or God of Freedom. We did not use the terms "God as Mother" or "Mother God" throughout our ten-year history because we were not comfortable using those terms. "Mother God" came to us as a challenge from other feminist theologians, and we responded to this challenge in a 여성교회 drama worship. In this worship, we embraced the image of God as mother, protector, sustainer, lover, and caregiver.

SHARING A RITE

Here is one of our liturgies, a Thanksgiving drama worship service.[9] Almost all of the liturgies of 여성교회 are more liberal in interpretation than this one, which is basically rooted in a biblical message. When we created this drama liturgy we had not yet heard the news of the famine in North Korea. However, we clearly had North Korea in mind in this liturgy. The liturgy held a message for rich South Koreans, especially rich South Korean churches, and for the First World, which largely controls the world economy. Our liturgies almost always hold a current message for people, connecting to current realities and calling for social justice. As such, many of our liturgies are not readily accepted in other Korean churches. We are trying to reenvision these liturgies to include an evangelical perspective so that traditional churches might also use them.

PULL OUT SOME HANDFULS OF GRAIN (RUTH 2:15–16)

The service begins with communal singing, lead by the music group. The pastor of 여성교회 then greets the community gathered for worship, and the drama director provides guidelines on the drama worship to follow. The drama worship itself begins with the ringing of a gong to signify the celebration of harvest. The biblical text is based on Psalm 65:9–13.

READER *(with drum beating)*	God visits the earth, waters it, and greatly enriches it; the river of God is full of water; God provides the people with grain, for so God has prepared it. God waters its furrows abundantly, setting its ridges, softening it with showers, and blessing its growth. God crowns the year with this bounty; God's wagon tracks overflow with richness. The pastures of the wilderness overflow, the hills gird themselves with joy; the meadows clothe themselves with flocks, the valleys deck themselves with grain, they shout and sing together for joy.
ALL *(singing with dancing)*	Look at the birds flying the sky, they are not farming nor harvesting. They don't store grains in their storeroom, because God in the heavens takes care of them. So don't worry about what you will eat and drink. Look at the flowers blooming in the field, they do not cultivate. They are more beautiful than Solomon's gown, because God clothes these grasses. Will not God also clothe the children God loves? Seek ye first the realm of God and the will of God, for God will give you everything. Do not worry about what lies ahead tomorrow. Do your best with the work of today.[10]
ENABLER	We not only harvest abundant grains and fruits grown in our land; we have also richly harvested from the efforts we have made in our own lives. We have had a fruitful harvest of our plans and hopes, even though some of our seeds are not yet ripe, and others have failed to grow. We celebrate our harvest today and thank the God who has given us all of this.

Different people stand up or come forward with symbols of their harvest and give thanks, speaking about how they have sown seeds and received fruit. There is, for example, a prayer of thanksgiving for a farmer's harvest, a prayer of thanksgiving for women's ordination, a prayer of thanksgiving for health, a prayer of thanksgiving for happy families, a prayer of thanksgiving for the formation of 여성교회, and a prayer of solidarity with overseas friends.

ALL
(pray the prayer of 여성교회)

God of Creation, we praise your name. The realm of God will come to the world and the will of God will be done on earth. Give daily food to hungry people. As we forgive those who sin against us, forgive our sins. Lead us not into temptation and deliver us from evil. May Love, Peace, Justice, and Freedom be with God forever. Amen.

ALL
(singing with dancing)

Like the seed grows into new bud by meeting with the earth,
You and I will become new people by meeting each other.
Like the heaven creates a new day by meeting with the earth,
You and I will become a new creation by meeting each other.

Everyone holds God's Love by meeting each other,
Everyone holds God's Love by meeting each other.
They will meet again and again with love and hope,
You and I will create a new day by meeting each other.

We believe in the Love of God with endless hope,
You and I will become new people by meeting each other.
This land and our nation are the country of God,
You and I will become new people by meeting each other.

East and West will create Peace by meeting each other,
North and South will embrace in Love by meeting each other.
You and I will become new people by meeting each other,
We will make a new nation of unification.[11]

At the end of the above song, "seeds" come forward and in dancing express their identities. They dance to express the birth of their lives. The "seeds" are grain, fruit, soil, pure water, an embryo, democracy, peaceful unification, etc. All sing the following "Song of Seeds," based on Psalm 72:16. This song is sung with dancing, with the seeds singing the main lines and the people singing the response ("Olshiguna chotta, Chiwhaja chonne" is a Korean expression of joy).

The earth is full of all kinds of grain.

It's full, it's full. *Olshiguna chotta, Chiwhaja chonne.*

There are abundant grains on the mountains.

It's full, it's full. *Olshiguna chotta, Chiwhaja chonne.*

There are all kinds of fruit, as many as the trees of Lebanon.

It's full, it's full. *Olshiguna chotta, Chiwhaja chonne.*

There are many people in the cities.

It's full, it's full. *Olshiguna chotta, Chiwhaja chonne.*

There is lots of food in poor people's communities.

It's full, it's full. *Olshiguna chotta, Chiwhaja chonne.*

The earth is alive, flowing with oxygen.

It's alive, it's alive. *Olshiguna chotta, Chiwhaja chonne.*

All the water in the wells is living water.

It's living water, it's living water. *Olshiguna chotta, Chiwhaja chonne.*

Fruit is delicious because it is without pesticides.

It's delicious, it's delicious. *Olshiguna chotta, Chiwhaja chonne.*

People join hand in hand, rejoicing.

They rejoice, they rejoice. *Olshiguna chotta, Chiwhaja chonne.*

The embryo is dancing in its mother's womb.

It's dancing, it's dancing. *Olshiguna chotta, Chiwhaja chonne.*

We all practice democracy.

We practice, we practice. *Olshiguna chotta, Chiwhaja chonne.*

We create peace on the earth.

We create, we create. *Olshiguna chotta, Chiwhaja chonne.*

We dream of the unification of North and South.

We dream, we dream. *Olshiguna chotta, Chiwhaja chonne.*

In what follows, the drama group dramatizes the "suffering of the seeds."

PERSON 1   Look at me, everybody, life's not easy. There are many conditions that disturb and bother our peaceful lives. But maybe we shouldn't be bothered, because hard times also tempt and train us, don't they? . . . Hey! See what's coming. Look at the dark cloud and the typhoon with whirlwind.

Two persons holding poles with big black flags walk around the stage and through the assembly. Person 1 runs offstage. Person 2 runs in, with two blue flags following her, which will eventually overpower her.

PERSON 2   It's a big storm! It's rain. *Oop, oop, Ko Roolook!* It's a flood! The flood is coming over us. Help! Help me!

PERSON 3   Is there anybody who was drawn under the floodwaters? Did we lose anyone? Phew, the flood is over at last, but we are not safe yet. What is that sound? Listen to it.

Person 4 coming into the center, almost crawling, with two red flags following her, which eventually overpower her, while person 3 barely escapes.

PERSON 4   Water! Water! Give me water! I will die of thirst. We have had no rain. Huh! Huh! If there is no rain by tomorrow, we all will dry and die.

Person 5 praying, on her knees, but eventually also overpowered by the red flags which then leave to find other victims.

PERSON 5   Please help us! I will never sin again. Honestly!

Person 6 holding a water bowl and trembling, initially escapes the red flags but eventually is also captured. Her water bowl is taken and thrown to the ground. The red flags continue to subdue their victims.

PERSON 6   The sky god, our brother who will not give any rain, please help me! This is the last water that we have. We will all die without water. Please forgive us and pass by us.

PERSON 3   After the flood, all the earth was dried by the Sun, and there was no rain.

ALL	Flow, flow, years and months are flowing.
(singing)	From morning to night, from spring to winter.

ALL
(singing)

Flow, flow, years and months are flowing.
From morning to night, from spring to winter.
We pray and pray, pray and pray.
The earth will not give us any blessings.
The flood and the dry are coming to us one by one.
Where is our hope? What is our joy?
The suffering one is my neighbor, the sighing one is my friend.
I am trying to love, trying to love, but my neighbor is my enemy.
Flow, flow, years and months are flowing.
From morning to night, from spring to winter.[12]

In what follows, the drama group dramatizes division, inequality, and frustration.

Person 1 presents a stock of wheat and opens it, only to find it empty.

PERSON 1   When I look around now, there are not many things. We sowed many seeds, but there is no harvest. It looks like a full stock of wheat, but no grain is in it.

Person 2 searches while people with masks, eager to steal, circle around the worship space.

PERSON 2   Remaining here will only bring deep sighing to us. We must seek something to eat from somewhere else. We have to find out: Is there anything to eat? Who has something to eat and has stored it for themselves?

Person 3 circles through the congregation, taking things from a couple of people.

PERSON 3   We are looking for food. If anyone has anything valuable, we will take it. Be careful, if there is a chance, we will steal!

Person 4 takes something from another.

PERSON 4   And if I can find people who are weaker than I am, I will take things from them by force, without asking or thanking or honoring them.

Person 5 comes out and grasps something from person 4 who begs with tears to have her possession returned to her. Instead, she is kicked and falls to the ground.

PERSON 5   Even though people cry and beg for mercy, we cannot hear it. We lost our sympathy, and our attitude is indifferent and cold.

Fighting breaks out, with people grasping and taking their masks off. There is confusion and then war. The result of the war is that the world is divided. The drama group is divided into two groups.

GROUP A   One part is the people who won the war and now possess a lot.

GROUP B   The other part is the people who failed to win the war and have lost all.

Groups A and B start a play of war. Group A ends up with all the possessions of group B.

Enabler goes around and eventually stops at group A.

ENABLER   Everybody, we have experienced temptation, suffering, and confusion. More time has now passed by. It is the thanksgiving season again. People are giving thanks to God for what they have harvested: some have a lot and some have a little. Oh, you have harvested a lot. Very good, let's celebrate the harvest.

PERSON 1   Look at us, everybody. We have a rich harvest because we sweated and worked hard. Please celebrate with us.

Group A agrees and begins to eat and drink, with exuberant dancing and singing. Initially, the enabler celebrates with them, but then leaves group A and joins group B, where everyone is sitting with sad faces. Group A continues its celebration.

ENABLER   What is happening? What are you doing here? It is Thanksgiving Day. Why don't you celebrate?

PERSON 2   Thanksgiving? Granted, it is a beautiful word. But for what can we give thanks? We don't have anything, not even a head of grain.

PERSON 3   Yes, if we had grain, we would thank God for it. But for what can we give thanks?

PERSON 4   We have nothing; should we thank God for that?

PERSON 3   Let's go to the others on that side. They have a lot and are celebrating. Let's ask them to share with us. Let's find out if they have eaten and have left something for us to glean.

Group B moves towards group A.

PERSON 5   Who are you? Why are you peeping at us? Don't disturb our joyful celebration.

PERSON 6   Send them away from us. How lazy they are! While we were working hard, these people became lazy and did no work. And they are now looking for their food by begging and peeping at what others have.

PERSON 2   What? What are you saying? That because we were lazy, we don't have food. Is that what you said? But we never had anything from the beginning!

GROUP A   What a noisy people! Go away.

GROUP B   Really, it is a dirty world. What kind of people are you?

PERSON 1   Don't you feel any sympathy for them? Let's help them. Let's give them some food so that they can escape from their starvation.

PERSON 6   Oh! It's not good for them! If we help, then they will ask again and we will have to help again, because they will not try to work by themselves. Then how long can we continue to help them?

PERSON 7   You are right. I also think that we have not examined this issue fully. Let's think a moment about our future. How long will we have this food? We don't know when we, too, will become empty-handed. I know that it is important to help others, but we need to store food for our own future.

PERSON 5   Right, that's right. Don't forget the severe damage a little while ago! We cannot know the future, so I agree we must store food for ourselves.

PERSON 6   To ensure our harvest for next year we celebrate this year's harvest and give thanks to God. We have worked for a better life for ourselves and saved enough food for next year, too. So those people who are coming and going with their requests for food are destroying our solemn celebration. Let's send them away.

Person 1, who is joined by her whole group A, says the following to group B, which eventually retreats back to its own position.

PERSON 1   Did you hear and listen to what we said? We want you to go away. Go, go!

PERSON 2   We were not lazy at all. We did our best, but we could not make it. What shall we do?

PERSON 3   We don't have any place to work or any occasion to participate in the growing of food. Where is our land to cultivate? What kind of techniques do we need to develop? How much money do we need? They have it all! We have only empty hands and dry mouths.

PERSON 4   We have only unhappiness and desperation here. There is no place to ask for help.

Everybody expresses desperation. The music group sings an adaptation of Psalm 121, "From Where Will Our Help Come?"

PSALM 121
We lift up our eyes to the world, but it avoids our eyes.
We lift up our eyes to the sky, but it is just dark.
We lift up our eyes to the mountains, but they close their eyes.
We look at the earth, but there is only dust.
Our shoulders loose strength, and our knees are crippled.

Our tears fall down upon the earth, but they dry soon,
And on the earth, only our footprints remain.
From where will our help come?
We lift up our eyes to the world, but it avoids our eyes.

From where will our help come? We are hardly breathing.
God will give God's breath to us by breaking open the
     dark sky.

God will open God's bright eyes over the eye-closed mountains.

The dry sprouts will come alive.

The golden light will change our tears into joy.

Our shoulders will recover strength,

And our knees will be straightened for dancing.

We will dance and stretch our arms high.

God will dance with us.

People who ran from us will come back, and we will dance
together.

We will sing and dance hand in hand, and shoulder to shoulder.

We will dance, 덩실덩실, 덩실덩실.[13]

PASTOR   We are in the midst of a joyful celebration of the autumn harvest. However, we know that we cannot simply celebrate in our
society, because our world is shaped by division, war, inequality, and frustration. We find our hope in Jesus Christ who came
as one who reconciles into this desperate society to bring unity
in times of division, peace in times of war, equality in times of
inequality, and reconciliation in times of frustration.

Then what do we have to do in order to actualize God's
unity, equality, peace, and reconciliation in our society? We
find clues in the story of Ruth. We find clues in the relationship between Ruth, a foreign widow, and Boaz, a landowner in
the motherland. Here is an example of sharing by the haves; it
is not a story about the haves getting more. There are obviously many issues to ponder in the story of Ruth, but today we
will concentrate on one part only. In Ruth 2:15–16 we read,
"When she got up to glean, Boaz instructed his young men,
'Let her glean even among the standing sheaves, and do not
reproach her. You must also pull out some handfuls for her
from the bundles, and leave them for her to glean, and do not
rebuke her.'" According to Jewish law, widows and orphans are
protected and supported through gleaning, but gleaning itself
is not enough. The haves deliberately need to pull out some
handfuls of the heads of grain. They do this not out of sympathy or pity, but because it is important to share. This is the
sharing of their lives through giving up their own possessions.

We understand that people who want to give thanks to
God for a good harvest do pull out their own heads of grain.

To work hard is part of the joy of harvest. But the full benefit of the harvest is expressed in the sharing of life by "pulling out" grain for others to glean. Because of the nature of the gleaning process, the one who gleans does not know the people who "pulled out" the grain for her. To be able to glean is the legal right of the widows and does not depend on chance. In this kind of sharing the "have-nots" are not indebted to the "haves." It is their right to participate in the harvest God has granted. What do you want to "pull out" for others? Many gleaners are waiting for you. Your "pulling out" will create the reconciliation of our society. Let's "pull out" the food that we prepared. Please also "pull out" your possessions through our offering.

All then share in a time of reconciliation and community. Church members bring out the food to share with everybody. The offering box also passes. During this time, the music group sings the song "Sharing" and stories are exchanged among the congregation. Then the community divides into small groups and shares its thoughts and reactions to the drama. At the end, the pastor takes time for announcements, news, and the introduction of visitors.

PASTOR   The sharing of this bread and cup is a sharing of our love. You and I are friends; we have the same smile. You and I come from the same heaven; within us flows the same blood, and under the same heaven, we live. And we all have the same way to go. We are sharing a meal of potatoes that were boiled in the same pan, and apples and oranges that grew on the same land. Our eating is a sign and testimony of our reconciliation. And while we are eating, let's greet each other and reflect together on the drama message.

ALL   ADAPTED FROM PSALM 150
(singing) 아하라디아 산사디아

Praise in the holy place, praise in heaven.

아하라디아 산사디아.

The great work is done.

아하라디아 산사디아.

The great sound of the trumpet echoes afar.

아하라디아 산사디아.

캥맥캥 캥맥캥.

아하라디아 산사디아.

All living things that breathe, praise God.[14]

All stand in a circle for the communal blessing and share something that they are willing to "pull out." The pastor closes this communal blessing. All then join in the closing song, the "Song of 여성교회."

We are the daughters of God, Women Church.
It's a small church gathered by the least.
It's a community standing by the side of the oppressed.
We are filled with hope and joy.

We are the disciples of Jesus, Women Church.
It's a small church with neither high nor low.
It's a community sharing our stories in the circle.
We bless each other with hand in hand.

We are the daughters of Mother, Women Church.
It's a small church bringing people to life.
It's a community of loving and caring.
We work for justice and peace in this world.[15]

Ritual That Transforms

The Women's Centre at Brescia College, London, Ontario, Canada

PATRICIA MCLEAN

> Above all, ritual should transform its participants.
> It should heal us so that we can take part in the world's healing.
> Katherine Zappone, *The Hope*
> *for Wholeness: A Spirituality for Feminists*

 **WOMEN'S CENTRE**

Our Women's Centre is located on the campus of Brescia College, Canada's only university-level women's college. The College is affiliated with the University of Western Ontario in London, Canada. The Women's Centre opened its doors in 1990 as a unique resource and program center for students and women in the wider community. Familiarly known as The Circle, the Centre has become a part of the vibrant women's network on the Brescia and University of Western Ontario campus, and in the London region. The Circle exists to raise the consciousness of women in social, economic, and spiritual issues, and focuses on contemporary feminist spirituality. This focus of the Centre's work is best captured in our mission statement:

> The Circle
> affirms the experience and hopes of women
> and the unique process we employ
> to explore and reflect
> the sacred in our lives.
> The Circle is a forum
> where the richness of our experience,

personal and collective,
the seed of the sacred
can be uncovered, shared and celebrated.
The Circle desires to link with other women's groups
and, with them, to be agents of transformation
for women everywhere.
The Circle sponsors courses and events
and communicates through its newsletter.

The Centre's logo, a dynamic spiral, signifies the two-directional movement of a spirituality that is feminist, inward to the soul, and outward to the world.

Our programs annually attract the interest of some thousand women in the community. The interest of students in our resources and programs has been limited to certain projects, but there is a steady growth in desire to become knowledgeable and active. This educational process is slow. It seems that when students' study or research or some personal interest or crisis brings them to our door, they become enthused. Our resource center provides books, videos, journals, and tapes for research and for self-development. We also offer a credit course in Feminist Spirituality. All of our members enjoy free access to these resources, to the college library, and to our Centre newsletter, which is published three times a year. Most of the staff and all of our "working circles" are volunteers, except for students who are employed through a funded work/study program.

As stated in our mission statement, the Centre tries to collaborate with other women's groups to strengthen the network. We support women's projects and work with other groups in planning events such as International Women's Day or the World March of Women and in coordinating women-sponsored programs. In the London region, there is a loosely knit group for coordinating local activities. Women from various organizations, health care agencies, academia, unions, and student groups meet regularly for planning sessions. Our Centre values its connection with this group. These women influence us, and we see our influence with them in promoting the spiritual life and in integrating ritual into various activities. This network is a powerful locus for change.

RELIGIOUS TRADITION

Brescia College was founded in 1919 by the Ursuline Sisters of the Chatham Union, a religious community of Roman Catholic women with a long tradition in the education of women. In the many years that the Ursulines have administered the College, they have provided possibilities for alternate learning experiences and, just as important, have fostered an ethos of truth and beauty, respect for the dignity of persons, and concern for social justice—all constitutive elements of Roman Catholicism. Brescia College has always welcomed faculty and students from all religious traditions. Likewise, the Women's Centre, though deeply shaped by Catholic tradition, works beyond the boundaries of any particular religious denomination. The Centre's mission is to reflect the sacred in our lives. The women who are involved in programs and events of the Centre come from various religious backgrounds or none at all. Many of the women who participate have left their churches but have not relinquished or squelched their hunger and thirst for the sacred. A strong Christian inspiration remains implicit.

What our Centre fosters is an eclectic spirituality, a way of life in the world that is cultivated from diverse sources and expressed in many different ways. The impulse of this spirituality is a feminist consciousness. This is a spirituality that is concerned with the inner life and with worldly relationships. It is personal and political. From this broad context, it was natural that our Centre would respond as it did to a particular issue that profoundly affected women's lives in Canada.

OUR CONTEXT: VIOLENCE AGAINST WOMEN

The horror and the pervasiveness of men's violence against women reached a crisis moment in Canadian history on December 6, 1989. On that day, a young man enraged by the numbers of women in the School of Engineering, whom he perceived to be threatening his admittance, entered L'Ecole Polytechnique, a university campus in Montreal, and massacred fourteen young women, most of whom were engineering students. This event sent shock waves through the country and beyond. It was the worst massacre in Canadian history, enacted on women who were taking their rightful place in society by a man who, as he said, hated feminists. This event soon took on symbolic proportions.[1] For some, it was the culmination of all violent acts against women by men. It gave rise to a passion for action to end all forms of violence against women, a passion for action such as Canadians had never known before. The need for new consciousness, for support of women's shelters, and for people to act together was never so strong. Others, however, denied the import of this event. These people preferred to see the massacre as the isolated action of one madman. For us at the Centre, it became important to take action with other groups to counter the latter view that was widely proclaimed in the media.

In the months following that memorable day, the Women's Centre—which had opened its doors in the wake of the massacre—became part of the network of action for change. The Centre would act out of its particular mission. For the Centre staff and volunteers, this event and the subsequent action had moral significance and invited a spiritual response. We decided to plan a communal Service of Re-Membering for the first anniversary of the Montreal Massacre on December 6, 1990. We would invite the participation of women and men, students (including those from the School of Engineering at Western), those working in agencies or activist organizations, and people from the general population, who would remember the fourteen women and together with them all women victimized by men's acts of violence. We believed that our solidarity would be strengthened to act for change to end violence against women through this prayerful remembering.

CLAIMING OUR RITES

In her book on feminist ritual thealogy, *To Make and Make Again*, Charlotte Caron writes about the purpose of rituals: "Rituals have the power to help people find solutions to their problems. Often they give space to think about things that are troubling, to hear principles of action, and to gain perspective by moving outside one's own limited interests and viewpoints." [2] We wanted to create sacred time and sacred space for listening and reflection in order to make sense out of our existential situation. We wanted to create a ritual, but we knew the "danger" lurking in that word. Though firmly rooted in Christian tradition, the more popular understanding of "ritual" connected the term with so-called pagan events or devil worship. Because of the many dubious meanings of the word "ritual," we opted, in the following two years, to call our event "A Service of Re-Membering." Boldness grew with experience, and soon we named it what it was—a ritual. For us it was a political act to claim the word, shape its meaning, and exercise our right to create ritual and enact it in the public domain using new symbols and gestures. Rosemary Radford Ruether has underlined the importance of symbolic action in effecting change. She claims that it is not enough to engage in critical reflection and social action: "One needs communities of nurture to guide one through death to the old symbolic order of patriarchy to rebirth into a new community of being and living. One needs . . . deep symbols and symbolic actions to guide and interpret . . . the journey." [3]

SHARING A RITE: "IN RITUAL, WOMEN EXPRESS THEIR HOPES"[4]

Nowhere is the revolutionary quality of feminist spirituality more clearly expressed than in the rituals that women create—rituals that are symbolic enactments of the personal inward movement and the outward dynamism of that spirituality. Ritual has been compared to poetry, both helping us to access that deep place within "where hidden and growing our true spirit rises"[5] and to express that creative spirit for radical change in our world. In feminist ritual, that inner movement toward personal awakening and the outer movement toward action are held in intrinsic relationship.

The "Ritual of Re-Membering" has been held at Brescia College on every anniversary of the Montreal Massacre since the event occurred in 1989. The elements of that ritual, though modified each year, have become familiar to those who participate year after year. Participants have come to expect certain things. The chairs will be arranged in circles, fanning out from the central sanctuary, and covered in multicolored cloths. Fourteen empty chairs will surround the centerpiece, draped one year with colored scarves and another with unfinished dress patterns in rough cloth. The haunting sound of drums will open the ritual with the rhythmic heartbeat. All the symbols chosen have a particular significance in women's lives. For some people, these symbols seem ordinary; for women they are anything but ordinary. They signify what we consider sacred. They also describe the new paradigm that we envision with wholesome patterns of relationship to replace those that have been damaging in our experience.

Feminist rituals are usually planned around an issue or a rite of passage that touches women. The murder of the fourteen young women in Montreal was such an event, shattering us so thoroughly that it was difficult to express in words. It was a personal violation, a violation that resonated in our experience. It was not an isolated event; it was the tragic culmination of the everyday violence against women that is still tolerated in our society. For us Canadians, it was a watershed event, moving us together with an intensity we had never known before. Tears were not enough. We captured the energy of our brokenness, tears, and anger and let them be transformed into action for change—to end violence against women in all its forms. Both women and men became part of the action, but women needed to act on their own and to do it their way.

In feminist ritual, there are gestures that take us into the grief and sadness and lift us into hope and power. It is poignant when women engineering students light a candle when a murdered woman's name is read and when participants name women they know who are victims of violence. The pervasiveness of violence is overwhelming. Those present sense the brokenness, the "dismembering," but spoken words and a time of silence create the milieu for transformative activity within persons and the community. This transformation is no more poignantly embodied than in the gesture of dance. The beauty, the strength, the rhythm, the power of one woman's body as she moves is representative of all that is hoped for. In such a dance, there is an appreciation of women's bodies, moving freely and fearlessly, the body "re-membered."[6] Dance is a revolutionary gesture. It fuels the action of women and men as they return to their homes and workplaces.

Feminist ritual encompasses many varieties. Some rituals take place in small groups and are much less structured than our "Ritual of Re-Membering" and not so public. All feminist rituals have certain commonalities. They are occasioned by issues and events that are close to women's hearts. They are expressed through symbols, gestures, and words that are significant for women—naming and choosing what represents "life" for them. In making their choices, women are claiming their authority in the public domain, an authority that has so often been denied. They are reclaiming their power and becoming agents of change in the world. This is a slow and arduous process in which there is often burnout, backlash, and loss of hope. But our impatience for change remains. In ritual, we are strengthened personally and communally. In ritual, our passion is ignited "to make and make again where such unmaking reigns."[7]

Following is a description of the program that we follow in our ritual. There is a conscious effort in this ritual to create solidarity, to move the community through grief to action. A special effort is made to use few words and to let symbols and gestures "speak" for themselves. After all, they are a language of their own. We always use a woman's work of art that is expressive of the theme for the poster and program. People have remarked that in our ritual, we make no mention of God. For some this is a gross omission! However, it is our strong intent to create sacred time and sacred space—in which we know that God (the divine or whatever you wish to name the presence) is present and active without necessarily being named. Thus, the participants, who come from various religious backgrounds, feel at home and free to name the sacred presence in their own terms.

THE RITUAL OF RE-MEMBERING

Our ritual is always held on December 6, the National Day of Remembrance proclaimed by the Government of Canada in 1993.

Drumming marks the beginning of the ritual with the rhythm of heartbeat.

Welcome and Opening Statement

The welcome and opening statement provide the context for the gathering, recalling the history behind our ritual and introducing the theme, "Feel the pain, find the power." (It is important to note that any person who speaks does so from a different location in the circle).

Remembering the Women

The names of the fourteen young women murdered on December 6, 1989, are read aloud. As each name is read, a candle is lit and carried to the central altar. Being affiliated with the University of Western Ontario, we also name and light a fifteenth candle for Lynda Shaw, a University of Western Ontario engineering student who was murdered in 1990. Then people in the assembly name and light small candles to remember other women, victims of violence. After the reading of each name, the assembly responds with "Feel the pain, find the power." Here are the names of the fourteen young women murdered in the Montreal Massacre:

GENEVIEVE BERGERON
HELENE COLGAN
NATHALIE CROTEAU
BARBARA DAIGNEAULT
ANNE-MARIE EDWARD
MAUD HAVIERNICK
BARBARA MARIA KLUCZNIK
MARYSE LAGANIERE
MARYS LECLAIR
ANNE-MARIE LEMAY
SONIA PELLETIER
MICHELE RICHARD
ANNIE ST. ARNEAULT
ANNIE TURCOTTE

Meditation

A three or four minute period of quiet follows. Music plays in the background, namely, "Ancient Pines" by local Canadian musician, Loreena McKennitt.[8]

Speaker

An active and committed woman from the community speaks, underlining the progress toward change, the possibility that is in this community, and action that we must take.

Quiet Reflection

A time of quiet reflection follows, allowing the participants to integrate the message.

Dance

A woman, in dance, evokes the spirit of hope and the power of change.

Closing Remarks and Announcements

Closing Song

We always close with the song "This Tough Spun Web"[9] by Carolyn McDade, inspiring a sense of power in community as we leave:

> This circle opening moves with deepened faith
> Our lives to birth a living dawn
> As love renewed turns in our common way
> Creating hope we carry on.

CONCLUSION: THE POWER OF RITUAL

Each year as this closing song is sung, more and more voices sing together in chorus. In fact, the chorus gains momentum through each verse. Perhaps this rising chorus speaks for the power of ritual—a power that is alive in the ritual planning committee as it goes through its long process of working together that is a ritual in itself. It is present in the assembly as it attends with utmost reverence and deep emotion in the presence of "terrible beauty" that permeates its consciousness—a power that emanates outward to women and men. Because of this power, women and men keep living courageously to replace symbols, gestures, and words that are exclusive and oppressive with those that truly touch our strength and the great Power that works in us and among us—a power that can transform us as individuals and communities and can effect the social and political structures in which we live. Ritual does, indeed, hold the power to transform, "to create the possible."[10]

Springtime:
September in Chile

The Collective *Con-spirando* in Santiago, Chile

UTE SEIBERT[1]

We are a community of women who have been meeting since 1991 to share our intuitions concerning the sacred, concerning life. Our community, *Con-spirando*, was born in the postdictatorship years in Chile, in the so-called period of "transition to democracy." This process of transition in Chile began in 1990, after seventeen years of a military dictatorship associated worldwide with the name of Augusto Pinochet. Pinochet had come to power in 1973 in a bloody military coup that ended the elected socialist government of Salvador Allende. The transition from Pinochet's military dictatorship to democracy, begun in 1990, was the result of an agreement with the military; this agreement thus relied heavily on the state apparatus and on the political establishment. The progressive social movements, on the other hand, that had been a vibrant presence during the years of military dictatorship became fragmented and less visible during this period of transition. These movements are coming together only very slowly once again. The political climate during the transition time can be characterized as a search for consensus, above all in regards to the massive human rights abuses under the military dictatorship. The hope was that with the passing of time, Chile would become a modern democratic society and macroeconomic indicators would stabilize—at least such was the hope of neoliberal economics. These developments, although accompanied by sustained unemployment, would lead Chile to have an "advantage" for its exports on the global market. This reigning neoliberal economic logic has produced many forms of social injustice in Chile. Overcoming this logic and its effects on the Chilean people demands the reconfiguration of the progressive social movements and, indeed, of all organizations with a vision for sustained local activism. But such efforts at reconfiguring and articulating a new progressive social politics are not legitimized by or recognized in the wider public sphere. Without a public voice, however, these efforts remain invisible as political actors.

Within the culture of consensus that marked the period of transition to democracy, little room was left, in practice, for debate and argument. This fact—perhaps initially justified because of the relief associated with the peaceful transition toward a more democratic state—slowly gave rise to passivity, indifference, and a growing individualism. The majority of Chileans either seeks to survive within the system of consumption or to have nothing to do with *este país*, "this country, Chile" (with its traditions, customs, etc.), which has undergone momentous changes without stable points of reference by which to understand and to confront the great crises at the turn of the millennium.

THE WOMEN'S MOVEMENT IN CHILE

The period of transition to democracy and the political, social, and economic processes just described also affected the women's movement. This movement had been a vibrant and articulate presence on the political scene during the military dictatorship in the 1970s and 1980s. In the larger context of the military repression of civil liberties the voices of women had surfaced, first defending and demanding human rights in general, and then detecting and defining specific issues of gender.

In this period,[2] numerous women participated in organizations in defense of their human rights, in labor workshops, and in communal kitchens. All these were organizations created by women to defend life. Many of these groups existed within the churches or functioned under the churches' eaves. These groups of social involvement and struggle were also the places where women became aware of their situation as women. The awareness of gender thus developed in the context of the political struggle against the military dictatorship and out of social justice, solidarity, and self-help groups. In many cases, this process of conscientization was also closely related to women's religious commitments. It was their faith commitment that motivated many women to get involved in social struggles and at the same time offered interpretive lenses for such involvement. Liberation theology was especially important here. On the other hand, women's increasing conscientization also led them to question the roots of the oppression they were living through and the theological and ecclesiastical justifications for this oppression, especially in relation to sexuality, family, motherhood, reproduction, and decision making.

Throughout the 1980s, a time of relative liberalization during the military dictatorship, many nongovernmental organizations also supported and facilitated the growing conscientization and political organizing of women. Popular feminism emerged with greater strength and articulated its demands in the well-known slogan "Democracy in the country and in the home." The women's organizations participated on a large scale in the ensuing process of transition to democracy. Together with the advent of democracy, however, a process of public institutionalization began within the women's movement. The most visible expression of this institutionalization in the formal political sphere was the creation of the government agency SERNAM, *Servicio National de la Mujer* (National Women's Service). This ministerial-level organization introduced and implemented women-friendly public policies, especially on issues such as domestic violence, equal employment opportunities, and labor rights. The implementation of these policies, however, was marked by numerous limitations, such as the fact that in Chile, conservative sectors and the Catholic Church still carry much weight in any discussion related to family, sexuality, and reproductive rights. At the same time, other women's groups have emerged that are more autonomous and have resisted all attempts that would compromise that autonomy. Among women's groups and organizations formed during the military dictatorship, one notes a move from social and political struggle towards self-help, women's spaces, gender analysis, and an insistence on the importance of women's everyday lives.

WOMEN AND THE CHURCHES

During the military dictatorship, the churches, and especially the Catholic Church, presented themselves as a safe haven for solidarity groups, self-help groups, and human rights organizations. The churches were thus also a privileged space for women, who for the most part formed these groups of resistance. In these groups, women began to alter and expand their traditional roles as mothers, protectors, and nurturers of the family, and to claim new spaces and roles for themselves. At the same time, however, this process was not antagonistic to the teachings of the church: woman continued to be "mother," the one who sacrificed herself in service of others. The fact of now having a "job," of joining other women in the struggle to guarantee the survival and well-being of their families (through communal child care, handicraft workshops and the making of *arpilleras* [wall hangings with a political connotation], solidarity work with the victims of political repression, and health groups) legitimized the active presence of women outside the home and in traditionally male-dominated spaces.

But beyond providing legitimacy and work outside the domestic sphere, these women's groups also became a space where many women became aware of their situation as poor women, as urban slum dwellers, or as working women. An awareness of gender-specific oppression emerged, that is, a sense of being discriminated against specifically for being a woman rather than simply for being poor. Professional women working with women from the popular sectors underwent similar processes of conscientization. Within Christian communities also women began to emerge as women and to define themselves and their women-specific needs. In the process of searching for joint solutions to common social problems, these women forged paths of solidarity and trust. Soon they began to share other problems, concealed initially as "private": women began to speak of women-specific problems, of domestic violence, of their own sexuality, and of their relationships with their partners or spouses. The normative narrative of what it meant to be "woman"—namely, mother, wife, and homemaker—came under intense scrutiny. Women recognized that in this narrative, they had been defined as dependent, that is, solely in reference to others: to children, to husband, and to the family and the home. As women began to question the givenness of this normative narrative of womanhood and acknowledged themselves as subjects with other possible narratives, they recognized the social and cultural constructions of gender. A painful process of conscientization was set in motion, simultaneous with an intense antidictatorial struggle.[3]

Christian women were part of this process. Often, however, they discovered that in the church and in their parishes, they could not address these women-specific topics. Sexuality, unwanted pregnancies, birth control, violence, incest, and partners living together (Chile has no divorce law) were all matters that women could not freely raise within the confines of the church. Christian women began to question ecclesial teachings that silenced and marginalized women, teachings built on the dichotomy between Eve (the evil woman who allowed herself to be tempted and thus became responsible for the expulsion from paradise) and Mary, the Virgin Mother (the impossible model of what it means to be a "good woman"). Women questioned the condemnation of sexuality and the denigration of pleasure. They pointed out that theologies with a negative view of the body are often the same theologies that perpetuate and justify violence. In the 1990s, the turn of the churches to their traditional concerns of doctrine and morality and a renewed emphasis on evangelization rendered more difficult the participation of women in the life of the church. These women, after all, had experienced themselves as protagonists of a vibrant social struggle, as fighters for life; they now wondered how they could also be protagonists of their own life and their own faith in the church.

For almost twenty years, then, women had, in different contexts, actively and critically reflected on their faith and their spirituality. They read and reread the Bible, tackled ethical and theological topics, and created their own liturgies and celebrations. Churches and religious congregations now had women's groups and pastoral teams; different women's programs[4] existed within the religious realm, and some of them integrated a critical perspective of gender in their work. There are, however, few written records of women's activism in the churches, in social organizations, or in the women's movement. For the most part, this women's history is an oral tradition.[5] Nevertheless, some shared insights from women's activism and struggles during this time are readily evident. There was, for example, the realization among activist women of the relationship between their social and political commitments and struggles, on the one hand, and the discovery of themselves as individual persons with rights on the other. There was also the growing interest among these activist women in reconstructing their own personal, communal, and collective history—of the country, of their gender, and of the human species—in the appreciation of the present and the insistence of living in it; in the discovery of the personal and the collective body; and in a commitment to women's health and bodily integrity. This reconstructed history would also reflect an interest in ecology; a search for spirituality in everyday life and for celebrations, rituals, and safe spaces of and for women; a will to shape one's own symbolic and linguistic universe in women-friendly ways; an emphasis on ecumenical sharing; and the discovery of other religious and spiritual traditions—Asian, for example—and of the indigenous roots both of Chile and of other regions.

AND SO WE WERE BORN:
THE COLLECTIVE *CON-SPIRANDO*

It was within this context that at the beginning of 1991 some women suggested that we begin to gather with the express purpose of celebrating women's rituals. The suggestion was open-ended; there simply was a desire and an urge to gather in this way. The response was overwhelmingly positive, and we began to gather as a group of women every other week for the next two years. Sometimes five women would come, sometimes fifteen. Slowly we began to develop an appropriate shape and space for our women's celebrations. Initially we rotated among different spaces but kept to the bimonthly round of our celebrations. We shared our celebrations with women from different walks of life—Christian women; women with indigenous or feminist roots; women coming from other women's groups, from the human rights movement, and from ecumenical groups. Based on its own needs and creative energies and intuitions, each group prepared the celebrations we shared in our fortnightly meetings. Typically, one or two women would prepare a celebration. At times, the celebrations were created especially for that particular moment. At other times, the women drew on rituals that had been created by other women in and for other contexts. This process of ritual production and adaptation opened up to us a diversity of symbols, movements, music, texts, and silences.

Much later, other needs appeared in our conversations. The fact that we had opened ourselves to sharing this ritual space, that the number of new women who attended our celebrations had increased, and that we desired to create new rituals made us wish for a place of our own. Here we could delve deeper into our experiences of the sacred and share the knowledge gained from our experiences within the churches and with ecumenical organizations with whom we were in contact (many of them tied to liberation theology), with the prophetic church, and with those struggling for human rights and engaged in the struggle for democracy in Chile. Many of these groups had left little space for women and for our specific questions. We confronted our own grow-ing unease with patriarchal institutions, with macho attitudes, with the silence and invisibility of women, and with our ambivalent experiences in the churches.

One day, this unease received a name. We had just finished one of our rit-uals and were standing in a circle, holding hands. One of the women said, "Do you know what we are doing? We are *con-spirando*.[6] We breathe together, we all share the same air, and that connects us with every living creature. We also share the same dreams of so many women and their experiences in the churches, the same utopia of justice and of change. We are *con-spirando*." Women in a circle, breathing together and joined with others, sharing a vision and connected with everything living—this was a very powerful image for us. When it was time to name ourselves, we affirmed this experience: we are *Con-spirando*.

Within the space of discovery and experimentation we had claimed for our-selves, a desire to share our celebrations, reflections, and insights with other women began to grow. We also felt the need for a means of communicating our insights in Chile and other parts of Latin America as well as ways to hear the voices of women from other parts of the world where feminist theology and women's rituals flourished. The idea emerged to publish a journal, so that we Spanish-speaking women might be able to connect with the reflections of women from the United States, or Africa, or Asia. Our dream was to create a space for networking that would allow us to communicate safely and freely. On International Women's Day, 1992, we launched the first issue of the *Revista Latinoamericana de Ecofeminismo, Espiritualidad y Teología: Con-spirando*. The preface to this first issue continues to express many of our intuitions and desires:

We are a group of women joined together in Santiago, Chile, who want to invite and to incite our sisters, our Latin American companions, to unite with us, to recognize each other, to speak our own word, to weave a web in which our energies, our creations, and our insights can circulate.

We know that there are divisions throughout our continent . . . women come from distinct faith traditions, be they Catholic or Protestant Christians, be they from Asian faith traditions, or aligned with the indigenous faith traditions of the native peoples of these lands. Women may be nuns, ex-nuns, pastors, theologians, lay missionaries, or simply women who are developing their spirituality, constructing their theologies from their bodies, their spirits, their lives, and their experiences as women, thus looking at the world from a feminist perspective which integrates the dimensions of class and race that so sharply mark our continent and the dimension of gender. We women—never absent from the struggles for liberation from all forms of oppression—some time ago started to become aware of a particular form of oppression constructed on the basis of sexual difference. This oppression is patriarchal or androcentric culture, that is a culture centered on the male. We have begun to name this system which, when it subordinates more than half of the population simply because of its sex, mutilates and impoverishes in ways which have scarcely begun to be recognized, the development of humanity in its entirety.

We have also begun to discover that the same relationship established in a patriarchal and androcentric world between men and women, namely, a relationship of hierarchy and power, is also established between men and nature. This kind of relationship has led, in our own times, well beyond the limits of a moral crisis. It has become a question of survival.

We thus claim a feminist perspective. This feminist perspective—constructed within the diversity of class, race, age, and cultures—embraces also our anguish and our love for life on our planet. This life we perceive to be radically threatened at the present time. We embrace a deep ecological consciousness similar to that which our original grandmothers in this land most certainly had. This journey, this web we have begun to weave is the search for a spirituality that might speak to us and join us together, a healing and liberating spirituality. We thus begin developing new theologies in critical dialogue with the Christian tradition, exploring the submerged roots of the indigenous peoples, freely delving into our own experiences and our religious imagination. We women have been absent from the theology studied and taught in the universities, absent both as subjects of theological vocation and also as subjects of reflection. Our lives, our everyday practices, and our spirituality do not surface in theological reflection; our experiences of suffering, of joy, and of solidarity are not taken seriously there.[7]

Much of this summons in the first issue of our journal *Con-spirando* still stands. But today we also have a space of our own, the first floor of an old house in the center of Chile's capital city, Santiago. It is here that we produce our journal, gather, and celebrate. A patio with trees and plants is the favorite place for our rituals.

CLAIMING OUR RITES

Our beginnings were marked by our desire to celebrate together, and our celebrations continue to be a central feature of our activities. There are times when we begin our meetings with Asian meditative exercises such as tai chi or shibashi. There are also special moments that we celebrate: journeys, farewells, joy or sorrow, our friendship. Our ritual space is open to other women. We do not strive to act as priests or ritual experts. We rather think of ritual as part of the everyday life of a group and of people. We are interested in empowering, inviting, and inciting the participants to celebrate and develop their own rituals.

With time we have established a regular round of celebrations. We celebrate five rituals a year, namely, the four changes of the seasons, and, on October 31, the memory of women burned as witches. These rituals are open to all women who want to participate in them. It is a sacred time and space for us. Several years ago, some men also began to participate, at first men who were friends and husbands of women from within *Con-spirando*. We then opened two rituals a year for men. After a while, the restriction to two rituals was lifted for men and youth who did not find a spiritual home in the churches. They are now welcome to participate in our rituals and find their place in our journey.

In the process of creating our rituals, we have noticed that there are elements, moments, and situations that recur in all our celebrations. The first such element is the intentional making of sacred space, of a sacred circle. Through various means, we establish a space separate from everyday life. Often, recovering ancient indigenous traditions, we invoke the four elements, earth, air, water, and fire. We search for our rootedness in the earth. We also often begin by breathing together, thus experiencing the energy that begins to flow in our midst. Depending on the particular reason for our celebration, we choose specific symbols, movements, and sounds to express our emotions, feelings, needs, and desires. The power of our shared energy circulates and creates room for the expression that each of us is seeking. We make room for sharing laughter, fun, playfulness, lament, silence, and emotions. We trust enough to let ourselves go. The sacred space contains us. When drawing a ritual to closure, we give special attention to returning our energy to the earth, before opening the sacred circle. The celebration always continues in the sharing of food and conversation.[8]

The seasons of the year, the cycles of nature, and the elements—air, water, fire, and earth—are fundamental to our celebrations, especially since in a large city such as ours, the relationship with nature has become so fractured. But our ritual recourse to nature is never decontextualized and dehistoricized. The beginning of spring, for example, gave rise to a ritual we called "September in Chile." This ritual not only celebrates a particular change of season but summons the different events and memories that this month evokes in Chile (September 11, 1973: the military coup; September 18: Independence Day). Our ritual by no means is timeless but rather seeks to integrate the cycles of nature and the events of history and to allow their symbolic and ritual expression. Other celebrations of ours might challenge the defining power of Christianity and its characteristics as a religious tradition coming from the Northern Hemisphere. An example is December 21: in the Southern Hemisphere, this is the day on which we celebrate the summer solstice, the longest day and the shortest night of the year. In Chile, this is the height of summer. Ripe fruits, summer aromas, and colorful flowers abound. The school year ends, and the holidays draw near. Christmas, on the other hand, comes to us accompanied by symbols such as the snow-covered Christmas tree and candles representing Christ as the light that appeared in darkness. These are fitting symbols for the cold winters of the North but not for us at the height of summer. So we look for other symbols from within our own reality that express the promise of abundant life born with the birth of Jesus. Fresh fruits might be such a symbol for us. We also draw on Chilean traditions from colonial times when Christmas was a time of carnival, a time of turning the world and its social hierarchies upside down.

There are also more personal celebrations that connect with our lives and with "death—life from the other side," as the *Con-spirando* issue on death was called. We created this ritual at a moment when a number of friends and companions of *Con-spirando* had died. Some of us had been out of the country at the time of these deaths and thus were unable to attend the funerals. We realized that we needed a ritual to say goodbye to our friends who had died: Susan, Dolores, Christa, and Madonna. We remembered each of them by gathering and celebrating a simple ritual in our backyard garden. We gathered photos of our friends and objects that had been significant to them; we listened to music that they had liked; we shared memories and stories that brought our friends' skills and weaknesses to life, and with these their smiles and their strength. We planted flowers, jasmine and bougainvillea, and our patio now continues to bring forth the memory and presence of each of these women.

SHARING A RITE

This ritual forms part of our regular round of celebrations. Every September when spring begins in the Southern Hemisphere we celebrate it. It is, however, not only the beginning of spring that we thus mark ritually. September in Chile is also the month of the military coup of 1973. September 11 marks the bombardment of the presidential palace, the death of President Allende, the beginning of the arrests and disappearances, the torture, the repression, the exile, the struggle for justice. Another important date in Chile is September 18, Independence Day, with its national festivities and the memory of the country's independence from Spain. Traditionally, this has been a feast day where the national dance, the *cueca*, is danced, and traditional foods, such as *empanadas*, and red wine are consumed in abundance. However, the festive character of this celebration changed markedly during the years of the dictatorship because it came too close on the heels of the anniversary of the military coup. These dates with their significance and their histories are written into our lives. With all this in mind, then, we created our ritual.

SPRINGTIME: SEPTEMBER IN CHILE

In the patio of our house we join together on a night in September. In the center of our circle a large bonfire is lit. There are small flower pots filled with soil, a water bowl with seedlings of medicinal plants, and a pitcher of water.

Welcome

> We begin our celebration in a circle, our circle of equals, as we prepare to journey together along the path of memory and hope, to con-spire, and to plant together. We are grateful for this possibility to gather together so that we might know that we are not alone in September in Chile.

Invocation

> Embracing one another, with our eyes closed, let us listen to a beautiful melody.

A music tape is played. When the music ends, a speaker says,

> This is us; here we are; it is September in Chile. Let us make room for the words, memories, and feelings that come to us when we get in touch with ourselves, with September in Chile. Let us speak these words, be it in a loud voice, in a soft

voice, in a low voice, at the top of our voice, as the words may come.

Words are then called out:

solitude, death, fear, silence, the *cueca*, flying kites, a new dress, the disappeared, feeling powerless, the Spring Circus, trees in full bloom; my daughter was born in September; little white shoes that I received as a gift when I was a little girl, silence, *empanadas* and red wine, pain.

Women speak these and other words in different voices and with varying degrees of loudness. Our words are accompanied by drumbeats that begin very softly and move into a mounting crescendo, until one person says again,

This is us; here we are; it is September in Chile.

Holding hands, we begin a rhythmic movement that soothes and calms us. We give expression to what our bodies experience at that moment. One woman sings; another remembers her native country where the seasons are different; another recalls other peoples who also live through a September that breaks their spirits. From memories we then journey to desires.

Invocation to the Fire and to the Air

We ask the fire to transform our powerlessness into vision, our pain into energy for change.

We conclude the invocation, breathing (con-spirando) *together: inhaling, we move forward and raise our arms; exhaling, we move back, lowering our arms. These movements, which fill us with energy, are repeated several times.*

We have asked the fire to transform us, and we have experienced our connection in breathing together. We have shared the feelings, the memories, and the thoughts that are evoked in us by "September in Chile." We are in touch with our personal and collective histories.

Thanks to the Earth and to the Water

September is also the beginning of spring, and today we celebrate this beginning. For several days now, we have been able to see the signs of spring: the trees in bloom, the new buds, the brighter and warmer days, the new energies, sensuality, and desires that arise in our bodies. Spring is arriving, a new turn in the wheel of life, part of a cycle that develops independently of us, but that involves and envelops us.

We want to join this cycle. In a moment we will be sowing; we are going to plant medicinal plants today—mint, rue, and balm—which also are awakening and putting forth leaves again this spring. We want you, at the end of the celebration, to pick up the plants and to take them to your own home, to your women's centers, to your workplace or to your organization. We invite you to plant these plants and to put into them your desires and your hopes. When we have planted the seedlings, we know that they need care, watering, light, and time in order to grow. They have their own rhythm and time, just like our projects and desires.

Accompanied by cheerful music, we go to plant the seedlings in small flowerpots that we had placed at the center of our circle, next to the fire. Each person plants and waters her seedling. Some women share the hopes and desires that they connect with this planting.

We form our circle again, holding hands. The same beautiful music with which we began this ritual is played again.

We are grateful to the earth for the opportunity it offers us each spring to witness the miracle of its renewal. We are grateful to the water, which makes it possible for us to continue trusting in the power of life, which recycles itself infinitely, washing over many forms of violence. We put our hands upon the earth, returning energy to the earth.

As a way of bringing closure to our circle, we pass a kiss one to the other and open the circle. Then we begin to dance among the trees of our patio that have just begun to bud, and we share food and drink.

Women Gather for Worship

The Catholic Women's Network in Clapham, London, United Kingdom

VERONICA SEDDON

IN THE BEGINNING

"Women gather for worship on the first Friday of each month, 7:30 p.m., at 7 Nightingale Lane, Clapham, London: bring food to share"—so reads the flyer. The initiative for this venture comes from Catholic Women's Network. The aim of Catholic Women's Network is to provide a network of support that will empower women to grow and mature in their spiritual lives; encourage and enable women to engage in theology; work toward participation of women in every aspect of church life; and create new ways of worshiping together.

Catholic Women's Network has its roots in a 1984 conference entitled "Called to Full Humanity." Rosemary Radford Ruether participated in the conference and supported the formation of our network. Sixty-six women from different Christian traditions who attended the conference went through a process both of "denouncing" aspects of church that inhibit women's partic- ipation and of "announcing" a new vision of how church could be. The group identified strategies for bringing about change in ourselves and our church institutions and identified "networking" as the organizing principle: that is, we seek to bring together like-minded women but leave them free to structure their activities as seems best to them. The main way of being in touch with each other was through a newsletter that has grown over the years into a quar- terly journal, *Network*. We decided to name ourselves Catholic Women's Net- work although we wanted to include, as at the conference, women from other traditions. However, our Anglican sisters advised that if we were intent to bring about change in the Roman Catholic Church, we should include "Catholic" in our name in order that our church would listen to us.

LEARNING FROM EXPERIENCE
AND FROM EACH OTHER

At the beginning we organized day-long gatherings around a theme to experiment in theology and liturgy based on our experience. The very first gathering we held in October 1984 was entitled "Difference and Diversity." Dodi Donnelly of Berkeley, California, facilitated the gathering. In hindsight, the theme of the gathering proved to be prophetic because this emphasis on accepting our difference and diversity has become increasingly important as we start a new millennium and the Roman Catholic Church becomes more rather than less entrenched in its views. In other sections of religion and society also, fundamentalism is on the rise.

At Easter 1985, following the inauguration conference, three of us traveled to the motherhouse of the International Grail Movement for women at *De Tiltenberg* outside of Amsterdam in the Netherlands. Here we joined an international group of women to spend Holy Week as "Women Celebrating Death and New Life." The program for the week was planned by Grail members Mimi Marechel and Carol White. In small groups we reflected on our own experience and then in the light of that experience looked at Scripture and how it spoke to us. We devised special liturgies for each point of the Holy Week story. It was a week of complete integration of the so-called sacred and secular. This Easter had a profound effect on the three of us and subsequently on Catholic Women's Network. The experience at *De Tiltenberg*, for example, encouraged Catholic Women's Network to have similar celebrations of the Easter story here in England, and these have now become regular events lasting three to four days. Also, whenever we gather, we light a candle at the beginning as a sign that Christ is present, and we see the entire day as part of a liturgical whole. "For where two or three are gathered in my name, I am there among them" (Matt. 18:20).

We had experiential days of learning regularly in the initial stages of Catholic Women's Network. Each time there would be three women to plan the process of the day. Two of these would take on the task of planning the next event but would be joined by a new woman. In this way, women were able to have the confidence to take on this task even though they had no previous experience of planning such a day. In the mid-1980s, there was still little opportunity to theologize from a woman's perspective and no opportunity for women-only liturgies. But as time has gone by, feminist theology has become more available and accessible here in the United Kingdom. As we became more aware, the worship provided by the institutional church, in this case the Roman Catholic Church, became less and less satisfactory, and some women and even some men were looking for alternatives. So some of us began to gather in London in a mixed group of women and men to create our own liturgy. We met in each other's houses early on a Sunday evening once a month. We found that planning a liturgy needed only the expertise we had gained through planning day-long gatherings; the time frame was, of course, much more limited.

As time went on however, attendance decreased. Not to be deterred, a few women decided to try again but in a different way. We would meet as women only on the first Friday of each month in each other's houses. This choice of date was based on a Roman Catholic tradition of holding novenas on the first Friday of a month. With this format, the gatherings flourished, and by the autumn of 1992 we were offered space in the house of the Sisters of Notre Dame in Clapham, South London. I acted as coordinator of the group. This involved producing an advertising flyer every six months and ensuring that there was always a planner for the liturgy. We advertised through our journal *Network*, by word of mouth, and by leaving flyers at the house of the sisters of Notre Dame, our meeting place. We found that women from other Christian traditions were attending our gatherings on a regular basis. They wished for an informal liturgical format, which their own churches did not necessarily provide even if they did have women ministers.

We have never found the ecumenical nature of our gatherings to create any problems; it has rather given an added richness to them. Catholic Women's Network has always been open to and welcomed women whatever their tradition or practice if they feel in tune with what we are doing. We also recognize the tension between those who seek to change the church from within and those who feel there is no longer a space for them within the institution. Thus, women come who still see themselves as members of the Roman Catholic Church or of other Christian sister churches, while other women see themselves as no longer belonging to any official church structure.

CLAIMING OUR RITES

Sixteen years after the initial start of Catholic Women's Network, there are many opportunities for Christian women to gather to share experiences and to do theology together. But the space to gather for liturgy in a smaller, more local setting is still not so easy to find. Our liturgical format has been the same from the beginning. One or two women plan the liturgy. They provide an appropriate visual centerpiece including a candle or candles to express "Christ with us." This centerpiece sets the scene and provides a focus for reflection and meditation. The centerpiece is usually on the floor. The women sit on chairs in a circle around this centerpiece. We always begin by going around the circle saying our names and where we have traveled from. This seems to be a simple but important way of immediately including any woman who has not come before. It also reminds us of each other's names and makes us all "present" to each other and of equal value.

After the name sharing, the liturgy proceeds as the planners have devised it. They are responsible for planning a process that enables all to give something of themselves. Every liturgy is different, although usually there are poems or sacred readings—not always from Scripture. Whatever the source of the reading, we consider it to be sacred in this context. In fact the boundaries of what we perceive to be sacred have grown with time. There is often sharing of experience, thoughts, and ideas in a group of two or three and also reflection in the full group. The "sermon" has become communal. Sometimes we make a piece of art together. In a liturgy with the theme "Anger and Peace," we were invited each to contribute to a collage expressing anger. Sometimes we create something individually. For example, on one occasion we each drew a mandala with colored pens to express "what is important in my life now." We always have a ritual sharing of food and drink but not always bread and wine. Again, our eucharistic boundaries have grown with time. We try to make the elements that we share come from the theme or the readings. In the autumn, for example, we shared fruits, and in a wilderness liturgy we used bread and water. In a midsummer liturgy we had summer pudding, a traditional English summer dish made from bread slices enclosing cooked soft fruits. It is usual to have a space where we can each pray for others. We often but not always sing and circle dance. Whatever the planners offer, we accept.

The space we use has a large kitchen/dining room adjoining our comfortable meeting room, so we are able to sit around the large table and eat a meal together from the food we have all brought to share. There is opportunity over the meal to get to know each other in a different way again while eating. There is also an opportunity for the coordinator to ask for volunteers to plan future gatherings. Often two women will plan together, thus enabling a more experienced woman to pair with someone who has not planned a liturgy before. In this way everyone can be empowered to plan and act as leader or take on the priestly function. While eating there is also the opportunity to network and tell each other of other meetings of interest to Christian women. We do not see this part of the evening as an extra but as an integral part of our liturgy. Afterwards we wash up and tidy the rooms.

This whole process of planning and/or participating in the liturgy is about integrating personal spirituality with religious belief. It is a living creative theology, a woman's theology. It is not a disaster if the liturgy is not perfect or some part does not work well. It is as important to learn what does not work as what is satisfactory. Our gathering is a place, a space to learn how to create liturgy. Between twelve and twenty women usually come to a gathering. The group is thus quite small, although the number of women attending throughout any one year will be about forty. Not every woman attends every gathering. Women come because they want to but may not be able to come every time. The planners must thus create a process that works as well for half a dozen as two dozen.

So that they might speak for themselves, we asked the twelve women present on one particular occasion to describe who they were and why they came. This is what they wrote:

> I am a woman, a wife, a mother, a Catholic Christian, a manager, and a pilgrim. I come to be in a warm, sacred space: to stretch and strengthen and grow my relationship with God, to pray, to share, to love and be loved, to be me. I come because there is nowhere else like this.

> I am a woman in my late sixties and a committed radical feminist—"until all women are free, no woman is free."

> I come because these liturgies nurture me. They and the Catholic Women's Network Easters have been totally transforming. These liturgies are church to me.

> I come as a religious scientist constantly searching, constantly asking.

> I am a Christian feminist, a communicator and writer, with one foot in the institutional (Roman Catholic) church and one in the prophetic and spiritual church. I have been coming regularly to these liturgies since they began, to experience liturgy that is relevant to me as a woman and that reflects a real community that supports me and helps me to develop.

> I am a woman wanting to grow and mature in my spirituality, and have let go of institutional religion. I come here to hear and be with women and share their insights about life, the world, and God; about what moves and motivates them.

> I am creative, articulate (sometimes too talkative) and feel deeply about many things. I love literature and the arts. I come because I want to find out about many things and need to know why; need plenty of space to question dogma when it suffocates me and interferes with my quest for and relationship with God. I want to be a free spirit.

> I am Sue, a radical Catholic feminist who also seeks deeper sharing and contemplation. I come because it represents a vital sharing and participation at a very deep level. It renews and refreshes me, and I also hope I give something to it through occasional leadership (planning). It is one of the most creative spaces I have ever experienced, and everyone brings something through their group sharing. I have begun to learn what liturgy really means through this experience.

I am a sixty-year-old cradle Catholic, always interested in theology and liturgy and Catholic social action. I find the mass repetitive but here at this Catholic Women's Network liturgy, God comes among us. We pray; we are free to express our needs and hopes and listen to others who are seeking, searching, and sharing. These monthly meetings give me sustenance and make me feel *alive* to God and others. *Deo Gratias*.

I am a composer, hymn writer, university lecturer, mother of two boys, divorced, writer, researcher, performer. I enjoy feminist liturgy and think feminist insights need to be encapsulated in it. I wish to see the church change, and I see our gathering as being part of this. I enjoy the friendship, the chance to discuss, and the knowledge that other people are engaged in the same struggles as me. To find that solidarity is very important.

I am a feminist. I have been all my life. I am a circle dancer. I am in my seventieth year; a widow, and the mother of three sons, the grandmother of two grandsons. I am responsible for the care of my ninety-four-year-old mother. I am an administrator. I come to these liturgies because they use inclusive language; they encourage us to be creative whether we are taking part in or leading liturgies. There is no hierarchical structure, and it is a safe place to be and to share. It is an oasis in an unsatisfactory institution (the church!).

My name is Sinead. I come to this liturgy as it is an oasis, a spring of fresh water to nourish me on my journey, to nourish women together. It is an oasis which allows for discovery and remembering and moving on.

"I am searching
feeling and sensing
struggling
remembering."

What the women wrote sums up what liturgy should achieve. If I myself had tried to describe who the women are and why they come, the answer would have been my perspective, although I would have tried to be true to the women. But by allowing the women to speak for themselves there is the sense that the whole is much more than the sum of the individual parts. And that is certainly what strikes me about creating liturgy in the way that we do. When all are contributing, there is a great richness because every individual matters and affects the whole. If one repeated the same liturgy the next week with another group of women, the experience would be different, just as rich but different. Each gathering produces a unique experience.

Some of the women who come to our group are content that we are "doing it for ourselves." Others would like our kind of liturgy to shape what is happening in the mainstream of religious practice. There, mostly, the church and clergy have assumed the role of performing the liturgy. Once established, such a pattern is hard to break. After all, it is much easier to have a ready-made formula with a priest or minister as celebrant. I would like people to realize that it is not nearly as difficult as they may think to create liturgy. I also wish for more groups similar to ours (I know of other groups both for women only and for women and men together, but there are still very few). Liturgy can take place in the formal church setting, in the more intimate home or family environment, or in another chosen place: wherever it takes place, the process should enable each person to be both a participant and contributor rather than just an attendee. My personal vision is that we will each grow and learn to devise liturgies and rituals when we need them for both the everyday moments and the special moments of our lives.[1]

NEW MILLENNIUM LITURGY FOR THE EPIPHANY

In preparation for the liturgy, the two long tables in our gathering space are moved to make one large square table. The table is set in a festive manner. In the center stands a small decorated Christmas tree. Light comes from lots of tea lights on the table. There is a bowl of nuts and figs, gold foil-wrapped chocolates, one sachet of myrrh and one of frankincense, and colored papers and pens. A meal of bread and soup is ready.

We begin by lighting a third of the candles.

SPEAKER 1 Welcome to our liturgy, which is a meal to celebrate the new millennium and the feast of the Epiphany.

We go around the circle, each woman introducing herself.

Opening Prayer

(in unison[2]) This is the season of hope!
Let the Spirit of Hope surround you.
Let your spirit rise to bless this new millenium.

O Great Spirit of Hope, blessed be your holy seasons.
Blessed be this season when we move to a new millenium.
Blessed be this magical time for new beginnings and fond farewells.
Blessed be this "crack between the worlds" that we encounter at the New Millennium.
Blessed be this threshold place of transition between inside and outside.
Blessed be this transformation when spirits of hope and change gather.

Blessed be this passage from past securities to uncharted uncertainties.
Blessed be this shifting of emotions.
Blessed be this letting go of old hurts and pains.
Blessed be this reliable balancing act of nature.
Blessed be this rededication of values and meaning in life.

O Great Spirit of Hope, blessed be your holy seasons.

SPEAKER 1   A special meal at a special time with special women who have chosen or are able to be here on this first liturgy of the new millennium. So we shall eat together and look at the past, the present, the future, symbolized by the foods we shall eat and also by the gifts brought to the child Jesus, myrrh, frankincense, and gold. These were all very, very rare and valuable at that time, and we will learn a little about them by and by.

The past! In our opening prayer we said, "Blessed be the letting go of old hurts and pains." So what do we want to leave behind? What do we need forgiveness for? What have we learned and want to take forward? These are some of the questions we can share with our neighbor.

Women share their thoughts in pairs for ten minutes.

SPEAKER 1   We pass the nuts and figs and eat that which is good and to be taken forward and throw shells and stalks into the bowl as a sign of truly letting go of old hurts and pains.

We pass the figs and nuts and eat them, discarding the shells in a bowl.

SPEAKER 1   Myrrh was one of the gifts brought to the new child Jesus.

One of the women present, Lala, speaks of myrrh as one of the very precious gifts of the past and hangs the sachet of myrrh on the tree. Every third person takes up her plate and glass and moves on to find different neighbors. Some more candles are lit.

SPEAKER 2   Let us all together say Lala's Jubilee prayer.[3]

ALL   God of all ages, maker of time
mark of the alpha and point to omega.
Creator, Sustainer of everything living

touching us all who hold a hope
with a vision that breaks through boundaries
to grasp the blurred horizon.
You gave your promise. A blessing of joy
to those who've lost their faith in You.
Now time is poised with renewed expectation
of Emmanuel, God with us.
To know our time of proclaimed favor
we make again the pledge You ask:
"Share justly the good things I give you.
Reconcile with peace the rule of abuse.
Give courage to those who voice the words
of lives that have been silenced."
Send us to carry your "Good News"
to those burdened with debt.
Transfer their chains into clasps of love,
of prayer, concern, and then action.
Aware of your Spirit always among us
we sustain Your purpose with passion.
Increase our endeavor to do what You ask.
Of "where there are wrongs, they be righted"
Now is the time.
It will be achieved
in acting justly,
in loving tenderly
and in walking humbly with You, our God.

SPEAKER 2   The present! "Now time is poised with renewed expectation
of *Emmanuel*, God with us . . . Now is the time . . . walking
closely with You, our God."
Is God with you?
Are you walking with God?
How? Or maybe another sentence speaks to you?

Women share their thoughts in pairs, with new neighbors, for ten minutes.

SPEAKER 2   We break bread and eat soup as the food for the present.

We eat the rest of the meal. Lala speaks about frankincense as our symbol for the present and hangs the sachet on the tree. Again every third person moves. The remaining candles are lit.

ALL   This is the season of hope.
       Let the spirit of hope surround you.
       Let your spirit rise to bless this new year, this new millenium.

SPEAKER 1   What are your fears, what are your hopes for this new millennium?

Women share their thoughts in pairs, with new neighbors, for ten minutes.

SPEAKER 1   We have food for the future. What else but gold!

Lala speaks about the gold. We pass the gold chocolates around the circle, and each person shares a hope.

SPEAKER 2   At this time it is good to give and receive gifts. So we ask each of you to write a womanly attribute that you would like to give to another. We will put the pieces of paper in the bowl face down, and then everyone will receive from the "lucky dip"!

Each woman writes one attribute on a piece of paper. The papers are gathered in a bowl. Every woman receives one such piece of paper and reads out the "gift" she has been given. We then stand to say the "Millennium Resolution"[4] in unison:

ALL   Let there be
       respect for the earth
       peace for its people
       love in our lives
       delight in the good
       forgiveness of past wrongs
       and from now on a new start. Amen.

SPEAKER 2   Let us give each other a Kiss of Peace, for new beginnings, new hope!

God, Our Sister and Friend

Kvennakirkjan in Reykjavík, Iceland

Auður Eir Vilhjálmsdóttir

IN THE BEGINNING

It was an Advent evening in 1992. Forty women—six from a course on feminist theology I had been teaching, the others from Bible study groups—had gathered in one of the churches in Reykjavík, the capital of Iceland. We had brought cakes, made coffee, lit candles, and now anticipated spending a peaceful and rich evening together. We sang Advent hymns, prayed together, and began to share our stories. The first woman to speak, who belonged to one of the Bible study groups, voiced her disappointment with the church. She wanted the church to be more open, livelier, more caring. We talked about our lives, our hopes, and our sorrows. One woman had been fighting cancer and spoke of her joy in now regaining her health. The atmosphere was one of warm friendship as the gathered women shared their stories. The last woman to speak, Elísabet, one of the six feminists, finally said, "I have a dream. You have voiced your desire for a different church. Let us found that church ourselves, *Kvennakirkjan*, a Women's Church."

This dream was not new. Several years before this Advent meeting, another group of about thirty women had gathered to reflect on ways of renewing the church. The vision of a Women's Church had surfaced, but the women at that meeting were not ready to embrace that vision. They wanted to focus instead on increasing leadership positions for women and enlarging the space for creativity and the arts in the life of the church. Some women pastors and seminarians also had studied feminist theology together for several years, created feminist liturgies, and published some articles and a booklet based on various materials from the Lutheran World Federation and the World Council of

Churches, such as *No Longer Strangers: A Resource for Women and Worship,*[1] and the report from the "Community of Women and Men in the Church" Study.[2] As the first women who studied feminist theology in Iceland, we owe much to the Women's Desks of both the Lutheran World Federation and the World Council of Churches. A core group of us had continued to gather and work on common concerns, even after most of the women had scattered to various parishes around Iceland.

Some days after the Advent meeting described above, the six feminists gathered again. This time, we decided to start a Women's Church. The six of us— Rannveig Jónsdóttir, Guðný Guðmundsdóttir, Inga Hanna Guðmundsdóttir, Elísabet þorgeirsdóttir, María Bergmann, and Auður Eir Vilhjálmsdóttir—took upon ourselves the responsibility of forming the steering group. We decided to have a pastor, namely me, and extended an open invitation to women to bring their ideas, to invite other women, to preach, and to shape the music life of our new church. Two months later, we announced the first worship service of *Kvennakirkjan* to be held in one of the local churches, Kópavogskirkja, Kopavogur Church. When February 14 came, we were in the midst of a snowstorm, the organist came at the last minute, and some uncertainty filled the air, but the dominant feeling was one of joy and hope. About one hundred women had come to the service, young and old, some familiar to us, but most of them new faces. We used prayers from a booklet the Icelandic women pastors had previously published, read the Scriptures in our own inclusive translation, and reflected on the possibilities of feminist theology in women's lives, especially the possibility of weaving together our own personal faith and the shared faith in our common strength. The preacher was one of the first women ordained in the Evangelical Lutheran Church of Iceland. We claimed the desire for God and the desire for the rights and freedom of women in a society made for men. We imaged God as feminine, as our woman friend, sharing our lives: she was not a king or a judge, but a woman baking bread and seeking her lost treasure, that is, us. We experienced our community with the many women who longed for a liturgy that truly reflected women's lives. We shared our vision of writing and living our own feminist theology by gathering together in worship and in other meetings. We confirmed our rightful place in the National Church of Iceland, whose stability we appreciated and whose life we sought to enrich by our own vision. Was this the kind of vision the women gathered in Kópavogskirkja had come to hear? We were afraid some of them would be disappointed because they might have hoped for another message. But this was the message of *Kvennakirkjan* and our common gift.

In the beginning much of our energy in *Kvennakirkjan* was focused on the monthly worship services. We requested from various congregations in Reykjavík the use of their church buildings and were welcomed almost everywhere.

We then wrote a letter to all the pastors in our city, introducing our work and requesting permission to be allowed to hold a worship service in their respective churches once or twice a year. Most often the women from *Kvennakirkjan* who brought the letters to their pastors were well received, but some of the pastors also argued that feminist theology was heresy.

Kvennakirkjan now has its own home in the center of Reykjavík. Its two rooms double as offices and meeting space for our seminars and other gatherings. Our liturgies, however, are celebrated elsewhere, in churches and outdoors. Every year, on June 19, we hold an outdoor worship service with other women's groups to commemorate women's suffrage, which became law in Iceland in 1915. We have close ties to women in the wider feminist movement, closer ties than with the traditional women's groups in our own church. We have not sought the official sanction of the bishop or leading committees of the Icelandic Evangelical Lutheran Church, but the church leadership is well aware that we consider ourselves part of this church, which looks back to a thousand-year history in our land. Christianity first came to Iceland from Norway and was adopted by law in the year 1000. At the time of the Reformation in the sixteenth century, Iceland adopted Lutheranism, embodied to this day in the state church, the Evangelical Lutheran Church of Iceland.

In 1999, I, the pastor of *Kvennakirkjan*, who up until then had been a parish pastor, moved to a new position in the church. My current job description includes work on feminist theology, which means I can give more of my time to working with the women of *Kvennakirkjan*. *Kvennakirkjan's* current leadership consists of a group of committed women who form the steering group— Elísabet þorgeirsdóttir, Elína Hrund Kristjánsdóttir, þóra Björnsdóttir, Steinunn Pálsdóttir, Guðrún B. Jónsson, Ásdís Ólafsdóttir, Auður Eir Vilhjálmsdóttir—the choir, and the core members of the church. All of us together shape the life of the church. Everything is intentionally open and aboveboard. We are committed to offering each other the riches of Christian feminist theology, to be lived and enjoyed in our daily lives.

CLAIMING OUR RITES

Kvennakirkjan holds its monthly worship services on Sunday evening at 8:30 p.m. We offer coffee and cake after each liturgy. For us, this is a part of the overall worship experience and gives us both an opportunity to mingle and enjoy each other's company and a chance to raise money by selling each others' coffee and cakes. We are proud to use this particular method of fundraising that women traditionally have employed in our culture. In fact, in some parts of Iceland, the congregation is customarily still invited to the pastor's home for coffee after the worship service; in other parts of the country the congregation itself is the host.

As of yet, *Kvennakirkjan* does not have a specific, well-established liturgical tradition, but we are moving in that direction. So far, we have created a new liturgy for each service. There are, however, constants that shape all of our worship services. We pray, sing, read from the Scriptures, and preach. The sermon typically weaves together faith in God and our faith in feminism. The Scripture readings are in inclusive language, and we speak the biblical texts in our own words. We use visual aids as homiletic material—for example, colors that speak to us of pessimism or optimism and joy, thereby colorfully visualizing for us God's forgiveness in our lives. We create our own Icelandic blessings and confessions of faith but also draw on sources of feminist spirituality from other parts of the world. We appreciate the liturgies of our sisters in other countries but also create our own texts. Thus, we might use as a eucharistic prayer the poem "Bakerwoman God," by Alla Bozarth-Campbell (U.S.A.),[3] and in the same service confess our sins in our own words by saying, "We confess our sins, our mistakes, and failures" with the simple communal response "We confess forgiveness."

We use inclusive language throughout and image God as our sister and woman friend. We do, however, always refer to Jesus of Nazareth as male and use the Lord's Prayer in its original form. But this prayer is put in perspective when, for example, in another part of the service we refer to God as our mother in heaven. Whenever we have guest preachers, we leave the decisions on inclusive language to them. We have long dreamt of new hymns and new music. In order for this dream to become a reality, we needed women willing to take charge of the music of *Kvennakirkjan* and to renew our liturgy through their musical skills. Several wonderful women worked with us in the early years of *Kvennakirkjan*. They formed our choir, mostly to lead the communal singing in worship but also for the occasional choral piece. In Icelandic churches, the hymnic tradition is strong and well-established, and it is exceedingly difficult to introduce something new. We began to search for new melodies and new hymn texts, written in inclusive language and speaking feminist theological convictions. Slowly, we gathered such new hymns and new music, drawing especially on hymns we heard and sang at international women's gatherings, but also on hymns from a Canadian hymn book, *Voices United*, that a Canadian friend of ours had brought as a gift. Some of us also have a gift for writing new hymns. Our current music leader, Aðalheiður Þorsteinsdóttir, is steeped in both classical music and jazz and also well-connected with other musicians whom we invite to our services. We continue to nurture our choir, write new hymns, and gather every week to sing and prepare the next worship service.

Our liturgies differ from one service to the next. We try to discern and respond to the needs of the women who gather. These women themselves are the subjects of the liturgy of *Kvennakirkjan*. They themselves are the celebrants by being present, by praying, by listening. The presence of each woman, with her hopes and her joys, her worries and her anxiety, her trust and her openness, is of vital importance for the community as a whole. Prayers are a central part of every service, and we practice a particular form of communal prayer: as the community gathers, each woman is invited to take a piece of paper from a basket in the foyer of the church and to write a prayer on it. The prayers are then gathered and read aloud during the service. This reading of the women's prayers is interspersed with music.

Typically, about a hundred women gather for our worship services, young and old, from different professions, among them several teachers, nurses, and social workers. Some of the women have attended *Kvennakirkjan* from the beginning; some joined us later but now come regularly. Some women come for a while and then stop attending, only to pick up again later. We welcome the ease with which women come and go as they desire. As a part of the Icelandic Evangelical Lutheran Church, we are free to design our own liturgy. We gladly share our liturgical vision with others and participate in wider church discussions when invited. We have also taken the initiative and written to the pastors of our church, encouraging them to use inclusive language in their own worship services.

VENTURES IN FEMINIST THEOLOGY

From its beginning, *Kvennakirkjan* eagerly engaged feminist theology. Our first seminar on feminist theology took place in the summer of 1994, a year after the initial formation of our church. We organized a two-day retreat outside of Reykjavík to reflect on feminist theology, liturgy, and our daily lives. We dreamed of regular seminars on feminist theology and feminist theory, and their meaning for our lives. The women had chosen three topics when asked what concerned them most deeply: "Feminist Theology," "Depression," and "Relaxation, Prayer, and Health," and these became the subject matter of the initial regular seminars. One of us had studied relaxation techniques, and we incorporated these into each seminar. This spurred the creation of a tape, now on sale in the office of *Kvennakirkjan*, that guides the listener through a time of relaxation and prayer. Other seminars focused on the role of leadership, on story writing, on faith in everyday life, and on the Scriptures, their origin, and their use today. The Bible is fundamental to all our work, and we are constantly amazed to see how women are empowered by its message and eagerly share this biblical message with each other.

We continue to go on retreat together and enjoy each other's company. We have also begun seminars and worship services outside of Reykjavík. We have traveled together internationally and made contact with women beyond our own context. For example, *Kvennakirkjan* attended the Nordic Forum, a forum for women and feminism, in Abo, Finland, in 1994 and held a worship service there. We also held a worship service during the Baltic-Nordic Conference on Women and Men in Dialogue, which took place in Valmiera, Latvia, in 1997. The Latvian organizers had suggested that the service be held in the Church of St. Simon in Valmiera, and, in preparation, *Kvennakirkjan* had sent the Latvian organizers a copy of the proposed ritual together with information on *Kvennakirkjan*. As it turned out, the ruling body of the Lutheran Church of Latvia subsequently forbade the holding of the service in the church. Arriving in Valmiera, we found the door of the church locked. The conference organizers and the mayor of the town offered us an alternative site, and, in the end, our worship service was held in the open air, among the ruins of an ancient castle. *Kvennakirkjan* also attended the European Women's Synods in Gmunden, Austria, in 1996 and in Svendborg, Denmark, in 1999. From all these meetings, we have brought back new ideas and new music. Indeed, *Kvennakirkjan*'s membership now extends to women beyond Iceland. Two of our members are Norwegian and one is Finnish. Seven women in Sweden also support our work while continuing as members of their churches in Sweden.

We are attentive to women's issues in the larger society. One autumn, for example, a group of fifty women, some from *Kvennakirkjan*, some from other groups, visited all the striptease establishments in Reykjavík. We wanted to see with our own eyes what was going on there, since we suspected that some of the young women entertainers were victims of the global sex trade and trafficking of women. We subsequently wrote a letter to the prime minister and took part in discussions in the media to raise awareness of the global sex trade and how it manifested itself in our country.

In our seminars in feminist theology, we are venturing out into new territory. We are in the process of preparing a study guide on feminist theology as our lifestyle, a process open to all the women of *Kvennakirkjan*. We are also putting together a booklet for the two girls in our midst who are preparing for their confirmation. Last but not least, we are gathering in a mentoring group all those theological students willing and eager to preach in *Kvennakirkjan*. The church newsletter appears monthly, offering information about the next worship service, news, and words of encouragement for each other. *Kvennakirkjan* has published two books: my book, *Vinátta Guðs* (The Friendship of God), is the first book written in Icelandic on feminist theology. It was published in 1994. *Vinkonur og vinir Jesu* (Women and Men and the Friendship of Jesus) is a collection of texts from the New Testament in inclusive language that we published in 1999.

OUR FAITH IN GOD, IN OURSELVES, IN OTHERS, AND IN LIFE

As all gather, a well-known hymn is played at the piano.

MEMBER   Tonight we are in my parish church, and I bid you welcome. Thank you, to each of you, for coming to the service tonight. It is very important to us that you are here and that you participate in the prayers and songs and everything we do together. We want you to know and remember that this service would not be the same without you, and that you, indeed, are the ones celebrating this service. May God bless you and give you what you need to hear and feel in your heart tonight.

Prayer   Let us pray together: God, our sister and friend, we thank you for being with us tonight and always. Bless our friendship with you and with each other; bless each one of us tonight. Amen.

Hymn   "BREAD AND ROSES"[4]

Reading   Our theme for this service is forgiveness, joy, and power, our own strength in our faith in God. God, indeed, needs us; she needs us to be free and strong with a warm heart and warm hands, as she herself is. She says, "I forgive all your mistakes, heal all your wounds. I take your sins as far away from you as the east is far away from the west."

Jesus said, "I give you my own peace. My word, my truth makes you free. Go on growing in me and I will grow in you. If you live your life in me and my words live in your hearts you can ask for whatever you like and it will come true for you."

Hymn   "SISTER, CARRY ON"[5]
Sister, carry on.
Sister, carry on.
It may be rocky and it may be rough,
but sister, carry on.

Sister, don't lose the dream.
Sister, don't lose the dream.

Don't sell out for no short time gain.
Sister, don't lose the dream.

Sister, don't settle too soon.
Sister, don't settle too soon,
till everybody's got their rights.
Sister, don't settle too soon.

Sister, we share the way.
Sister, we share the way.
Heart to heart and hand to hand,
Sister, we share the way.

Stand in solidarity.
Stand in solidarity.
Together bring a brand new day.
Stand in solidarity.

Sister, carry on.
Sister, carry on.
It may be rocky and it may be rough,
but sister, carry on.

MEMBER   As always in our services we come to God to tell her about
            what has happened to us since our last service. We all have
            something we want to talk about with her, sorrows, guilt, joy,
            and hope, something we would like to forget, something we
            would like to remember. God has said she is always willing
            to forgive us, therefore we can be ready to forgive both our-
            selves and others. Our faith in God gives us faith in ourselves,
            in others, and in life.

Sketch

*A woman enters the church and walks toward the altar, carrying three big bags or
pushing a shopping cart. She stops in front of the altar and starts speaking with God.
Another woman is hiding behind the altar, and her voice becomes the voice of God as
a conversation takes place between the two.*

WOMAN   I am so angry, God, so very, very angry.

VOICE OF   Why are you so angry?
GOD

WOMAN   The people at my workplace want me to do a lot of work they
               should do themselves. Most often they ask me politely and
               friendly, and I always do what they ask me. Nevertheless, I
               feel I should stop, but I can't. And I am angry with them and
               with myself for being so weak.

VOICE OF   You want me to take your anger away from you? I shall, my
GOD   dear.

The woman in front of the altar places one of her bags in front of the altar.

WOMAN   And I am worrying about money. My salary is too low, or
               maybe I spend too much. I have great difficulties in paying
               the bills every month. I don't know how to deal with my
               debts and give myself some pleasure at the same time.

VOICE OF   I have seen you are worried. Shall I take care of your debts?
GOD

Woman places the other bag in front of the altar.

WOMAN   Oh, thank you God. You are so good to me. Now I feel much
               better. But I am still a bit worried. I have not visited my old
               Aunt Margaret for a long time. I feel guilty. I always feel
               guilty because of her. It is a very bad feeling.

VOICE OF   Shall I take your guilt and bear it for you? You know I came
GOD   and carried all your guilt up to the cross. I came and I was
               Jesus, your friend and Savior. I can take this guilt too.

Woman places her third bag in front of the altar.

WOMAN   Yes. Yes. Thank you. Thank you. How free I am now!

VOICE OF   Yes, I want you to be free and full of joy and energy. I want
GOD   you to enjoy life, and I need you to be free and joyful. I need
               your strength to help me to continue my creation in the
               world I created so beautiful. So, are you really sure you don't
               want to handle the situation at your workplace? I could teach
               you to say no and yes at the appropriate times. Would you
               like me to do that?

WOMAN   Yes, maybe that is a better idea. Yes, I think so.

She takes one of her bags back.

VOICE OF   And I can teach you to handle your finances, too. I think your
GOD   salary is good. I think you need to find more appropriate
    ways to manage your finances. Shall we try together?

WOMAN   That would be wonderful. That would really make me feel
    good and give me security and strength. Thank you. I accept
    your offer.

She takes another bag back.

VOICE OF   And don't you really want to take care of Aunt Margaret? She
GOD   was always so kind and warm to you when you were a little
    girl and has always been there for you since. She needs you
    now. Are you sure you want to stop seeing her?

WOMAN   No, of course not. No, no, I want to continue seeing her. I
    owe that to her, and it makes me happy when I can find the
    time to visit her. Thank you, God, for reminding me.

She takes the third bag back.

VOICE OF   How good. You know I will help you. I will always be with
GOD   you.

*The woman behind the altar comes forward. The two women either push the shopping
cart together, or they carry the three bags between them out of the church.*

MEMBER   Let us thank God for helping us to take care of ourselves and
    our lives, for giving us the ability to share our lives with oth-
    ers, to accept the love of others and to give them love and
    friendship. One of the most precious gifts from God is to be
    allowed to stay near really good people, to work in a group
    of good and strong women and men and to feel that we are
    doing good work.

All rise and sing the African-American spiritual "I've Got Peace Like a River."

We confess our faith together in the words of Rachel Conrad Wahlberg's "Woman's Creed" (spoken by one member).[6]

Musical Interlude

Sermon

Hymn "STAY WITH US THROUGH THE NIGHT"[7]
Stay with us through the night.
Stay with us through the pain.
Stay with us, blessed stranger,
till the morning breaks again.

Stay with us through the night.
Stay with us through the grief.
Stay with us, blessed stranger,
till the morning brings relief.

Stay with us through the night.
Stay with us through the dread.
Stay with us, blessed stranger,
till the morning breaks new bread.

Prayers

Upon entering the church, everyone had been invited to write a prayer on a piece of paper. The prayers were collected in a basket and are now read aloud from the pulpit. The individual prayers are interspersed with the song "Holy, Holy, Holy," which we sing in Spanish. In conclusion, all pray the Lord's Prayer.

Music

(played by a soloist)

Announcements

The leader shares information about the next service, choir rehearsals, upcoming seminars, and other meetings and activities. Thanks are expressed to all, women and men, for celebrating this service together. All are invited to coffee in the community hall, which is a part of the worship service and gives an opportunity to sit together, relax, and talk with each other. The leader expresses her hope that each will be able to reconnect with the strength present in this worship service in the coming days, that we will remember that we gathered in a warm and strong group of good women and men who trust in God and want to be her friends and helpers.

LEADER   May God who created you to be free, bless you.
May Jesus, who freed you so you can create with God,
   bless you.
May the Holy Spirit who wakes you with a kiss in the
   morning
and stays with you the whole day,
so you can be the wonderful person
God created you to be and Jesus freed you to be,
bless you.

Closing Hymn "WE SHALL OVERCOME"

10

Air Moves Us

Frauenstudien- und -bildungszentrum in Gelnhausen, Germany

HERTA LEISTNER[1]

"Women's Center—Witches' Inferno," these words were written on a sign held by conservative Christians protesting at the opening worship service of the *Frauenstudien- und -bildungszentrum der Evangelischen Kirche Deutschlands*[2] in the summer of 1994. What led to this opening service, and which role did feminist liturgies play in this development?[3]

IN THE BEGINNING

At the end of the 1960s, students in West Germany rose up and revolted against their forefathers, who had constructed a post–World War II authoritarian and hierarchical society, with a deafening silence about the National Socialist past and the horrors of the Holocaust. Students took to the streets, calling for new democratic practices and politics. In connection with these student demonstrations, the women's movement developed during the 1970s. Women students had begun to actively participate in the student movement and demonstrated and fought together with their male counterparts. These women became aware, however, that they were prescribed specifically "female" roles: they were to make coffee for the men, do all the secretarial paperwork, and care for the children. This was a far cry from the revolutionary vision of these women students. Out of these contradictory experiences arose distinct women's groups that analyzed critically the situation of women in society, demonstrated in the streets for women's safety, called for women's rights to control their own bodies and the legalization of abortion, stood up for same-sex relationships and equal pay for equal work, and started co-op women's bookstores and women's cafes—to name just a few of the concerns of the German women's movement.

In the churches, women initially remained quiet, or became involved in the autonomous women's movement. However, the momentum of the women's movement in the wider society, and the 1974 Berlin Consultation of the World Council of Churches on "Sexism in the 1970s" caused church women such as Elisabeth Moltmann Wendel to look at the equality of women from a theological perspective.[4] In 1979, the first consultation on "Feminist Theology" took place. The women's movement in German churches had begun. More and more women met in groups, seminars, and consultations. With the tools of feminist critique of the patriarchal system, we scrutinized our church structures and theological interpretations of the Bible. A new image emerged of the church sustained and moved forward by women, however controlled and determined by men (today, we tend to forget that it was only in the 1970s that women's fully valid ordination was accepted in the Protestant churches in Germany). Thus, one of our goals at that time naturally was to place women in more leadership roles in the church.

As we analyzed the content of our faith and the forms of our worship, we realized that our symbolic universe was male-dominated. God was Father, judge, and ruler; the key disciples, apostles, and church fathers were all male (and as Protestants, we were not supposed to venerate Mary). Our prayers, songs, texts, and Gospels were full of such male-dominated images. With growing awareness came growing irritation. For many of us it became increasingly difficult to attend traditional worship services, since they evoked little more than our critique and protest. It took some time for us to develop the contours of our own alternative vision. At times, we almost felt like the heretics our fundamentalist critics had made us out to be—for example, when we looked to the early Christian witnesses whose texts, rather than being accepted into the New Testament canon, were instead rejected as heretical, or when we looked to the early worship of goddesses and the feminine side of God that played an important role for women and that we wanted to reclaim as part of our Christian tradition.

We not only looked at women within our church but also took a closer look at how women in our Western industrialized society actually live. Women's lives had changed tremendously in comparison with the lives of their grandmothers. We recognized a multitude of possible lifestyles and narratives of what it meant to live as a "woman." As women in society and in the church, we made these differences the foci of our own work. In contrast, our church, for example, even today holds in high esteem the traditional model of the heterosexual married couple as **the** normative Christian lifestyle. But the lives of many women in our society no longer conform to this pattern. Some women live alone, with or without children; some women are divorced; some are remarried; couples live together without being married; women love and live with other women as couples and as families. These discrepancies between official church teaching and women's actual lives demanded our attention and response. In the process of developing alternative visions, we went through many trials and tribulations with our church. There are the conservative Christians with whom we struggle, but there is also the public voice of German theology and its male authors who assume they are the final arbiters of all truth.

FRAUENSTUDIEN- UND -BILDUNGSZENTRUM

In 1987, a group of Protestant women began to draw up plans for a national church women's center. They wanted to create a center in which women themselves could work on their own concerns. This group of women sought to pave the way for a more just community of women and men in the church. The project was submitted to the church authorities, and in 1991 the Synod of the Protestant Church in Germany voted to set up such a center for women's study and education. In 1994, our *Frauenstudien- und -bildungszentrum* opened its doors. The church recognized it as a contribution to the World Council of Churches' Ecumenical Decade of Churches in Solidarity with Women (1988–1998). We found a house for the center in Gelnhausen, near Frankfurt. The site was owned by the *Burkhardthaus*, an educational institution of the Protestant Church of Germany. Originally, *Burkhardthaus* had been an education center for women in the social services fields. The Girl Scouts, Girl Guides, and the YWCA also had their headquarters there. *Burkhardthaus* is thus a place with a strong women's tradition. The site is located at the edge of Gelnhausen, with the main house, a nineteenth-century stately white villa, overlooking the medieval town center. Our own building is much more modest, with eleven bedrooms, three meeting rooms, and our offices. The house has a bright, airy atmosphere that women enjoy. We named the building *Anna Paulsen Haus* in honor of Anna Paulsen (1893–1981), one of the first women in Germany to receive a doctorate in theology. Anna Paulsen also had taught theology at *Burkhardthaus*.

The city of Gelnhausen itself offers an opportunity to connect with women's history. Gelnhausen is a picturesque town, with a fascinating and terrifying past. As in other parts of northern and western Europe, for a period of roughly four hundred years from the late Middle Ages to the eighteenth century, women were hunted, accused, and executed as witches.[5] Gelnhausen was one of the sites of such witch-hunts, and the city's *Hexenturm*, the "witches' tower," where women were imprisoned and tortured, still stands today. In the sixteen years from 1583 to 1599 alone, more than thirty women were arrested, tortured, sentenced to death, and executed as witches in this small town. The most famous victim of these witch-hunts in Gelnhausen was Maria Elisabeth Strupp, widow of a pastor and daughter-in-law of the Protestant reformer of Gelnhausen, who was accused as a witch, tortured, beheaded, and burnt on August 3, 1599. The witch-hunts not only targeted midwives and women healers but also the young, the old, the social misfits, the woman who had evoked someone's jealousy or contempt—any woman could become a target. This persecution of women as "witches," of course, is not unrelated to the Christian tradition and its image of woman as seductress and sinner. For us at the *Frauenstudien- und -bildungszentrum*, confronting and indeed living next to this part of both church history and women's history challenges us to ensure that no human being is pushed to the fringes and excluded as these women were. Even in our increasingly multicultural society, we still have deep problems in living with people from other cultures. But the birth pangs of a multicultural society also provide us with many opportunities to struggle to live with one another.

WE ARE CHURCH

Our center is an official part of the Protestant Church in Germany, and we are grateful for our existence and the funds we receive from the church. We are called to empower women to become visible in the renewal of the church. Our church, on the one hand, views this contribution of women as an enrichment but, on the other hand, experiences uneasiness and questions some of our liturgical practices, such as our choice of symbols, themes, texts, and interpretations. Here lie the roots of the attacks on our *Frauenstudien- und -bildungszentrum* from conservative Christians. On the theological side, they accuse us of syncretism and neopaganism, since we emphasize our connection with nature and the cosmos (see the "Ritual of the Elements" that follows) and draw on pre-Christian traditions—for example, the lunar cycle and seasonal feasts—in the celebration of our liturgies. On the ethical side, conservative Christians accuse us of destroying the bases of our faith and our society, since, for example, we do not accept marriage as the one and only Christian lifestyle, and render gay and lesbian Christians more visible in the life of the church, including its liturgies. Despite these conservative attacks, more and more women continue to say ever more clearly, *Wir sind Kirche*, "We are church; we ourselves take responsibility for our spiritual lives."

The Protestant and Catholic churches are still very influential in German society, but their influence is weakening, and for some people the Christian faith has lost its vitality. One of the reasons might be that living in an affluent society and "being full" immobilizes us. At the same time, there is a noticeable spiritual hunger since other religious traditions (for example, Buddhism) and esoteric groups are gaining adherents. There are also many independent women's spirituality groups that function outside of the Christian tradition or any other organized religious structure. Since we share with these women a commitment to the women's movement and together form the feminist base, we seek to stay connected with these groups. We are committed, however, to the flourishing of women's lives from within our Christian tradition. We also strive to be a sign for renewal so that women, children, and others on the edges will move to the center of the church. Whether all this can occur without our church breaking apart, we do not know, since conservative Christians are unremitting in their opposition. But for now, we continue to believe that we as women cannot simply rid ourselves of the 1,500 years of Christian tradition in our part of the world. The vision of a justice-filled reign of God is a crucial vision that we endeavor to make real in our lives and in our liturgies.

There are five women who work in the center together, including two administrative assistants and three women who are responsible for the scholarly and educational activities of the *Frauenstudien- und -bildungszentrum*. Our center came into existence in the midst of the reunification of East and West Germany. For forty years, there had been two German states, and even if the churches in East and West had maintained good relations, different agendas and different forms of church life had evolved on both sides of the border. These differences were very noticeable for women, too. Women from the socialist East Germany, for example, took equality for granted. They were used to working outside of the home and supporting themselves and their families. They thus had a difficult time understanding our West German women's struggles and the appeal of feminism for us. On the other hand, women from the East had the experience of living in a noncapitalistic society and of being Christians in a non-Christian society, something West German women knew little about. Building community between German women from East and West is an ongoing process; we still have different sensitivities and ways of going about our lives. At the *Frauenstudien- und -bildungszentrum*, we were clear that at least one of the women working with us had to be from the former East Germany (even if the center's vision and support had come entirely from the West). We also hope to strengthen the connections with and between East European women. We were, for example, very actively involved in the first European Women's Synod held in Gmunden, Austria, in 1996.[6] While taking part in this synod, we realized that we European women from the East and from the West have differing ways of expressing our faith and that, indeed, our worship services were foreign to each other.

Women from all over Germany come to the courses, seminars, and working groups of the *Frauenstudien- und -bildungszentrum*. Occasionally, we also have international visitors. One of our specific goals is to reach women responsible for the advanced education and training of other women. At the center, these women can exchange ideas and begin working on shared projects. One recent thematic focus, for example, was "Women—Economics—Ethics." We studied how and in which form theological reflection could intervene and contribute to this field, and how violence against women could be rendered visible as a social problem. The results of our shared learning have reached the highest governing bodies of our church. Women in leadership positions also meet together in the *Frauenstudien- und -bildungszentrum* to evaluate their situations and to develop strategies to bring more women into leadership roles. We draw on the newest insights of feminist theology for much of our work.

CLAIMING OUR RITES

Central to our work is the interest in new liturgical forms and spiritual practices. The women of the *Frauenstudien- und -bildungszentrum* share in the planning and leading of morning prayer services for those working at the *Burkhardthaus* and the *Anna Paulsen Haus*, as well as for our visitors and seminar participants. The center's women also regularly worship together in a smaller group. The *Frauenstudien- und -bildungszentrum* would like to offer a spiritual home for all women who wish to pray, celebrate, and gather together with like-minded women in one of the various weekend liturgical seminars. For the most part, these seminars occur at the beginning of the year, at Easter, at Pentecost, and during Advent. The seminar leaders decide on a theme, related both to the specific occasion and the overall program focus, which is then ritualized in feminist liturgies, morning and evening prayer, and other worship services. The services usually are planned by one woman or a team, but occasionally a service also develops as a group responsibility with all taking part in the planning.

Since we have been involved in the development of feminist theology and its particular expression in Germany since the early 1980s, we also offer, in cooperation with *Burkhardthaus*, basic and advanced training courses in feminist liturgy. Each year, we conduct a workshop called "Feminist Liturgy" where women with experience in their own liturgical groups come together and work on a specific theme, experiment, and worship together. We have focused on such themes as "Blessing," "Healed-Healing," "Ritual," and "We Are the Text." Two books have grown out of this liturgical work.[7]

We are grateful to the women's movement and to feminist theology for empowering and inspiring us to search for new expressions of our faith. We received inspiration from the World Council of Churches' Consultation "Sexism in the 70s" and the "Community of Women and Men in the Church." A wonderful experience for us has been, and continues to be, the Women's World Day of Prayer. In addition, we have learned theologically from women in the United States (Elisabeth Schüssler Fiorenza, Rosemary Radford Ruether), and we have been inspired liturgically by Diann Neu from WATER in Washington, D.C. The term *Frauenkirche*, "Women Church," best explains our identity. The Ecumenical Decade of Churches in Solidarity with Women was also very important for us and galvanized our energies.[8]

SHARING A RITE

We have chosen to share our "Ritual of the Elements" because it exemplifies our eco-feminist sensibilities, so very different from our received theological tradition in Germany. The ritual was celebrated at one of the Pentecost seminars at the *Frauenstudien- und -bildungszentrum* that have, for the last few years, been dedicated to individual women from the Christian tradition. One year, our ancestress Hildegard of Bingen inspired us. Hildegard, a twelfth-century nun who has received a lot of renewed attention, both scholarly and popular, was a visionary, a prophet, a composer, a physician, and a scientist. Her cosmic vision of life was combined with a holistic knowledge. She knew much about animals, herbs, and stones. Creation, and especially fire, wind/air, and water, are also elements interwoven into the story of Pentecost. With this background, and after a visit to Disibodenberg, where Hildegard of Bingen lived for forty-two years, we decided to celebrate the following "Ritual of the Elements." Hildegard Weiler, who had cooperated with the *Frauenstudien- und -bildungszentrum* for many years until her untimely death in 2001, created the design of the ritual. Hildegard prepared and led the ritual together with the women who participated in the Pentecost seminar that year.

AIR MOVES US: A RITUAL OF THE ELEMENTS

The site for this ritual was the grounds behind the Anna Paulsen Haus, *which hold one of the focal points of the* Frauenstudien- und -bildungszentrum: *a large natural wind chime. This wind chime represents the four basic elements: earth, fire, water, and air. The chime is made from a wheel from which long threads are hanging. Several objects are attached to these threads: snail houses (symbolizing the earth), pieces of pottery (for fire), shells (for water), and feathers (for air). When the wind blows, a beautiful music emerges. The wind chime's four basic elements are oriented towards the four directions, north, east, south, and west. Each direction is identified by particular sounds or instruments. To the north (standing for the earth) are drums;*

to the east (for air) are brass and woodwind instruments; to the south (for fire) are rattles; and to the west (for water) are rain sticks and ocean drums. For our liturgy, we had placed texts, quotes, and meditations on each of the elements next to the instruments, among them texts from Hildegard of Bingen.[9] Here are these texts:

Earth

"Soundness—Perseverance—Rootedness—Groundedness"

The north wind shelters contradictory tendencies. It holds back the darkness so that the darkness does not trespass its boundaries. "The earth with all her energy is contained in the flesh and in the bones of humans. Through the earth, the flesh is moist and grows." (Hildegard of Bingen)

Fire

"Spontaneity—Spirituality—Passion—Cleansing—Purification—Creativity—Inspiration"

The south wind has fire in its power; it prevents everything else from burning. "The fire is in the brain and marrow of humans. As the first human was created from the earth, a red fire burned through the power of God into the human's blood. That is why blood is red. The fire expresses itself as heat when seeing." (Hildegard of Bingen)

Water

"Depth of Feelings—Purification—Movement—Turbulence—Fusion"

The west wind wedges itself under the blowing clouds in order to hold in the water so the water does not pour out. "The water with its power is within moisture and in the blood of humans. This causes moisture to remain in humans in order that the power of life remains in them and so that the bones remain strong. The water nourishes the flesh with blood, so that it thrives, as well as also holding together the earth. It makes the body flexible." (Hildegard of Bingen)

Air

"Spiritual Energy—Thinking—Analytical Thinking—Intellect—Decision-making—Discipline—Creativity"

"The air with its power is in the breath and in the reason of humans. It achieves this through its lively aura, which is nothing other than the soul, which in humans is their duty, because the air carries them and it is the wings of humans' flight. When a human takes in air and breathes out, s/he can live. The air expresses itself, when it sends out the Spring thaw and encourages new growth, the wind blows and the human also grows and expands due to the warmth." (Hildegard of Bingen)

Forming the Circle

The gathered women are invited to form a circle around the wind chime.

SPEAKER   In order to form a circle and to strengthen the effects of the
            energy, I invite you to dance three rounds of the "Dance of
            the Elements." The following text accompanies the dance:

ALL   "AIR MOVES US"[10]
(*chanting*) Air moves us,
            fire transforms us,
            water shapes us,
            earth heals us.
            And the balance of the wheel goes round and round
            and the balance of the wheel goes round.

Drawing Near to the Elements

*All are invited to approach the different elements symbolized on the wind chime. The
participants walk around the elements, stopping by the different objects that represent
the elements, asking themselves, What draws me here? What is missing for me here?
What do I want to change? What is strange to me? What is comfortable for me? Each
person then decides which element she wants to place herself next to.*

The Power of the Elements

*The texts associated with each element are read aloud. The women are invited to reflect
on these texts and to share their thoughts on how they experience the power of fire,
water, air, or earth; what they receive from that particular element; what they need
from it; what they wish from it; and what they see in it.*

Bringing the Elements to Song

*The women are invited to practice on the instruments that are located near the ele-
ment they have chosen. They then play their elements, experimenting with sounds,
tones, and music. The others listen.*

Playing the Elements

SPEAKER   Hildegard of Bingen repeatedly pointed out that we humans
            live from the elements, that we are a mixture of them. She
            deepens this thought by claiming that this mixture is about
            movement, that the wind moves the elements, that the circle
            turns, that the people are "nourished" again and again from

this new energy, because we allow ourselves to become part of nature, part of life, part of the cycle of the year. In this way, our instruments play the elements—the fiery, the connecting, the earthy, and the airy. They can play with the other elements; they challenge; they answer.

Dance of the Elements

A spontaneous and improvisational "symphony" of sounds, tones, and music develops as each woman continues to experiment with her instrument. The improvisational music develops into the "Dance of the Elements," as a few women begin to play and chant again "Air Moves Us."

> Air moves us,
> fire transforms us,
> water shapes us,
> earth heals us.
> And the balance of the wheel goes round and round
> and the balance of the wheel goes round.

Promise

SPEAKER   Women, entrust yourselves to the earth,
may you have solid ground under your feet.
Women, entrust yourselves to the water,
may it connect you, let you move, let your life flow.
Women, entrust yourselves to the fire,
may it bring you passion and love, let your inner fire glow.
Women, entrust yourselves to the clear air,
may it allow your thoughts to come and go.

All then join in the following song (the text on which the song is based is by Hildegard of Bingen; it was set to music by Betty Wendelborn[11]).

Song   We are a wheel, a circle of life —
We are a wheel, a circle of power.
We are a wheel, a circle of light —
Circling the world this sacred hour.

Opening the Circle

SPEAKER The circle, our protection, is once again open. Each one of you may take with her what she wants and leave here what should remain. Open yourself, just as the circle opens, to the new.

The women remain, standing silently for a moment, then open the circle and leave . . .

Lady Wisdom as Hostess for the Lord's Supper

Sofia-mässor in Stockholm, Sweden

NINNA EDGARDH BECKMAN

We are gathered in a medieval church in the small Swedish village of Sigtuna, one of the first places in Sweden to be Christianized by German missionaries in the eleventh century. A liturgical dance has drawn us together into a human spiral. Holding each other's hands, we come, step by step, closer to a total stop. Far above us, just under the roof, is a carving of the crucified Jesus on a huge wooden cross, a triumphal crucifix marking the victor of the battle of creation and the means by which this victory was won. Abruptly, the melodic *Kyrie eleison* which has accompanied our spiral dance comes to a stop. It is now impossible to move. We are locked in the human spiral we had formed in our dance. Unexpectedly, the silence is broken by a clear, female voice, praying with rich metaphors:

> You who in your bowl contain both lightness and darkness
> Hold the strength of your hand over near and dear, and far away.
> Comfort all who have despaired, all who have been trampled into wet
> stains,
> all who pine away imprisoned, oh their only crime, to collapse, for the lily
> of justice.
> Lead us, you God of mildness, lead the flocks of humanity to your reign in
> this world.
> Through our expectation of miracles.[1]

In the center of the spiral, someone lights a candle. A sudden movement surges through the crowd. The priest leading the dance raises a bowl with water, flowers, and a burning floating light high above her head. The music starts anew, this time with a *Gloria*, a song of praise to God. Led by the woman priest with the bowl of water and light, the human spiral begins to unlock and move outward. The event just recalled was part of a *Sofia-mässa*, a Sophia-Mass. This Mass was celebrated in August of 1998 with participants from a meeting of the Church Synod (the decision-making body of the Church of Sweden with 251 delegates from thirteen different dioceses). The Mass ended an evening organized by *Kvinnor i Svenska kyrkan* (Women in the Church of Sweden) and focused on Jubilee 2000, the international campaign for canceling the foreign debt of the forty poorest countries of the world. After a presentation and discussion focused on this campaign, the participants were invited to celebrate a *Sofia-mässa* with the theme "The Voice of Justice." About seventy people participated, more women than men.

SWEDEN: WOMEN IN CHURCH AND SOCIETY

The *Sofia-mässa* is a form of liturgy introduced by women as an alternative to traditional androcentric forms of worship. These masses emerged in the context of a society recognized for its efforts to minimize gender inequalities. In 1995, for example, Sweden was ranked number one in gender development and gender empowerment indexes by the United Nations Development Program. In the same year, Sweden received a special prize for extraordinary contributions in this area at the United Nations' Fourth World Conference on Women in Beijing. Despite the progressive politics, gender division and gender inequality prevail in manifold ways. Violence against women, segregation in the labor market (that is, women holding the lowest-paid jobs and doing the unpaid housekeeping), and numerous more subtle forms of gender oppression survive alongside the official progressive politics.

The Church of Sweden counts a large majority of the Swedish population as its members (84 percent in 1999). Until 1999, the Church of Sweden was closely linked to the state. In spite of the first ordination of women in 1960, theologies legitimating the subordination of women and claiming gender differences as divinely instituted still coexist with theologies aligned with progressive social movements towards gender equality. Church leaders have to negotiate between feminists demanding radical and immediate changes in worship and conservatives striving to preserve what may still be rescued of an eroding heritage. Meanwhile, great changes have taken place in belief patterns and customs in our society. Most Swedes nowadays go to church only for baptisms and burials. Many of them vaguely believe in some positive energy, present in all of creation, but use the church merely as a service institution at birth and death. Their faith is thus closed off from the nurture that participation in a living faith community might offer. Gender patterns collide both in the Swedish church and in Swedish society today. The same can be said of different ethnic, religious, and cultural patterns. A formerly homogeneous society, which for centuries embraced the motto "one people and one faith" (first stated in Swedish canon law in 1686), is trying to come to grips with growing diversity. More and more these conflicting developments have also become visible in worship.

CLAIMING OUR RITES

The *Sofia-mässor* represent an explicit effort to create an alternative to andro-centric liturgies—not a gynocentric alternative but a liturgy relevant for both women and men. In these liturgies, female images for God are allowed to correct male idolatry, and intentional body language compensates the "logo-centrism" of the traditional Lutheran liturgy. The original initiative for these alternative liturgies came from a couple of priests in Stockholm, who had growing difficulties with exclusively male God-language and the overall androcentrism of the ordinary liturgy. The women's organization of the diocese decided that it was time to offer an alternative. My own involvement had its background in my research on Sophia, that is, Lady Wisdom in the Jewish and Christian tradition, and on the newborn feminist interest in this ancient female figure from the Scriptures.[2] The feminist interest in Sophia soon became one major source of influence for the shaping of our liturgies. Another source was the experience of circle dance as a form of ritual prayer. One of our group was a priest who for several years had worked with introducing meditative sacred dance in Sweden. The interest in this dance form had been lively, especially among women, but there was no liturgical life to which the groups could naturally connect. The gap was too wide between the women meeting to dance and the ordinary services in the parish.

THE *SOFIA-MÄSSA* WITHIN
THE SWEDISH LITURGICAL TRADITION

In the fall of 1994, a group consisting of a number of priests, a musician, several other laywomen, and me worked out a plan for the first four *Sofia-mässor*. Our liturgical backdrop was the Swedish Lutheran tradition that focused on the Word, both read and preached (the priest is called *verbi divini minister*, servant of the Divine Word). As women we had found that the overwhelming amount of words written and traditioned by men had lost their power to evoke awe. Our desire was to create more space for the Divine Creative Word by focusing liturgically on the meal and on a theme, which could be embodied in dance, words, symbolic acts, and music. The first four Masses took "Creation" as their common theme, with each of the four elements, "Fire," "Water," "Earth," and "Air," being the focus of one Mass. The theological rationale was the fact that in the Old Testament, Wisdom appears as the voice of God calling on humanity in and through creation.

If the decentering of the liturgical Word was controversial, the inclusion of the Eucharist in the *Sofia-mässor* was not, though it would have been not long ago. Not only was the Church of Sweden's liturgy at the beginning of the last century centered on the Word, but the eucharistic tradition had almost died out and been replaced by a guilt-ridden atmosphere focused on human sin and penitence. Throughout the twentieth century this emphasis changed, largely due to the High Church movement with its stress on sacraments, doctrine, ministry, and church. Especially during the last decades, the Eucharist has become more common again in the Church of Sweden and is now celebrated weekly in most parishes. Unfortunately, the High Church movement, while being the carrier of many vitalizing factors in church life, has also embodied a firm and stubborn resistance towards women priests. Today, forty years after the first women were ordained in the Church of Sweden, one fourth of the male priests continue to think it wrong that women are priests, and some of them refuse collaboration with their female colleagues. The liturgical renewal influenced by the High Church movement clearly has been unreceptive to feminist thought. Interest in sacramental theology, liturgical theology, and ecclesiology, in return, have been associated with sexism to such a degree that these theological topics themselves tend to be regarded as "contaminated" by many progressive theologians.

The *Sofia-mässor* originated in despair over the liturgical standstill this situation had created. At the same time, the Masses clearly responded to more than the despair of the initiators. To our surprise, 250 people came to the first liturgy, celebrated on December 4, 1994, in Stockholm's Sophia-Church (which received its name from a Swedish Queen). There was also great interest from the media. The creation of an alternative form of worship thus met with a clearly positive response. Not surprisingly, many also felt that the *Sofia-mässor* represented something alien in the Church of Sweden. In a series of articles in one of the national daily newspapers, the Masses were described as a new "Sophia cult."[3] In the first article, a woman who had attended a *Sofia-mässa* was interviewed. She said with great relief that, at last, the church was welcoming back the witches, whom it once burned at the stake. From these "outsiders" the response was only positive. We also received positive reactions from within the church, but the welcoming attitude was, of course, not universal. In April of 1995, for example, the Chapter of the Diocese of Stockholm received a formal inquiry from a woman priest asking if these services were in accordance with the Christian faith. Personally she regarded them as heretical.

Today, the *Sofia-mässor* do not create big headlines or outraged accusations of heresy although the *Svenska kyrkans fria synod*, a High Church organization opposed to women's ordination, maintains that calling God Mother is not Christian and praying to God's Wisdom as Sophia is an error the church has always rejected. The greatest danger for the *Sofia-mässor*, however, is not the risk of being charged with heresy but the fact that all work with the liturgies has been done voluntarily and on the side. In Sweden today, there is, however, little space for voluntary work in people's lives. This is especially true for the busy life of a young priest with a family. But despite the workload, the Masses continue to be celebrated two to four times a year in Stockholm and have also spread to other parts of the country. People continue to attend the services, and a more fixed liturgical form has gradually developed. A musician has composed music specifically for the *Sofia-mässor*, and some liturgical components have developed into a regular pattern.

SHARING A RITE

A closer look at the service celebrated in Sigtuna in August 1998 reveals several traits typical for both the *Sofia-mässor* and for the Swedish variant of the feminist liturgical movement.[4] These characteristics include the celebration of the Eucharist, the use of a church building as sacred space, and the leadership of one or more women priests. The structure of the *Sofia-mässor* comes quite close to the structure of a High Mass in the Church of Sweden, which in turn is very close to the liturgical pattern common to most western eucharistic liturgies (a gathering rite, the reading and proclamation of the Word, the meal, and a sending forth into the world). Feminist adaptation of the traditional pattern is possible because women are priests in the Church of Sweden and thus hold at least some ritual authority. In the Church of Sweden generally, however, there are no great differences between services celebrated by male and female priests. Most women, as most men, follow the official worship manual of the church and the informal customs in the parish. But for those who have the will and strength to create a feminist setting, as in the group behind the *Sofia-mässor*, the worship manual does provide the opportunity of celebrating a "thematic Eucharist." The only requirement for such a Eucharist is the reading of the words of institution and the sharing of bread and wine. Other parts of the service can be shaped according to a chosen theme. This possibility is used in the *Sofia-mässor*. Granted a broad correspondence to the ordinary High Mass, these *Sofia-mässor* also reveal typical divergences from the ordinary liturgy. The main structural divergence is the absence of a distinct part of the service reserved for reading and proclaiming the Word from the Bible. But the gathering, the meal, and the sending also differ from the celebration of an ordinary High Mass in the Church of Sweden.

The gathering rite in a traditional High Mass in the Church of Sweden is quite solemn and focuses on repentance and confession. An opening hymn is sung while the priest and maybe one or two elected laypeople enter in solemn procession. In the *Sofia-mässa* in Sigtuna, all participants instead were invited to enter the church together in a dancing procession to the song "Jubilation and Joy" (whose text was adapted from the Song of Songs). The dancing procession meant a more participative and affirmative start than is common even in contemporary Church of Sweden liturgies. A set of responsive readings followed, with the texts alternating between the priest and the congregation. The parts read by the priest concerned women around the world exposed to, but also opposing, various forms of injustice and suffering. The parts read by the congregation came from the Book of Proverbs: Lady Wisdom praises herself and exhorts the ungodly and foolish. Words of God in female guise were thus placed in the mouths of women, who gave voice to God's protest against the oppression of women around the world. A specific understanding of God and humanity was thereby established, which differed significantly from the traditional image of a holy but distant Father, judging and by grace forgiving his naughty children. The responsive readings suggested an understanding of a present and loving God who collaborates with humanity. At the same time, the readings made visible the vulnerable and exposed situation of women worldwide. Only then was the question of the participants' share in evil deeds raised. But instead of a confession in words, this issue was approached by the spiral dance described at the beginning of my essay, in an enactment where everyone became at the same time victim and perpetrator. Packed into an unmoving mob, the dancers could in the final standstill only leave their lives to God, and then by grace receive a way out of the closed spiral. Having returned to the pews, the congregation and choir sang a song (in place of the traditional *Gloria*) whose text came from the Wisdom of Sirach, a book usually not read in the Swedish liturgy. In this text, which has traditionally been interpreted as alluding to Christ, Lady Wisdom praises herself in the midst of her people. The hymn was followed by a short sermon by the priest who had led the dance. No particular reading from the Bible preceded the sermon; texts from the Old Testament and from the Apocrypha had only been used in readings and songs. This freer use of biblical texts differs significantly from the traditional formal reading of two or three canonical texts, followed by a sermon.[5]

The Eucharist proper began with an offertory hymn, the words placed again in the mouth of Lady Wisdom who invites all to come and eat her bread and drink the wine she has mixed. In this way Sophia herself, as God in female guise, invited people to the table. The congregation gave voice to Sophia through their singing. The eucharistic prayer addressed "eternal Wisdom," who has set the table and "come to us in Jesus Christ to reveal the mystery of giving and sharing." The institution narrative with its invocation of Jesus as "Lord" was taken directly from the official worship manual. The final part of the prayer, on the other hand, was directed to "Wisdom's Spirit," whose presence in the sharing of the meal was invoked so that we might "praise and glorify your name."

This divine "name" is expressed in shifting human words. This is particularly clear in the *Sofia-mässa*. There is, for example, a shift from female to neuter to male in the invitation placed in the mouth of a female figure called "Wisdom," the subsequent addressing of God as "Eternal Wisdom" (a term that in Swedish is neuter), and then of Jesus as "Lord." Such a frank shifting between differently gendered words for God is a recurring phenomenon in the Sophia-liturgies. This intentional shifting means a break with the common symbolism building on gender complementarity (such as the church as the receptive bride and Christ as the life-giving groom). In Sigtuna, male, neuter, and female images were instead treated as interchangeable with equal but limited potential for representing God. From a liturgical perspective this usage may be interpreted as a feminist application of the principle of "juxtaposition." According to the Lutheran liturgical scholar Gordon Lathrop, such juxtaposition, that is, the placing side by side of components that criticize and thereby correct each other, is an essential Christian liturgical pattern.[6] A basic example is the juxtaposition of the traditional Jewish ritual bath and the Word of the Gospel in baptism. In a similar way, the *Sofia-mässor* employ female and neuter words as correctives to, rather than substitutes for, the male God-language of the official worship manual.

The eucharistic prayer was followed by the "Our Father," as is usual in a High Mass. The prayer, however, was not only prayed in unison but sung (to a melody borrowed from the Finnish Orthodox liturgy) and accompanied by gestures. Here is another example of a feminist appropriation of the liturgical principle of juxtaposition: the image of God as Father appeared for the first time in this *Sofia-mässa* with the Lord's Prayer. The ordinary way of praying was, however, altered by the singing and by the movements. The potentially negative impact of the Father-language was compensated by juxtaposing it with bodily, and in the experience of the participants probably "female," means of expression. After the "Our Father" followed the breaking of the bread, accompanied by a prayer that associated the action of breaking the bread with the broken world and the human longing for justice and healing. Bread and wine were shared. A sung prayer of thanksgiving likened God with a caring mother, turning her face to her beloved child. The sending forth invoked Holy Wisdom, and a concluding hymn included all of creation in its praise of God who gives birth to and nourishes all nature and who has also become human. A danced recession (to the melody of the entering procession) completed the service.

TRADITION RETRADITIONED

In describing the service I have identified new patterns, new language, and new meaning in the *Sofia-mässa* celebrated in Sigtuna. Taken as a whole, this Mass includes most components of a traditional High Mass. The new emerges in the understanding of God and humanity, of gender relations, and of the Bible. Both words and gestures are used to embody these new understandings. The most obvious sign of the new is the recurring Sophia- or Wisdom-language. This is also the issue that has aroused the most debate. It is a common experience in Western feminism that female names for God evoke deep feelings—in the case of Sophia both enthusiasm and accusations of heresy as well as a more vague uneasiness and doubt that this female figure really is "our God." The above-mentioned inquiry to the Chapter of the Diocese in Stockholm voiced these doubts. One year after the inquiry had been opened, the Chapter issued a four-page response that was distributed to the vicars of all parishes in the diocese. The response noted positively that the *Sofia-mässor* had been celebrated in accordance with the worship manual's order for a thematic Eucharist. The Chapter also insisted on the urgent need to include women's experiences in worship. Negatively, the response noted that use of the name Sophia, without interpretive guidelines, would lead people to perceive her as a distinct person and not as another name for Christ or God. The Chapter also stated, however, that such interpretive guidelines "should not be necessary in a liturgy used in the Christian community."[7] The Christian language of worship is supposed to be a communally shared language, as the liturgy is corporate. The Chapter maintained that feminine terms for God cannot be the bearers of communal meaning today but instead confuse people who wonder who is invoked. What the Chapter did not discuss was the fact that the old King-God-Almighty-Father-Protector-language[8] itself functions badly today as a carrier of communal adoration before the mystery of God. Part of the problem may simply be lack of faith in the God people associate with this language. As previously mentioned, new surveys in the Nordic countries show a decrease in belief in an external personal God, while belief in a God who is present within each human being and in a nonpersonal energy or power is increasing. For good or bad, an association of God with "woman" might actually be more readily adaptable to these changes in belief patterns, as femininity tends to be more closely related culturally to immanence than to transcendence.

The response of the Chapter seems to assume that language problems entered the room when the name Sophia was first uttered. The *Sofia-mässor*, however, were created to solve problems that were already present, such as the absence of any images associating women and God. I am convinced that the debate which the language has aroused is ultimately rooted in deep-seated patriarchal values that are touched when one tries to change God-language from "him" to "her," and from "he" to "she." After all, God is imaged almost exclusively male in a Western culture that has traditionally subordinated women to men. The two sides of this coin are related, as Mary Daly pointed out long ago: if God is male, then the male is God. The exact workings of the interrelationship are, of course, complex. In some contexts, male-imaged liturgies have allowed women to experience the Christian faith as liberating and as a source of resistance against oppressive structures. Any liberating potential in male-dominated liturgies, however, is unlikely to shine forth in a culture like Sweden, where the church is regarded more as a refuge for people with conservative views on women than as a haven for women from an oppressive society. Rather, both the interest in and the resistance to the *Sofia-mässor* reveal a crisis in the language, and thus in the theology and self-understanding of the contemporary church. This crisis is closely related to the profound cultural shifts in women's lives in recent decades. In poststructuralist terminology, the *Sofia-mässor* represent efforts to destabilize dominant patriarchal liturgical patterns by establishing an alternative liturgical discourse built on feminist commitments. At the same time the *Sofia-mässor* obviously are dependent on the dominant discourse. The ease with which female images of God can be adapted to a more immanent understanding of the divine, for example, depends on gender constructions within the dominant discourse. The dependence on the biblical image of God as Lady Wisdom may, to take another example, suggest a contradiction with the free relationship to the biblical text manifested in the *Sofia-mässor*. Read against the background of a strong focus on the Word in the Swedish liturgical tradition, however, the adoption of a biblical—and thereby legitimized—female image is understandable.

The members of the Church Synod attending the *Sofia-mässa* in Sigtuna became involved not only in a liturgy but in an ongoing struggle within the Church of Sweden over the right to interpret the Christian heritage. It is a struggle against injustices performed against women. It is also a struggle taking sides with the poor all over the world who experience God as the "Voice of Justice," inviting humans to partake in the creation of a better world where justice and peace will reign. Last but not least it is a struggle for the relevance of Christian faith and Christian liturgy in the lives of ordinary Swedes who value solidarity and the equal worth of women and men but who in their daily lives are again and again caught up in spirals of evil.

THE VOICE OF JUSTICE: A SOFIA-MÄSSA[9]

All enter the church in a procession-dance to the song "Jubilation and Joy."[10]

The biblical texts are from Proverbs 1 and 8.

A Responsive   "Justice Cries in the Streets"
Reading
(between people   **Wisdom cries out in the street, in the squares She raises**
and priest)   **her voice. At the busiest corner She cries out, at the entrance of the city gates She speaks: "How long, O simple ones, will you love being simple? How long will scoffers delight in their scoffing and fools hate knowledge? Give heed to my reproof, I will pour out my thoughts to you, I will make my words known to you."**
She stands outside the metro station, shabby and hoarse, and sells *Situation Stockholm*, the newspaper of the homeless:

To you, O my people I call, and my cry is to all that live. O simple ones, learn prejudice, acquire intelligence, you who lack it. Hear, for I will speak noble things, and from my lips will come what is right.

She walks with the mothers in the Plaza de Mayo, her white headcloth shimmering like mother of pearl, as she demands to know the truth about the vanished sons:

For my mouth will utter truth, wickedness is an abomination to my lips. All the words of my mouth are righteous; there is nothing twisted or crooked in them. They are all straight to one who understands and right to those who find knowledge. Take my instruction instead of silver and knowledge rather than choice gold. For Wisdom is better than jewels and all that you may desire cannot compare with Her.

She stands with a group of black-clad women on a pavement during the evening rush hour, in a silent protest against war, a plea for peace:

I, Wisdom, live with prudence, and I attain knowledge and discretion.
The fear of the Lord is hatred of evil and perverted speech I hate.
I have good advice and sound wisdom, I have insight, I have strength.

She walks along a village street in Egypt, gathering women for a meeting to discuss how they are going to stop the genital mutilation of girls:

I love those who love me and those who seek me diligently find me. Riches and honor are with me, enduring wealth and prosperity. My fruit is better than gold, even fine gold, and my yield than choice silver.

She stands in the middle of a human chain in Birmingham, one of the tens of thousands demanding the cancellation of debt for the developing countries:

I walk in the way of righteousness, along the paths of justice, endowing with wealth those who love me and filling their treasuries. Does not Wisdom call and does not Understanding raise her voice? On the heights, beside the way, at the crossroads She takes her stand. Beside the gates in front of the town, at the entrance of the portals She cries out: "Happy is the one who listens to me, watching daily at my gates, waiting beside my doors. For whoever finds me finds life and obtains favor from the Lord."

All join in forming a human spiral in the following dance.

Kyrie-Dance   PSALM 25:20 (SET TO MUSIC)
                   O guard my life, and deliver me:
                   do not let me be put to shame,
                   for I take refuge in you.

As the human spiral deadlocks, the priest, lifting a bowl of water with a candle swimming in the middle, prays the following prayer:

> You who in your bowl contain both lightness and darkness
> Hold the strength of your hand over near and dear, and far
>   away.

Comfort all who have despaired, all who have been trampled into wet stains,

all who pine away imprisoned, oh their only crime, to collapse, for the lily of justice.

Lead us, you God of mildness, lead the flocks of humanity to your reign in this world.

Through our expectation of miracles.[11]

The spiral deadlock breaks, with the priest leading the people out and back to the pews.

Gloria-Dance

Praise to God in the highest and peace to God's people on earth.

We sing to you, Creator, Redeemer, and Giver of Life. We dance with you, you who invites us into your eternal dance.[12]

Praise to God in the highest and peace to God's people on earth.

Responsorial Song

FROM SIRACH 24

Wisdom praises herself and tells her glory in the midst of her people.

I came forth from the mouth of the most high and covered the earth like a mist.

Wisdom praises herself and tells her glory in the midst of her people.

I dwelt in the highest heavens and my throne was a pillar of cloud.

Wisdom praises herself and tells her glory in the midst of her people.

Alone I compassed the vault of heaven and traversed the depths of the abyss.

Wisdom praises herself and tells her glory in the midst of her people.

Before the ages in the beginning God created me and for all the ages I shall not cease to be.

Wisdom praises herself and tells her glory in the midst of her people.

The priest shares her reflections.

Offertory   FROM PROVERBS 9:1–6
Procession   **Come, eat of my bread and drink the wine I have mixed (twice).**

Wisdom has built her house; she has hewn her seven pillars.

Come, eat of my bread and drink the wine I have mixed.

She has slaughtered her animals; she has mixed her wine; she has also set her table.

Come, eat of my bread and drink the wine I have mixed.

She has sent out her servant girls; she calls from the highest places in town.

Come, eat of my bread and drink the wine I have mixed.

You who are simple, turn in here! To those without sense she says,

Come, eat of my bread and drink the wine I have mixed.

Lay aside immaturity and live and walk in the way of insight.

Come, eat of my bread and drink the wine I have mixed.

Eucharistic Prayer

O, Eternal wisdom, we praise and worship you,
you who prepares a table for us
you who has built us a home in the cosmos,
you who came to us
in Christ Jesus
to reveal the mystery of giving and sharing.
In the broken bread we see the heart of existence
which is your being.

On the night when he was betrayed
he took the bread, gave thanks,

broke it and gave it to the disciples and said,
"Take and eat. This is my body which is given for you.
Do this in remembrance of me."
In the same way he took the cup, gave thanks,
gave it to the disciples and said,
"Drink of this all of you. This is the new covenant through
   my blood,
which is shed for many for the forgiveness of sins.
As often as you drink it, do this in remembrance of me."

We proclaim your death, Lord.
We acknowledge your resurrection
until you come again in glory.

Oh, you Wisdom's Spirit,
come to us as we share this bread and wine,
so that we become one in Christ,
willing to give of ourselves,
share our bread,
and so become Wisdom's children,
to praise and glorify your name.
Amen.

The Lord's Prayer

(sung to a melody from the Finnish Orthodox liturgy and accompanied by gestures)

While praying the following prayer, the priest turns in four different directions and breaks the bread four times. The fourth and last time, she breaks the bread facing the congregation.

The Breaking of Bread

We break this bread for sisters and brothers
who live in lands where war prevails
as a sign that we all share
both in the pain of war and in the longing
and fight for peace and justice.

We break this bread for brothers and sisters
of differing beliefs and religious affiliation
as an expression of the fact that we are all part of
the same humanity
and share this life on earth with one another.

We break this bread for our wounded earth,
for fields, forests, and seas,
as a sign that we belong together
with the whole of God's creation
and want to take responsibility for the healing of the earth's
    wounds.

We break this bread for the division
and brokenness we experience within ourselves
and in relationships between people
as an expression that we want to open ourselves
to wholeness and life
when we share the bread that is the body of Christ.[13]

The Peace

(*sung by all*)   Wisdom, the fullness of God and light of creation
Has built herself a dwelling place here
And offers us her peace.

Communion

Prayer of Thanksgiving[14]

(*sung by all*)   You turn your face towards me and smile at your child like a
    mother.
Your face shines like the sun; it is this that makes me believe,
that you smile at me like a mother.

Sending Forth

*The priest blesses all with a blessing created by Janet Morley that invokes "holy Wis-
dom" as the one who makes us "friends of God."*[15]

Closing Hymn

With space full of mystery and buds that burst open,
with meadows, with forests, and seas,
we cry out in joy to you, nurturer of all:
Gloria! Gloria! Gloria!

With cells that divide in continuing patterns,
in flowers, in children, and birds,
we cry out in joy to you, who became human:
Gloria! Gloria! Gloria!

With the people who seek and are woken by the wind
of truth and freedom and justice,
we cry out in joy to you, our creator:
Gloria! Gloria! Gloria![16]

*All leave the church in a procession-dance to the song "Jubilation and Joy," which
accompanied the entrance procession.*

African Woman: Arise and Eat, For Your Journey Is Long

The Ecumenical Seminars on African Women's Theologies in South Africa and Mozambique

PAULINE MUCHINA AND JANA MEYER

The Ecumenical Seminars on African Women's Theologies in South Africa and Mozambique are examples of the transformation possible when African women define and contextualize their own theological and liturgical realities. Both of the 1999 seminars were facilitated entirely by African women, each using a slightly different format: the South African seminar brought together a small yet diverse group of men and women; the Mozambique seminar was comprised primarily of Mozambican clergywomen.[1] The Mozambique seminar gave birth to the Lusophone Circle of African Women Theologians, which initiated, organized, and facilitated a third seminar on African Women's Theologies, held in Maputo in September 2000. This seminar, organized entirely by Lusophone African women, broke the myth that African women need outside help to lead and train them. Together, the three seminars demonstrate the urgent importance of providing resources and support for theological training and liturgical experiences contextualized by and for African women.

African women's theologies are no new phenomena. African women have always theologized about the relationship between God, nature, and human beings. In the African churches, however, women's theologizing has often been ignored. Certain theological presuppositions and cultural practices have excluded African women from decision-making processes in church and in society. Because of the linguistic and cultural diversity of the African context, and because of barriers to communication and information, African women have often not had access to experiences and reflections of other African women theologians in spite of the ongoing efforts of the Circle of Concerned African Women Theologians. Women in Lusophone or Portuguese-speaking

Africa, in particular, have been excluded from discussions and resources of African theology, which has focused primarily on contributions from Anglophone and Francophone regions.

The Ecumenical Seminars on African Women's Theologies were designed to equip African women with theological resources to enable them to claim their place within African church and society. The two original seminars in 1999 were envisioned and coorganized by Pauline Muchina and Jana Meyer and sponsored respectively by the Kalahari Desert School of Theology at Kuruman, South Africa, and by the United Methodist Church of Mozambique, with the support and collaboration of the Circle of Concerned African Women Theologians. African women from Mozambique, Angola, and South Africa were invited to facilitate and lead the seminar, along with Pauline Muchina. The Rev. Olga Maria Raimundo Choto was involved from the early stages as a coorganizer of the Mozambique seminar. The seminars combined theological formation, empowerment and leadership exercises, reflection, prayer, and celebration, all set in the context of African women's experiences. Pauline brought together her course on African Women's Theologies with modules from a grassroots leadership training program designed by Women in Mission and Ministry of the Episcopal Church, U.S.A. Part of the preparation for the seminars also involved translating articles into Portuguese so that they could be available to women theologians in Mozambique.

The objectives of the Ecumenical Seminars on African Women's Theologies were broad-ranging: first, to develop an understanding of African women's theologies as transforming and empowering theologies; second, to explore and analyze the sources of these theologies and to examine the cultural, religious, political, and economic contexts in which African women theologize; third, to explore African traditional values that might empower women and to critique those values that subjugate; fourth, to strengthen African women's leadership skills; fifth, to contextualize African women's theologies in the light of the Mozambican and South African experiences; sixth, to create practical means of conveying the insights of African women's theologies in the church and the wider community through sermons, Bible studies, teaching, and reflections and to compile these in written form; and seventh, to strengthen the connections between Mozambican and South African women theologians, pastors, and laywomen, on the one hand, and the Circle of Concerned African Women Theologians, on the other.

The daily meditations, led by the participants, focused on the experiences of African women. These meditations provided the spiritual foundation for the seminar. Each day also included presentations by facilitators and participants, discussion, empowerment exercises, and projects to implement the content of the seminars. Discussions in both small and large groups ensured that each person had an opportunity to contribute. The topics of the seminars addressed the African context, African culture, religion, church, Scripture, sociopolitical conditions, violence against women, and other women's theologies, all in relation to and as sources for African women's theologies.

THE 1999 SEMINAR AT THE KALAHARI DESERT SCHOOL OF THEOLOGY

The South African seminar was a unique experience, bringing together a small yet diverse group of people to share worship and reflection focused on the experiences of African women. Eighteen participants gathered at the Kalahari Desert School of Theology housed at Moffat Mission Station, Kuruman, South Africa, in late August 1999 for the first Ecumenical Seminar on African Women's Theologies. The women and men who attended the seminar came from black, colored, and white communities, and included pastors, seminarians, lecturers, missionaries, and members of parish councils. They came from five different countries: the host country South Africa, Botswana, Namibia, Kenya, and the United States. For the majority of those gathered, this was their first encounter with African women's theologies, although the Circle of Concerned African Women Theologians has been active in South Africa for many years. Pauline Muchina from Kenya and Daphne Maphuti Majapie Madiba from South Africa facilitated the seminar. Daphne Madiba had to travel for over twelve hours to Kuruman. Some of the other participants traveled as much as fourteen hours by bus to attend.

Each day began with reflections on a biblical text in light of the experiences of African women. From the beginning, music was a constant part of worship as the participants shared spontaneous choruses in their own languages. On the first day, we built an altar together using different objects that the participants had brought to the seminar. We used this building of an altar to share our hopes for the seminar. The experience was very moving. One participant brought seeds as a symbol of growth and fruitfulness. Another brought a pen signaling that the time had come for African women to write themselves rather than to be written about. One person brought thorns symbolizing the distancing of men from the experiences of women. One brought a rock as a sign of Jesus Christ, the rock upon which African women's theologies should build. There was a shell signifying the shell African women were coming out of, a pencil symbolizing the hope of being sharpened, a match to light the way for women, charcoal as a sign of the fire of the Holy Spirit, and a water bottle pointing to our thirst being satisfied. As we built the altar, the Spirit of God moved us forward to struggle for the liberation of African women and never to look back.

In the presentations and discussions we reflected on the many contexts for African women's theologies. African women live in multilingual, multicultural, and multireligious environments, rich in resources yet devastated by poverty. How do we proclaim abundant life in the midst of abject poverty? We faced the stark statistics that testify to the political and economic crises of the continent. As we do theology as African women, we are confronting these issues and ask whether our theologies bring hope in these situations. African women are writing prayers and wondering: God, have you forgotten us? God, are you listening to us as African women? Do you hear our cry? The question we must ask ourselves as theologians is, Do we hear the cry of African women?

Creating space to focus on the relationship of African women, culture, religion, and church was central to the seminar's worship, reflection, presentations, and discussions. One morning, for example, Daphne Madiba invited the participants to join in an African form of worship. She began by invoking the presence of the ancestors, requesting them to bless the day, the discussion, our families, and our congregations. Daphne noted that usually water or snuff is used when communicating with the ancestors in Africa and that one person leads the ritual while all participants kneel. This particular form of worship is not used every day but at particular moments to communicate with the ancestors: in times of problems, at the start of a journey, in times of happiness, or at the birth of a child. Daphne Madiba invited those of us who chose to gather around the altar to participate in this ritual, which she led. This was a powerful moment, challenging African and non-African Christians alike to position themselves as observers or participants with respect to African traditions. For some participants, this was an empowering moment, enabling them to practice openly a traditional African form of worship as Christians. For others it was a contradiction to what they had been taught by their churches. Yet others seemed unsure how to react. In her presentation, Daphne Madiba emphasized the importance of African culture and religion for women: "Yes, we are Christians but in Africa we have ancestors." She stressed how in African traditional religions, women's leadership is recognized, especially in the ritual veneration of ancestors.[2]

The seminar participants also discussed, with differing perspectives, traditional practices that undermine the well-being of women, such as polygamy, female genital mutilation, the subordination of women, and the failure of the church to provide adequate guidance in the area of sex education and human sexuality, especially in relation to the HIV/AIDS pandemic sweeping the continent. We spoke about violence against women and ways in which the church had been complicit with such violence and with shrouding in silence the violated women. Yet, in Africa, sixty to seventy percent of Christians are women.

They are the ones who nurture the church while being excluded from decision making and leadership.

One of the objectives of the seminar was to create meditations on biblical women—based on African women's experiences—to use as resources for parish worship. One powerful example was Wendy Esau's reflection on Hagar from the perspective of a Cape colored woman theologian. Wendy noted that like Hagar, colored people in South Africa are an uprooted community experiencing high levels of violence against women. She asked,

> How do we keep hopeful, how do we become healthy and whole human beings in this multifaceted situation of oppression, suffering, and violence? One of the things we can do is to go back, just as Hagar, in order to move forward. We need to know our history—why are we such a fragmented, violent community? Why do we have such low self-esteem? We need to know our tradition and cultures, which for so long have been suppressed and denied. We need to learn from the struggles and victories of other colored women, to say boldly that colored people too are created in the image of God. It is when we go back, when we understand why we suffer, that we can go forward and partake in the blessings and promises that are there for us.[3]

Malebogo Mothibi shared the story of the Hottentot woman Vehettage Tikkuie, an early African woman convert and church leader whose story has been largely forgotten. Vehettage Tikkuie came into contact with Christian missionaries in 1739 and was baptized in 1742. She is described as the first indigenous person in the region who could read the New Testament. When the missionaries returned home, they left responsibility for the indigenous believers in the hands of three men. When these disappeared, Vehettage Tikkuie, renamed Magdalene at her baptism, took over responsibility for this community of faith. Malebogo Mothibi concluded her presentation on this woman by emphasizing both Vehettage's legacy and the church's silencing of her contribution: "Today, we are a church in Africa thanks to Vehettage! But how much is said about her?"[4]

One of the male participants, Nathan Isaacs, chose to write a text in honor of his mother, a colored woman. His text argued that violence against women is a sin against God and challenged the church to confess and to change its attitude toward women, to eliminate sexist language and liturgies, to recognize the humanity and experience of African women, and to draw colored women into the power-holding structures of church and society.[5]

For the participants, the seminar motivated change by critically looking at culture, church, and society from the experiences of African women. At the same time, the seminar created a place of inspiration and challenge for the struggle for women's place in church and society. One participant stated that the seminar had awakened in her the need to rediscover herself and a contextualized theology, to look at her culture in order to choose what was relevant, and never to give up in the struggle for the rights of African women. The participation of men in the seminar was a particular opportunity for transformation. One of the men, a twenty-eight-year-old intern pastor, acknowledged a growing sensitivity for women in his ministry, and a seventy-six-year-old farmer said he had learned about the sufferings of women to which he had been blind.

In a closing ritual at the end of the seminar, we took down our altar. As we took away each of the objects we had brought on the first day, we named what we were taking with us. One of the men who participated said he had heard the cry of African women and been deeply moved. While the seminar in South Africa was not an African women-only space, the experience demonstrated that creating African women-centered reflections and prayers in a small but diverse group of women and men from black, colored, and white communities planted seeds of liberation and transformation for communities and the church.

THE 1999 SEMINAR IN MAPUTO, MOZAMBIQUE

The second Ecumenical Seminar on African Women's Theologies took place at the invitation of the United Methodist Church of Mozambique and with generous support from the Ecumenical Theological Education Program and the Women's Desk of the World Council of Churches as well as from the Women's Division of the United Methodist Church, U.S.A. Preparations for the seminar nevertheless were complicated. To begin with, twenty-five articles by different African women theologians had to be translated into Portuguese. The Rev. Olga Maria Choto, an ordained minister of the United Methodist Church of Mozambique and our coorganizer in Maputo, began the process of identifying women pastors to invite to the seminar. This was no easy task since the churches were unable to provide us with a complete list of their women pastors. We also invited laywomen from those churches that do not ordain women, such as the Anglican and the Wesleyan Methodist Churches in Mozambique. Sending invitations to women who had no telephone or mail service was another challenge. And we felt overwhelmed when comparing the financial resources designated for the project to the monthly salaries of women pastors in Mozambique. These women serve their churches on seventy dollars or less per month. Despite all the difficulties, however, the twelve-day *Seminário Ecuménico de Teologias de Mulheres Africanas* took place with over fifty participants in mid-September in Maputo, the capital of Mozambique.

"African Woman: The Spirit of God is upon you to announce all of these things to the others" (Luke 4:18; 24:9) had been chosen as the theme of the gathering. Five African women theologians from Kenya, Mozambique, and Angola facilitated the seminar. Participants included fifty-five women from eleven different denominations, mostly from Mozambique and Angola. The majority of participants were women pastors, with a range of theological backgrounds from no theological training to postseminary education, and from both urban and rural areas. Some laywomen were also present, with professional training in education, theology, and journalism. During the seminar, most of the worship and music were led by the participants themselves, rather than by the facilitators. Ample time was allowed for discussion in small and larger groups to ensure that everyone's voice was heard. The diversity of geographic contexts and educational levels added both richness and challenge to the seminar. Women pastors valued the exchange of diverse experiences, but the diversity also brought the challenge of ensuring everyone was included in the discussions. Men had not been specifically excluded from the seminar but had also not received invitations, except for the opening and closing worship services.

The linguistic diversity of Lusophone Africa permeated the seminar. There was no common language in our gathering. Pauline Muchina, one of the facilitators, spoke English and other regional languages from Kenya. The three Angolan facilitators all spoke Portuguese but different local languages. Some of the participants spoke local Mozambican languages only, such as Xitswa, Bitonga, Ronga, Chope, and Changana. Throughout the seminar, therefore, there was a constant humming due to all the simultaneous interpretation efforts. The ability of women from different African cultures to transcend linguistic barriers as they shared their experiences, sermons, and prayers bore witness to the power of the Spirit and to the sacredness of the space being created.

As had the first seminar in South Africa, the Mozambican seminar also began with the construction of an altar out of objects women had brought. Placing these objects on the altar, the women shared their hopes for the seminar. We then invoked our ancestors, especially the women who walked the same paths before us. As the altar building drew to a close, both the objects on the altar and the music reminded us of our African context: there were African cloths, drums, and a calabash, among others. Many of the objects were those used by women in their daily lives. The ritual of constructing the altar and the manner of sitting around the altar in a circle gave structure to the integration of the liturgical, theological, and educational aspects of the seminar. One of the participants said in her final evaluation that both the altar and sitting in a circle (in contrast to the usual sitting in rows for a conference or presentation) were among the most important things she learned.

Issues of African culture and African church life in relation to African women proved to be of paramount importance. In her presentation, Olga Maria Choto pointed to several intertwined realities for African women, such as the effects of colonization and family and church socialization. In Sunday school, for example, a girl will be taught to yield her chair to her brother and to sit on the *esteira*, the traditional straw mat, instead. Choto also noted, however, that in traditional African religion, women took on the role of priestess (*Massingalacate*). Today in Mozambique women still function as traditional healers in larger numbers than men, and the first person called upon in the rite of invoking the ancestors (*Kuphala*) is a woman.[6] Pastor Eva das Dores Benedito Gomes spoke from the perspective of the Kimbanguista Church of Angola, an African Independent Church in which women have exercised leadership positions from early on; Mama Muilu, although illiterate, was one of the most important leaders of the Kimbanguista Church. Both Gomes and Muchina challenged the women from mainline churches to reflect on the question "Is the culture of our church African?"[7]

There were several other powerful moments in this seminar. One came in the spontaneous burning of all negative statements about African women. Several participants referred to this ritual as deeply cathartic (although we were charged twenty-five dollars for the trash can used in this ritual burning!). Positive statements, on the other hand, were written on papers and remained around the altar for the rest of the seminar. The daily meditations led by different participants also were important, as we reflected on Esther, Vashti, Tabitha, Deborah, and Mary Magdalene as inspirations for African women today. Music played a principal role, often in the form of spontaneous choruses, usually of African origin. These choruses were used to gather and center people. The music was almost always a capella. Participants organized several smaller choirs during the seminar to provide music during the liturgies and meditations. Usually hymns were sung during the liturgies and meditations while choruses were used to gather, celebrate, play, and revive.

The Mozambican organizing team had decided to select a theme for the seminar, a common church practice in Mozambique. The theme, "African Woman: The Spirit of God is upon you to announce all of these things to the others," focused the seminar. Pastor Telma Armindo's morning meditation was an example of how the theme of the seminar was woven together with prayer and meditation to form a liturgy. The morning meditation began with hymns sung by two different groups. Then Pastor Telma invited us to approach and circle the altar we had made with our own hands out of objects of our daily lives. She reminded us that circling the altar is part of our African way. As everyone sat down around the altar on the floor, she led us in a song: "God I Want to Feel Your Presence in My Heart." The biblical text (Luke

4:18f) that provided the theme of the seminar was read. In her meditation Pastor Telma exhorted African women to undertake the difficult but important mission entrusted to each of them with the conference theme: to announce salvation and liberation to their African sisters. She told the women to give themselves to God in prayer and to trust God for strength, courage, and guidance, leaving fear behind them. She led the participants to pray for their sisters who had preceded them in this work even to the point of martyrdom, for African countries at war, and for those devastated by AIDS. Pastor Telma concluded by encouraging the women never to give up but to take on the mission to announce all these things to the others, knowing that the Spirit of God is upon them.[8]

On the last day of the seminar, bishops and other ecclesial representatives were invited to the closing worship, which was planned and led entirely by participants rather than facilitators or organizers. The celebration of the Lord's Supper was a deeply meaningful event that contextualized communion in the experience of Mozambican and African women. The women pastors had chosen to come in African dress rather than their clerical garb. African elements of cassava and orange juice were used as elements for the Lord's Supper. The elements were laid out on an *esteira*, the straw mat on which women traditionally sit and eat, in the center of the circle in front of the altar we had constructed. The participants invited us to prepare for the celebration of the Lord's Supper by kneeling in a circle in prayer. The women pastors leading the service knelt on the *esteira*. At the time of communion, they served the cassava and orange juice. For most of us, whether African or non-African, this was the first time we had received African elements for communion. At the end of the worship service, participants who represented different continents took objects from the altar to symbolize our taking the message of African women to all parts of the world. We concluded with a festive meal with music and dancing, culminating in the cutting of a cake in honor of the Lusophone Circle of African Women Theologians, which had formed during our seminar, and its newly elected leadership.

The Mozambican seminar created an impact beyond the immediate participants. The media gave the seminar much publicity. The weekly newspaper carried an article and featured interviews with the facilitators. The local television station included the seminar in one of its evening headlines. Some men in the church complained about having a seminar just for women. One of the men who attended the final worship (and holds a position of responsibility in the church) insisted, however, that he saw God calling the church to make changes and that one should not resist but rather cooperate.

In their final message, the participants stated that the seminar "strengthened our vocation, awakened us and encouraged us to a challenge to conquer our lost values and to recognize our capacity within the culture in which we live and work. We discovered and rediscovered the identity of women in the Sacred Scriptures, in society, and in the church." Many of the participants in their evaluations of the seminar cited a renewed confidence in their value as women in the church and society and as African women theologians. One of the seminary students, for example, learned that "I too am an African woman theologian." A fifty-four-year-old pastor said, "It took away the difficulties I had not believing in myself, but now I feel secure. I learned that the African woman is equal to the man." The discussion about the values and practices of African culture prompted for many the recovery of their culture as a resource for ministry. As one participant affirmed, "I will put into practice African culture as a source for theology."[9]

The influence of the seminar on the participants carried beyond the actual seminar, sometimes in small but powerful signs. We heard later that one of the seminarians who had attended the seminar caused a stir when she began a prayer at her school's chapel with "God our Mother and Father." We also heard of participants giving presentations on African women's theologies in their parishes and schools. Still, no one imagined then how the seeds the participants had planted would continue to grow.

THE 2000 SEMINAR IN MAPUTO, MOZAMBIQUE

The second seminar of the Lusophone Circle of African Women Theologians took place in September 2000.[10] The Lusophone Circle, under the leadership of the Rev. Olga Maria Choto and the Rev. Benedita Mabjaia, organized the entire seminar. The women solicited and obtained funding from the World Council of Churches' program on Ecumenical Theological Education and from the Women's Division of the United Methodist Church. The seminar, originally planned for June, had to be postponed until September due to the catastrophic flooding and cyclones that hit Mozambique, cutting off north-south transportation and occupying all of the church's resources. Yet the significance of the seminar for women theologians in Mozambique was evident when Pastor Olga began receiving telephone calls from women all over Mozambique, asking in advance to be invited to the seminar.

The theme of the 2000 seminar came from 1 Kings 19:7: "African Woman: Arise and Eat, for Your Journey Is Long!" Fifty women from approximately nine denominations in Mozambique and Angola gathered in Maputo in September of 2000 for the seminar. The women, according to their own descriptions, had come to claim their rights in church and society, to increase their knowledge in order to serve their communities better, to exchange ideas as well as experiences of discrimination, and to unite and strategize in the battle against women's marginalization. The women came from all over Mozambique, including urban and rural districts of the provinces of Tete, Sofala, Gaza, Inhambane, and Maputo. Linguistic diversity again was an issue. Xitswa, Bitonga, Maronga, Mashangana, Maxope, and Portuguese were spoken by the Mozambican participants. Two of the Angolan participants spoke Portuguese and a third spoke French, as well as their maternal local languages. Portuguese was chosen as the language of the seminar, with multilingual participants interpreting for those who could not understand or speak Portuguese. Prayers, hymns, and meditations were often in one or more languages other than Portuguese.

One challenge was the fact that approximately thirty participants had attended the previous year's seminar and about twenty had not. It took time to introduce the newcomers to all that had taken place the year before. This was particularly the case for some of the rituals that had become established for the group, such as the construction of the altar and the use of a candle on the altar. The 2000 seminar began, as its predecessors had, with the ritual of constructing an altar together, thus creating a worship-centered and an African-centered space for the gathering. After biblical readings, each participant brought the object she had chosen to the altar and explained its significance. A candle was lit on the altar. Some of the newer participants, however, had difficulties understanding what the altar represented and thought that they had to place something of extraordinary value on it. In addition, some women were hesitant about using candles in worship since this was not practiced in their church. Thus, conflicts between denominational practices and the seminar liturgies had to be addressed. The previous year's participants explained that the candle was a symbol for God's presence and not an object of worship. But it took a few days and the intentional efforts of the leadership of the seminar to bring everyone together in these liturgical practices.

The use of a theme continued as a major characteristic of both seminars. The September 2000 theme, "African Woman: Arise and Eat, for Your Journey Is Long," exhorted the women to wake up and to eat in order to begin a long journey that would continue to their places of residence and work. The theme was woven into the meditations, reflections, Bible studies, and prayers and became the spiritual foundation of the seminar. Other biblical texts related to the theme were also used, such as 1 Samuel 3:8: "This is the moment of the call of women pastors," and Romans 8:3: "If God is for us, who is against us?" Liturgical texts were chosen that spoke particularly to women and that valued women, always in light of the Mozambican context. The seminar included workshops on Scripture that highlighted biblical women as inspiration for women today, such as Judith, Vashti, and Esther. These workshops also gave women resources to challenge biblical texts that subordinate women. One workshop specifically addressed such texts (e.g., 1 Cor. 11:7–10; 14:34–35; Eph. 5:21–24; 1 Tim. 2:11–15). The organizers also facilitated a debate about "Hagar in History and Today." The participants discussed positive and negative values in these biblical passages. The important leadership roles of women theologians in raising consciousness about the equality of women and men were emphasized.

When asked if the experience of the seminar affected the way she conducts worship in the parish, Pastor Olga said she had to be subtle in her parish: "Since we women are just beginning, we cannot 'exaggerate' or we will not bring people along with us because they will say we don't like men." The women clergy face criticism and accusations of excluding men as a result of the seminar. Because she does not want to be perceived as favoring women over men in her parish, Pastor Olga focuses on valuing everybody. Thus, when her youth group submits its list of officers, she insists they elect girls as well as boys. Pastor Olga cannot deny that the seminar's feminist theology has affected her ministry and her vocation, not least of all because of the invitations she now receives to speak about African women's theologies. When asked to define the difference between the liturgies celebrated in the context of the seminar and those celebrated in her parish, Pastor Olga said the principal difference is related to the seminar's themes. These themes center on African women's ministry: "The seminar is like fasting. We separate ourselves, as if for a fast, to pray specifically for ourselves, our families, and our ministries as women." In the parish, on the other hand, women pastors must strive to speak more broadly and to include everyone.

When asked to choose a liturgy that was significant for the 2000 seminar, Pastor Olga highlighted the liturgy on the beach of Bilene. Bilene Beach, approximately one and a half hours away from Maputo, had been chosen as the site for the women to gather for a special time of prayer. The seminar participants traveled together and arrived around noon at the beach. They shared lunch and then gathered for prayer. Bilene Beach was a deserted and "desert" place, where the women would not be disturbed. The liturgy began with an opening prayer and a hymn. The participants then dispersed along the beach for ten minutes of individual prayer, for themselves, their families, and their ministries. They came together again in a communal prayer and the singing of a hymn. The women then divided into groups of five and prayed for the Lusophone Circle of African Women Theologians, for women's ministry, for women pastors who belonged to the Circle but were absent, for the leaders of their countries, and for themselves. Each person was asked to share a personal problem in her pastoral ministry, in her family, or in her society. In response, two others in the group led everyone in prayer for this particular need. All then sang "Here I Am, Lord" in Xitswa (*Oh Hosi hi mina loyi*) and came together in one group. The women knelt in a circle and proceeded to a time of alternating psalm reading, singing, and prayer. Psalm 133 and portions of Psalms 24 and 25 were read first. The hymn *"Ku Khongela ka nanziha"* ("To Worship God Is Good") followed, then portions of Psalms 121 and 109. The next hymn was in Portuguese, *"Senhor, eu quero sentir a tua presença no meu coraçao"* ("Lord, I Want to Feel Your Presence in My Heart"), followed by the reading of Psalm 133 both in Tsonga and in French. The liturgy closed with the Hymn of Africa sung in Xitswa, *"Hosi Katekisa Africa"* ("God Bless Africa"), and a final prayer.

According to Pastor Olga, this was a time for the women to dedicate themselves to prayer for their particular vocations and ministries and for themselves. Pastor Olga had experienced this type of liturgy outside of Mozambique and wanted to share it with the women from the seminar. The participants were very moved by the experience of this liturgy on the beach; many of them cried during the prayers. They had never experienced this kind of prayer. Some told Pastor Olga that they would not be permitted to pray in that way in their own churches, but that if they could, it would renew their communities.

For the final worship service of the 2000 seminar, the women clergy came in their usual clothes instead of African clothes. The clergywomen who presided at the Lord's Supper wore clerical collars; the other ordained women did not. As in the previous year, African elements of cassava and orange juice were used for communion, but a table was used instead of the *esteira*. The prayers were taken directly from the Bible, not from a prayer book or traditional liturgy.

For Pastor Olga, the significance of the 2000 seminar lay in the unity it created among different women. This included women pastors from different churches but also women pastors from the same denomination who did not know each other. During the seminar these women got to know each other and bonded with one another. They had the opportunity to strategize together for their ministries. Pastor Olga said that the Christian Council of Mozambique was amazed at the ability of women pastors to organize and unite across denominational lines, when the council itself had had difficulties to bring together pastors from different churches. The council had never seen an experience like that of the seminar. In Pastor Olga's words, "The seminars bring unity. And unity makes strength." But not only did the seminars bring unity, they also brought recognition and visibility for the women involved. Even churches that to this day do not ordain women now acknowledge the existence of these seminars.

One of the new visions that emerged for the Lusophone Circle with the

2000 seminar was the networking with women involved in women's issues both in nongovernmental organizations (NGOs) and in the government. Dr. Alicia Mabote from the League of Human Rights and representatives from the Ministry of Women and Social Services had all been invited to speak about human rights, African culture, and African women at the 2000 seminar. These speakers urged clergywomen to partner to educate themselves and others about human rights, specifically the rights of women. As a result, the possibility of promising collaboration with the League of Human Rights and other NGOs emerged. The League of Human Rights offered to provide training on the issues of women's rights. The department of conflict resolution wanted to cooperate in the area of domestic violence. This cooperation is particularly important because women clergy are confronting violence in their own lives and families as well as in their congregations and communities. The Ministry of Women and Social Services wanted to join with women clergy in the area of fighting poverty.

The Lusophone Circle of African Women Theologians plans to continue with the seminars. In the making are an ecumenical seminar for Mozambican women pastors and a regional seminar of the Lusophone Circle in Angola. In addition, the United Methodist clergywomen as well as the Presbyterian women are scheduled to meet. Among the priorities of the Lusophone Circle are funding for theological education for women, support for widows and their children, education about women's rights, and the fight against violence against women, in collaboration with human rights organizations.

The journey is long, and the task facing the women theologians of the Lusophone Circle is great. The merging of African women's theologies, rituals, and empowerment activities has produced a vibrant space that is productive and transformative, making clear that African women are the hope for the future of Africa. Without support, education, and resources for African women, however, the hope for the future of Africa is threatened. Recognizing this reality, the Circle of Concerned African Women Theologians continues to solicit resources to facilitate training for African women and to encourage them to write from their own experiences. The women of the Lusophone Circle have demonstrated that they are able to nourish and train each other for the long journey; what they still need are financial resources, continued support for theological education, and opportunities for continued exchange and collaboration with other African women theologians. In order to curb the isolation that existed earlier, we have facilitated Mozambican women's participation in various activities in different countries in Africa, for example, during the Spring Ministries' HIV/AIDS seminar in Kenya, the World Council of Churches Young Theologians Conference in Ghana, and the African Theologians Conference in Kenya. A representative of the Lusophone Circle was also part of the World Council of Churches' delegation to the African Regional Preparatory Conference for the United Nations World Conference against Racism. All these women are taking one step at a time. May the Spirit of God and the spirits of the ancestors continue to guide us all as we stand in solidarity with one another.

Pista-Lakbayan: Celebrating the Journey to Shalom in the Year of Jubilee

The Ecumenical Women's Festival in Quezon City, Philippines

ELIZABETH S. TAPIA

The liturgy at the center of the following story was celebrated during International Women's Month 2000 as part of a *Pista-Lakbayan*[1] of Christian women in the Philippines. The liturgy took place in St. Andrew's Seminary Chapel in Quezon City, which is part of metropolitan Manila, the capital of the Philippines. About three hundred women from different churches, denominations, and traditions gathered to participate in this celebrative event. The *Pista-Lakbayan* was conceived by Filipina women who had attended the 1998 Women's Festival in Harare that closed the Ecumenical Decade of Churches in Solidarity with Women. Jointly sponsored by the Women's Desk of the National Council of Churches' Program Unit on Ecumenical Education and Nurture and by the Women's Desk of the (Catholic) Association of Major Religious Superiors in the Philippines (AMRSP), this ecumenical *Pista-Lakbayan* was a very festive and celebratory gathering that included songs, dances, speeches, poetry, testimonies, skits, colorful banners and streamers, and a table fellowship of native fruits, noodles, and rice cakes.

The liturgy on March 16 was the culmination of a series of women's fora and protest rallies in celebration of International Women's Day 2000. On Women's Day itself, a large group of Catholic and Protestant women—joined by laymen and children, pastors, priests, and some bishops—staged a protest rally in Plaza Miranda, a public square in Quiapo, Manila. The theme of the rally was "Reclaiming and Sharing the Priesthood of All Believers" (cf. 1 Pet. 2:5–9). A week prior to the rally, two major events took place: the official opening of the Women's Jubilee Month and a seminar on "Women and Ecology." Women also staged protest rallies against the United States' Visiting Forces Agreement and against capitalist globalization and its adverse effects on women and the environment.

The overall theme for Women's Month 2000 was "Celebrating the Journey Towards Shalom in the Year of the Great Jubilee." Our motto was "Courage amidst Struggle." We face many and difficult struggles in the Philippines today. Among these are the struggles for human rights and for economic justice, for land and jobs, for self-determination and people's participation. Issues of particular concern for the seventy-five million Filipinos today include increasing poverty (75 percent of the population live below the poverty line), unemployment, ecological crises, sex trafficking of women and children, the presence of multinational corporations, gambling, graft and corruption, kidnapping for ransom, and massive labor migration. These struggles and problems are situated within the larger context of capitalist globalization that controls the economic and sociopolitical life of our nation. Looking toward the third millennium and the Christian churches' celebration of the year of Jubilee, Filipina women had declared a Women's Jubilee Year—a year-long series of education, liturgical celebration, mobilization, and organization of women—as a way of involving all people in the struggle for justice and freedom.

The Philippines is the only Asian country that for centuries has been Christian, having been colonized by Spain in the sixteenth century. Over 80 percent of the population is Roman Catholic. Protestantism was introduced in 1898 through American missionaries. The United States colonized the Philippines for fifty-five years, and neocolonialism is alive and well today. The Philippines is one of the countries from the South that struggles because of the death-producing debt crisis. Hence, Filipina women joined the Ecumenical Jubilee 2000 Campaign Network, a nationwide ecumenical movement aiming for debt repudiation and a just economic order. The Jubilee 2000 Campaign calls for freedom from foreign control, from feudal bondage, from land abuse, from indebtedness, and from modern slavery. Most importantly, ecumenical women in the Philippines sought to reclaim this biblical feminist principle: "There is no longer Jew or Greek, there is no longer slave or free, there is no longer male and female; for all of you are one in Christ Jesus" (Gal. 3:28). Our rallying cry as ecumenical women in the Philippines is "Courage amidst Struggle in the Continuing Journey towards Shalom . . . Abundant Life for All!" Our *Pista-Lakbayan* was one of the active expressions of women's ways of doing theology in the Philippines. Our festival-journey is also an invitation to women and men in other parts of the world to enter a journey of solidarity with us.

IN THE BEGINNING

If the festival drew together initiatives centered on women's issues in the year of Jubilee and grew out of the need of women to mobilize and celebrate together amidst struggles, these initiatives themselves have roots that go back many years. Since 1978, through the initiative of the Women's Desk of the National Council of Churches in the Philippines (NCCP), of the Ecumenical Association of Third World Theologians (EATWOT), of the Association of Women in Theology (AWIT), and of the Asian Church Women's Conference (ACWC), Christian women in the Philippines have charted a new course, new paths of partnership, solidarity, and ecumenism. The Association of Women in Theology in particular has linked its doing of theology with gender and justice issues. AWIT is a nonhierarchical group of women, lay and ordained, who do theology in their own contexts, all over different islands in the Philippines. AWIT members continuously struggle with the questions of why and how women doing theology should be involved in transformation in church and society.[2]

SHARING OUR RITE

The printed invitation to our liturgy (with a beautiful piece of art work in purple) began with a call to celebration: "Let us celebrate women's creativity and their caring, nurturing, transforming, and life-giving gifts. . . . Let us celebrate the mutuality and partnership among women and men. . . . Let us celebrate our *Diwang Katutubo* [the Indigenous Communal Spirit] that continues to enflame our hearts and has never been quenched by centuries of colonization." The liturgical setting of our *Pista-Lakbayan* was the Chapel of St. Andrew's Theological Seminary, an Episcopal seminary in Quezon City. This chapel is an open space, surrounded by plants and trees. Large pews are arranged in a circle. Since our liturgy took place at the beginning of Lent, the altar was almost bare, and the cross was veiled. The women liturgists, however, had created a liturgical space in the middle of the aisle: with traditional mats and malong cloth, baskets full of tropical fruits, and flowers. There was a bowl of water, incense, and purple cloth to one side. Banners lay on the floor and hung outside. Around the chapel, outdoors, a group of women had mounted a display of women's handicrafts and a pictorial documentation of women's activities. During the worship service, the women sat in a semicircle. The music came from guitar, piano, a tape, and the traditional gong. The liturgy was celebrated both in Pilipino and in English.

Twenty-five different women's organizations participated in this ecumenical liturgy. The event was primarily organized by the Women's Desks of the NCCP and of the AMRSP, the Board of Women's Work of the United Methodist Church, the Women's Concerns Desk of the Ecumenical Bishops' Forum, the Association of Women in Theology (AWIT-DIWA *ng Kababaihan*), and the Filipino Indigenous Women's Spirituality. Dr. Konrad Raiser,

the General Secretary of the World Council of Churches, who was on an official visit to the Philippines and Indonesia at the time, had been invited to give
an inspirational message.

In what follows, I invite you to relive with us the *Pista-Lakbayan* with its
theme "Celebrating the Journey to Shalom in the Year of Jubilee." The core
group that prepared this liturgy included the following persons: Sr. Rosario
Battung (Roman Catholic), Deaconess Emma Cantor-Orate (United Metho-
dist), and the Rev. Lydia Niguidula and Jane Montenegro, both of the United
Church of Christ in the Philippines.[3] The main liturgists were Emma Cantor-
Orate and Maningning Tiquia. The emcees in the multimedia program were
Bernadette Aquino and Rose Mallaman.

PISTA-LAKBAYAN:
CELEBRATING THE JOURNEY TO SHALOM
IN THE YEAR OF JUBILEE

Our Pista-Lakbayan *begins in the early afternoon with the community gathering.
Early comers are able to watch a video of the 1998 Harare Decade Festival and to
appreciate the exhibits mounted around the chapel walls. At 3:00 p.m., the sound of
a gong signals the beginning of the liturgy proper. Several symbols of faith and life are
brought into the center of the assembly during the entrance procession: the Christ-
candle, delightful flowers and foods, the Holy Bible, pictorialized stories of women, and
banners expressing our common journey. The congregation is called to silent reflection
on the theme of our* Pista-Lakbayan: *The living, moving Spirit of God has gathered
us together to celebrate creativity, courage, and community amidst struggle in our
journey towards shalom.*

Call to Worship

> Blessed are you, O God Eternal, Creator of the Universe
> who empowers the Spirit-Stewards of the wind, rain, moon,
> sun, and stars and the whole cosmic energy, that we, women,
> children, and men, can gather at this sacred time and in this
> space.

> **ALL**   Bless us, O God, Creator, Redeemer, and Sustainer. Breathe
> into us your breath of peace. Breathe into us your gentle
> stillness, as we pause together in our struggle for shalom.

All breathe meditatively in silence for a while.

Sound of the Gong

Invocation

The invocation is sung by all and consists of two well-known songs: "Come, Holy Spirit, We Need You" and "Spirit of the Living God."

Sound of the Gong

A Call to Bonding in Christ

Two Women Leaders	God is yesterday. God is today. God is to come! God is here. God is now!
All	Now is the time for celebration! Now is the space and time for *Pista-Lakbayan!*
Two Women Leaders	The community of Jesus Christ is where children bring ribbons and fruits where old women come to dance where the youth sing joyously where men lend their joy in festivity.

Singing and Dancing

Everyone is encouraged to sing and dance spontaneously, touching hands or shoulders, smiling, nodding, and moving as all give expression to what they feel.

Song of Praise "THIS IS THE DAY"

Sound of the Gong

Leaders	The community of Jesus Christ is where everyone breathes in God's grace where everyone breathes out God's blessings where the sick come to be healed where each child of God is received as beautiful and precious.

Sound of the Gong

The Rite of Individual and Communal Affirmation

Each person stands with one hand placed over the heart, saying,

> I am a child of God, molded out of Mother Earth,
> I am made in the image of God.

Each person reaches out to another, saying,

> You are a child of God, molded out of Mother Earth,
> You are made in the image of God.

With the left hand placed over the left shoulder of a neighbor, each person says,

> We are children of God, molded out of Mother Earth,
> We are made in the image of God.

Song   "JESUS LOVES THE LITTLE CHILDREN"

A time of welcome, greetings, and comments on the purpose of the gathering follows.

The Community Reclaims its Cultural Heritage and Herstory

Sound of the Gong

A child reads the following text:

> In the beginning, in the very beginning
> God gave birth to, God delivered, God created the light,
> The heavens and the earth.
> Yes, out of the womb of fertile divinity emerged
> Our Mother Earth.

Dance

Sisters from the Apostolic Christian Church offer Bulaklakan, *a communal floral dance.*

Reading   "THE ORIGIN OF THE FIRST WOMAN AND MAN"[4]
of the Filipino A beautiful bamboo grew on the spot of Captan's (the God
Creation Story of the land breezes) and Maguayen's (the Goddess of the sea
breezes) romantic love. Then one day, King Manaul, the
Eagle-God, weary from ceaseless flying, came to alight on
the bamboo. King Manaul was about to fall asleep when he
heard, first, a female voice, and, a little later, a male voice
from within the bamboo. King Manaul, who was very vora-
cious, thought that a chick was hidden inside the bamboo.
Just then a beautiful lizard appeared on the bamboo trunk.
Manaul lunged forward to peck at it, but the lizard escaped.
Manaul's peck, however, cracked the bamboo. Out of the
cracked bamboo emerged two beautiful creatures: Sicalac
(Silalaki) and Sicauay (Sibabai), the first man and woman.
The two greeted and thanked Manaul for setting them free.
Then they raised their hands skyward as if in prayer.

A Litany of Thanksgiving and Remembering

So God created humankind;
In the image of God, male and female, God created them.
God blessed them, and God said to them
"Be fruitful and multiply, and fill the earth . . .
and take care of the fish of the sea, the birds of the air."
And God saw everything that was made,
And indeed it was very good!
Let us give thanks to God for the creation of the universe;
for all that lives with which we share this planet earth;
for the mysterious interconnections that bind us to each
    other
and the elements of which all is composed.

Let us give thanks for the flow of human history
for the events that have shaped and molded us,
and all our courageous sisters who refused to be subjugated
by the colonizers and those who would subdue them.
We remember the silenced, the invisible,
the almost-forgotten sisters of ours.

Sound of the Gong

Remembering the Filipina Women Who Suffered From and Resisted Colonization and Domination

From the pre-Colonial period, we remember the Babaylanes (natural healers and spiritual leaders), the Balangiga Women of Samar (who hid bolos inside bamboo tubes), and the Eskayan women of Bohol (who kept the indigenous alphabet).

From the 333 years of Spanish colonial rule, we remember Gregoria de Jesus, the women of Malolos who fought for their right to education, Melchora Aquino, Trinidad Tecson, Teresa Magbanua, Rosario Villaruel, Trinidad Rizal, Gabriela Silang, and the prostituted women of the Spanish soldiers and friars.

From American colonial times, we remember the revolutionary women such as Salud Algabre, Rosa Alvero, and Constancia Poblete, the prostituted women of the American soldiers, the women leaders and priestesses of Mount Banahaw, and those Filipina women who were the first suffragists of Asia.

Sound of the Gong

From the time of Japanese rule, we remember the women who joined the anti-Japanese guerrilla movement, and the women forced into military sexual slavery for the Japanese Imperial Army.

Sound of the Gong

From the time of martial law rule to the present, we remember Lorena Barrios, the Rev. Vizminda Gran, Deaconess Filomena Asuncion, Pastor Hella Hoyle, and countless wives, mothers, and daughters who were tortured, raped, and killed.

Let us remember all women and men struggling for justice and peace, and working for food and freedom.

Sound of the Gong

LEADERS	God of Love and Justice, thank you for those who fought for food and truth, for freedom and love, for women's and children's rights, for the right and integrity of creation.
ALL	Praise and thanks be to God!

Musical Offering

Students of the Asian Institute of Liturgy and Music, Quezon City, offer music played on Asian and Filipino instruments.

The Community Listens to Women's Pains and Visions

In a short but powerful play, a group of Filipino migrant workers who have come home portray their painful experiences and the unjust situation of migrant workers abroad. Ruby's story is culled from the collective experience of about fifteen million Filipino workers in Japan. Cora's story portrays the harassment of a Filipina working as a maid in Taiwan. The Migrante International, a nongovernmental organization, helps these overseas contract workers regain their rights and dignity. At the end of the play, the women voice their own visions for a better future and their commitment to work for justice and peace.

Sound of the Gong

The Community in Penitence

For the lives and stories of women and children that shaped us . . .

for the grieving and the pain
for the oppression that lies deep in our own soul
for all that we know of ourselves
and for the shaking of the spirit, O God forgive us.

We pray for ourselves, where healing must begin.

Where disease has invaded our blood and bones,
let your Spirit enter with cleansing fire.

Where there are scars of hatred, resentment, and bitterness, soften them with your balm of love.

Where fears, anxieties, despair, and depression have
settled in like smog, let your Wind blow away the
pollution.

And we pray for our country's suffering from self-inflicted wounds of deceit, greed, drugs, and the victimization of the weak and the marginalized.

May your Spirit teach us justice, generosity, and compassion as we reclaim the call to Jubilee.

For your church divided, often intolerant, unjust, and unloving, we pray . . .

Send us your guiding light, your wisdom, and healing love. In the name of Jesus Christ, we pray. Amen.

Assurance of Pardon

Sisters and brothers, let us thank God for sending Jesus Christ to us, living the truth of God, bringing good news to the poor, proclaiming release to the captives, and recovery of sight to the blind, to free those who are oppressed, and to proclaim the year of God's favor, the year of the Jubilee!

Reflections   "WOMEN'S VISIONS FOR THE TWENTY-FIRST CENTURY"

Sr. Emelina Villegas ICM works and lives with women factory workers in Rosario, Cavite. She shares her experience of living with the exploited factory workers and doing theology and reflections with them, and their education-mobilization campaign to make their working conditions better. Elizabeth S. Tapia shares her poetic letter to her niece outlining women's struggles as well as her lyrical portrayal of the church of the future.[5]

Song of Jubilee

A Jubilee song widely used in Roman Catholic parishes in the Philippines is sung in both Pilipino and English.

The Community Resounds the Jubilee Call

Silent Reflection of the following text, prepared by the Pista-Lakbayan *Organizing Committee on the theme "Courage amidst Struggle in the Continuing Journey towards Shalom":*

Women, along with men from the basic sectors of peasants and workers, have long suffered from historically entrenched oppressive structures.

Reclaim the feminist principle: "There is no longer Jew or

Greek, there is no longer slave or free, there is no longer male and female; for all of you are one in Christ Jesus" (Gal. 3:28).

In the Philippines, the call to reclaim the feminist principle and the freedom from patriarchal control forms part of our observance of the Jubilee. Recent global developments, summed up as "globalization," have exacerbated the oppression of women, who along with children bear the brunt of the suffering.

In the year of Jubilee, land is given rest, slaves are set free, property is restored to the dispossessed, debts are forgiven, and each person is enjoined to return to one's family. . . .

This biblical vision of freedom to the captives coincides with the historic aspirations of our people to rid the nation of foreign and domestic oppression, enjoy full national sovereignty, obtain land for the landless, break the chains of modern slavery, including the slavery of women, and cancel unjust and onerous debts.

God's promise of deliverance from enslavement empowers us women to overcome our limitations, gather strength and courage, and break free from bondage. It gives us hope to look beyond our individual suffering, to be in solidarity with one another, and, together with other similarly oppressed sectors, harness our inner strength and spirituality for the service of church and society.

The Scripture Lessons

LEVITICUS 25:8–10
You shall count off seven weeks of years, seven times seven years, so that the period of seven weeks of years gives forty-nine years. Then you shall have the trumpet sounded loud; on the tenth day of the seventh month—on the day of atonement—you shall have the trumpet sounded throughout all your land. And you shall hallow the fiftieth year and you shall proclaim liberty throughout the land to all its inhabitants. It shall be a jubilee for you: you shall return, every one of you, to your property and every one of you to your family.

GALATIANS 3:28
There is no longer Jew or Greek, there is no longer slave or

free, there is no longer male and female; for all of you are one
in Christ Jesus.

Reflections

*Priscilla Padolina introduces Konrad Raiser, General Secretary of the World Council
of Churches, who offers some reflections. Raiser emphasizes how he himself is inspired
by the ecumenical women gathered. He speaks of the church as a sanctuary, a tent, a
roundtable with unlimited space for all, a place that is open and protected, celebrative,
mutual, and inclusive. "The true shalom is built on mutuality," Raiser says.*

Musical Offering

*A song, "Harana," is offered by Lei Garcia, a member of the Youth Advisory Group
of the World Council of Churches. During the musical offering, Emma Cantor presents Konrad Raiser with a purple women's scarf bearing the theme "Courage amidst
Struggle."*

The Community Celebrates its Commitment

A Reading of the *Pagsanjan Covenant* and Ritual Signing

The assembly reads and signs the Pagsanjan Covenant, *produced by an ecumenical
gathering of women held in Pagsanjan Garden Resort in November 1999.*[6]

> We are mothers, sisters, aunts, teachers, legal practitioners,
> housewives, religious sisters, pastors, deaconesses, and church
> workers—each one taking a personal and communal journey
> into the recesses of our beings and discovering how violated
> we are as women. As this millennium ends, our search for heal-
> ing and bonding has led us to Pagsanjan Laguna.
>
> **We are angered**
>
> by the systemic collusion of global powers to impose their
> economic and political agenda on developing countries, like
> ours, through a deceptive scheme called globalization;
>
> by the subtle way in which religion is used to legitimize patri-
> archy in order to obliterate women's voices of protest and
> suppress women's wisdom and giftedness;
>
> by the senseless—both subtle and obvious—cultural rape of
> the indigenous peoples, making us strangers to one another
> and blind to our indigenous cultural heritage, which roots us
> in our Motherland;

by the alarming rate at which our forests, waterways, flora, and fauna are neglected to die each passing day and exploited in the name of progress and development;

by the heartless insensitivity of those who are in power and refuse to heed the people's searing cries for jobs and justice, food and freedom, shelter and sovereignty, or simply to be recognized as human beings created in God's image.

We are inspired

by the stories of Eve, Deborah, Miriam, Mary, and other women of courage in the Bible who dared to be different and did assert their rightful claims;

by the courage and tenacity of Jean, Farida, Josie, and Beth who crept out of the "hell" they found themselves in and commenced the painful journey for their liberation and on to shalom;

and now, by the resounding call of Jubilee, announcing our freedom from the crippling effects of modern slavery and inhumanity!

Pista-Lakbayan gave us a foretaste of Jubilee—the celebration of our humanity and womanhood as we endeavored to remove barriers that separated us women one from the other; as we feel in depth our inner agony—the sinned against—and to comprehend more fully and realistically our aspirations; as we made our own painful experiences, long buried within ourselves, the starting point of our reflections, meditations, and realizations; as we embraced one another to affirm each one's humanity. Imbued with this awakening to the collective woman consciousness,

We earnestly pledge

to commit ourselves to struggle for self-determination and the protection of our ancestral domain against the wanton exploitation of our natural resources;

to consistently study and update ourselves on the social patterns and trends of our society that we may carefully analyze and seriously critique them when necessary in the light of the Gospel of liberation of Jesus Christ our Savior, and of our Filipino cultural heritage;

to condemn the subtle harassment of workers at the Shoe-mart picket lines as we uphold these sisters and brothers in their legitimate demand for just wages;

to denounce as well the deprivation of the livelihood of Calamba fisher-folk due to the continuously diminishing shoreline of Laguna Lake, and the destruction of our fresh sea water resources there;

to earnestly support the existing programs of the churches, nongovernmental organizations (NGOs) and people's organizations (POs) for the promotion and defense of peoples' welfare and dignified humanity;

to share and witness to the positive effects of this gathering in our local congregations, parishes, and neighborhoods, and strengthen one another in our ecumenical efforts for women's empowerment.

Contemporary Song of Commitment   "IF WE HOLD ON TOGETHER"[7]

A Tiboli Worship Dance

Grace Odar Mamathola of the University of the Philippines, garbed in the colorful traditional Tiboli dress, offers an indigenous tribal dance ritual from the Southern Philippines.

The Blessing and Sharing of Food

All partake of food and refreshments as an integral part of this liturgy.

LEADERS   In this moment of sharing this food and drink, we remember folks in the fields, market places, kitchens, and streets. We remember children and women who feed the world, and we pledge to work for justice and mutuality as we journey towards shalom.

ALL
(lifting up the food and palms)

Yes, may the food we eat and drink
remind us to share God's abundance.
May the lives we lead be transforming.

May the unity of creation become our mission
for the new heaven and the new earth.
So be it.

Sharing of the Meal

Hymn of Commitment

"CALLED AS PARTNERS IN CHRIST'S SERVICE"[8]
Called as partners in Christ's service,
Called to ministries of grace,
We respond with deep commitment
Fresh new lines of faith to trace.
May we learn the art of sharing,
Side by side and friend with friend,
Equal partners in our caring
To fulfill God's chosen end.

Christ's example, Christ's inspiring,
Christ's clear call to work and worth,
Let us follow, never faltering,
Reconciling folks on earth.
Men and women, richer, poorer,
All God's people, young and old
Blending human skills together,
Gracious gifts from God unfold.

Thus new patterns for Christ's mission,
In a small or global sense,
Help us bear each other's burdens,
Breaking down each wall or fence.
Words of comfort, words of vision,
Words of challenge, said with care,
Bring new power and strength for action,
Make us colleagues, free and fair.

So God grant us for tomorrow
Ways to order human life
That surround each person's sorrow
With a calm that conquers strife.
Make us partners in our living,
Our compassion to increase,
Messengers of faith, thus giving
Hope and confidence and peace.

Closing Prayer and Blessing

Sharon Rose Joy Ruiz Duremdes, General Secretary of the National Council of Churches in the Philippines, prays a closing prayer expressing gratitude to God and to the community of women and men working for justice and peace, journeying towards shalom. Dr. Fe Villao, Vice Chair of the National Council of Churches in the Philippines, then thanks all organizers, participants, guests, and the sponsoring organizations.

Final Sound of the Gong

The community goes out to serve the people.

14

Like Water in a Desert

Women Church in South Africa

WILMA JAKOBSEN

CLAIMING OUR RITES

I was sitting in a circle of women gathered for a Celtic worship service. We were celebrating the life of Saint Hilda, the seventh-century learned abbess of Whitby. I felt as if I were drinking a glass of pure, clear, cold water, which was reviving my soul in the dry and thirsty depths of my being. The worship space, created between the front pew of our church and the chancel area, was lit by tiny candles in red glasses. The liturgy wove together the music of Carolyn McDade's song "This Ancient Love" and other Celtic songs, readings from the Psalms and from Proverbs about Wisdom, inspiring texts about the life of Saint Hilda, silence, and prayers. At the end of the service, I sat quietly, feeling enriched. I experienced keenly the reality of knowing the "ancient love":

> Long before the night was born from darkness
> Long before the dawn rolled unsteady from fire
> Long before She wrapped her scarlet arm around the hills
> there was a love, this ancient love was born . . .
>
> Long before the name of a God was spoken
> Long before a cross was nailed from a tree
> Long before She laid her arm of colors 'cross the sky
> there was a love, this ancient love was born.
>
> Wakeful our night, Slumbers our morning
> Stubborn the grass sowing green wounded hills
> As we wrap our healing arms to hold what her arms held
> this ancient love, this aching love rolls on.[1]

Just as "This Ancient Love" inspired us that evening, so did a prayer written by the coordinator of this particular worship service. The prayer gives thanks for the mothers of the church, the great women who blazed trails for us all to follow:

> We come to you, O God, our Mother and our Father,
> To give you thanks for all great mothers in the church.
>
> **We bless you for the witness of faithful women**
> **through the ages,**
> **and especially for those who have carried**
> **great responsibility and borne noble authority.**
>
> We celebrate the vision, the steadfastness, and the strength
> Of those who have gone beyond the restrictions of their
> culture
> And who have blazed new trails for women and men to
> follow.
>
> **We pray that we may be inspired by such women**
> **and that their example may be a beacon**
> **even in our own day.**
>
> Give us vision, give us nurturing care, give us faithfulness in
> our own responsibilities;
>
> **give us courage, hope, and a heart that can rejoice in**
> **the gifts of others,**
>
> **to make the way open for them to become all that you**
> **have called them to be . . .**
>
> **so that together we may rejoice in the fullness of your**
> **tender gifts.**[2]

Our worship service in honor of Saint Hilda was only the second gathering of a group of women that as yet has no name. The group was born out of a desire to use the text of a eucharistic liturgy created for the feast day of Saint Mary Magdalene on July 22. I had received this text from a women's group at All Saints Episcopal Church in Pasadena, California; the group had celebrated the feast day of Saint Mary Magdalene with this liturgy. Two South African women who had both the necessary scholarly resources and also the energy helped with trying to make this service a reality in Cape Town. As we talked with other women from our parish and from various women's networks, we discovered a desire for a space that was feminist, creative, and spiritually nurturing. Being one of the first women priests in the Anglican Church in Southern Africa, I had long felt the desire for such a space, but only now does it seem to come to birth. We gathered in July of 2000 to celebrate the life and faith of Mary Magdalene with this inclusive-language eucharistic liturgy. The worship service included a reading from the apocryphal *Gospel of Thomas* about Mary Magdalene and prayers and litanies focusing on the saint's life and witness. For the eucharistic prayer we used a beautiful text by Jim Cotter.[3] The intercessions also were based on the life and witness of Mary Magdalene, and the communal response to the petitions invoked God as our mother: "Amma, help us to see your face." The prayers focused on those dealing with grief and loss and on those in need of healing, and they celebrated the joy and energy of Mary Magdalene as she encountered the risen Christ.

Twenty women and one man attended our liturgy, which had received little advertising and took place on short notice. Some of the women came from the university parish I serve; some came from other churches; some from no church. The liturgy certainly met a need. Lay and ordained, theological students and professional women, all indicated that this was something we would like to do more often. Our fledgling group has now decided to meet four times a year, on Saturday evenings, on days closest to the feast days of women saints such as Hilda, Brigid, Cecelia, and Mary Magdalene. No pattern for worship is set; so far we have enjoyed celebrating our mothers in the faith and the inspiration they offer. The inclusive language of our liturgies has been a welcome alternative to regular church services: like water in a desert, it is scarce, yet longed for, and necessary for survival. Our worship is already a nurturing, soul-feeding space, even though its lifespan has been short.

IN THE BEGINNING

This worship, however, is not the first attempt in Cape Town for such a women-identified group to be born. During 1989, in the midst of the movement to ordain women as priests in the Anglican Church in Southern Africa, an informal network of women and men formed to pray and work towards this goal. At the same time, a group of women began to organize monthly women-church gatherings. During 1990 and 1991, the two groups met together and held inclusive worship services. These were either eucharistic services or liturgies of the Word focused on a particular theme. Different women took responsibility to coordinate and facilitate each of these worship services. We used liturgical materials from a variety of different sources. The prayers, poems, and litanies of Janet Morley of the Movement for the Ordination of Women in England were especially important for us. Alla Renée Bozarth, the American Episcopal priest and poet, also inspired us with her poem "Bakerwoman

God."[4] One of our services focused on a midrash of Lilith and Eve, written by Judith Plaskow.[5] Although we enjoyed the prayers, litanies, and other liturgical resources gleaned from England and North America, we also wanted to write our own prayers and liturgies. We were conscious, however, that at that particular point in time, we did not seem to have the energy, time, and freedom to create something that was uniquely ours and uniquely South African. The context of our gatherings was one of struggle—the struggle of the mass democratic movement against apartheid as it reached its peak in 1989, and the concurrent struggle for women's priestly ordination in the bastion of tradition that was the Anglican Church. Most of us who participated in the new women-identified liturgies were involved both in the struggle against apartheid (either directly or indirectly) and engaged in service-related work. We were seeking a space to vent our feelings and our anger about the oppression in our country both in terms of race and of gender. We needed a space that would tend our souls as women. We needed space to explore the possibilities for women and worship together.

The group that formed in the early 1990s consisted mostly of white English-speaking South African women, with a couple of black women participating. We were very conscious of the differences between us even as women together in the group. We were aware that it was difficult for women who lived in the townships to meet on a Friday night; transportation was always a problem. Issues of race and class thus clearly cut across issues of gender. We were conscious of being a group of mostly white, middle-class women and of the doubt this could cast on the group's credibility. Yet we also knew that we needed what Women Church gave to us. Life in South Africa—then and now, even after the transition to democracy—is draining and exhausting, as well as exhilarating. We needed the refreshment and the strength Women Church gave us to survive the gender struggles in the church and the larger struggles of life in South Africa.

One of the collects by Janet Morley, "O God, the Power of the Powerless," particularly spoke to us as South African women in the complexities of our struggles, and we used it frequently. Morley's images of persistence and power in the midst of powerlessness, and of God as the source of strength for those who are powerless, encouraged us to keep on proclaiming the truth.[6] Morley's collect is based on the Easter lectionary reading of Luke 24:1–11, the story of "women disbelieved," as Morley calls it. Like the women who were entrusted with spreading the good news of the resurrection, though they were "disbelieved," we, too, sought courage, their courage to continue. The prayer inspired us, women in South Africa, to persist in the struggle. We also found inspiration and included in our liturgies blessings that invoked God as Mother, or that highlighted women of faith such as Sarah, Hagar, and Mary, or drew on feminine images of God.[7] And we oftentimes used Rachel Conrad Wahlberg's "Woman's Creed."[8] Another favorite prayer of ours was an alternate version of the Lord's Prayer, written by Jim Cotter. This beautiful prayer invokes God as "Eternal Spirit, Life-Giver, Pain-Bearer, Love-Maker, Source of all that is and shall be, Father and Mother of us all, Loving God, in whom is heaven."[9]

About two years into the life of our women-church group in Cape Town, the woman who up until then had shouldered most of the coordinating and organizing took up full-time graduate work. She was thus unable to continue her role in our group. Sadly, no one else in the group felt they had the time and energy to shoulder the work, so the group faded out, and Women Church went dormant. Many of us bemoaned its demise year after year, but the simple reality was that we did not find enough energy within us to begin again. In 1992 the struggle to ordain women priests became the paramount issue for many of us. The never-to-be forgotten Anglican synod in Swaziland decided by the surprisingly high percentage of 79.8 percent to pass the resolution to ordain women as priests. Our church was never to be the same. It was a heady time of rejoicing and participating in the ordinations of those who had waited for up to seven years after their diaconal ordinations to become priests. Priestly ordination for women in the Anglican Church in Southern Africa was a sign of hope for the larger South African struggle to negotiate its way towards democracy. Many times the political negotiations faltered and were on the brink of failure. The Anglican vote to change, in an unequivocal way, the bastion of tradition that was the Anglican Church provided a clear sign of hope: if the most intransigent institution could be transformed, then perhaps even the apartheid government could prepare to negotiate towards democracy.

CELEBRATING NATIONAL WOMEN'S DAY

South Africa's apartheid struggle also provides the backdrop for another way in which South African women have come together to worship. Since 1956, South Africa has celebrated National Women's Day, and since 1994, this day has been a national holiday. The day potentially brings together the struggles of race and of gender. On National Women's Day, services are held throughout South Africa, and women of every race and class gather to commemorate women of the apartheid struggle, especially the women demonstrators of August 9, 1956. On that memorable day, twenty thousand women gathered outside the Union Buildings in Pretoria, the administrative capital of South Africa. The women had come from every corner of the country to protest the government's decision to extend the pass laws to women (this extension of pass laws to women would have meant that in addition to all African men, all African women could be arrested for being in white areas unless they had special passbooks carried on their persons at all times to avoid arrest). The women protesters simply stood in silence for half an hour, with their fists raised. A small group of women was then allowed to deliver the petitions. The slogan the women used to address the Minister of Justice has since become famous around the world: "Strijdom, you have struck the women; you have struck a rock." Although pass laws affected only African women, this did not prevent colored, Indian, and white women from joining the campaign. South Africa now honors all these women by holding a public holiday on the day of their protest march. In more recent years, the worship services held on this day have focused on the issues of violence against women and on bringing women and men together to pray and protest this violence. One particularly meaningful part of the service has been a litany for healing, with responses in English, Xhosa, and Afrikaans, the three major languages spoken in the Western Cape.

As a university chaplain, I have been able to hold National Women's Day worship services with college students. I use the opportunity to teach younger people about the history of church women and women of South Africa. It has been encouraging to see the young male students insisting on taking part as well, wanting to be involved in a worship service that celebrates the women of South Africa. Sometimes the students have lit candles to honor and name the women in their lives who have inspired them. Every year, we use the text of Ann Heidkamp's "Litany of Women's Power," which praises our ancestors and foremothers in the faith and asks for their courage, power, and perseverance. We have added our own South African materials to the original text of this litany, praising South African women who are our forebears in the faith, in the church struggles, and in the political struggles. Here is this "Litany of Women's Power":

> Spirit of Life, we remember today the women, known and unknown, who throughout time have used the power and gifts you gave them to change the world. We call upon these foremothers to help us discover within ourselves your power and the ways used to bring about the kingdom of justice and peace.

> We remember Sarah, who with Abraham answered God's call to forsake her homeland and put their faith in a covenant with God.

> **We pray for her power of faith.**

We remember Esther and Deborah, who by individual acts of courage saved their nation.

We pray for their power of courage to act for the greater good.

We remember Mary Magdalene and the other women who followed Jesus, who were not believed when they announced the resurrection.

We pray for their power of belief in the face of skepticism.

We remember Phoebe, Priscilla, and all the women leaders of the early church.

We pray for their power to spread the gospel and inspire congregations.

We remember the Abbesses of the Middle Ages who kept faith and knowledge alive.

We pray for their power of leadership.

We remember Teresa of Avila and Catherine of Siena, who challenged the corruption of the church during the Renaissance.

We pray for their powers of intelligence and their outspokenness.

We remember Annie Salinga, campaigner against the pass laws; Lilian Ngoyi, Dora Tamana, who led the women in protest; Ruth First and Dulcie September, assassinated for their beliefs; and all the women in our land who, through their lives, helped us to see the need to work together for a better life.

We pray for their courage and commitment.

We remember Nancy Charton, first woman deacon and priest in the Church of the Province of Southern Africa; Barbara Harriss and Penny Jamieson, first women bishops in the Anglican Communion; and all women deacons, priests, and bishops who with their courage and vision seek to create a mutual community within the church.

We pray for their power of perseverance.

We remember our own mothers and grandmothers, whose lives shaped ours, and the special power they attempted to pass on to us.

We pray for the special power they attempted to pass on to us.

We pray for the women who are victims of violence in their homes.

May they be granted the power to overcome fear and seek solutions.

We pray for those women who face a life of poverty and malnutrition.

May they be granted the power of hopefulness to work together for a better life.

We pray for the women today who are "firsts" in their fields.

May they be granted the power to persevere and open up new possibilities for all women.

We pray for our daughters and granddaughters.

May they be granted the power to seek that life which is uniquely theirs.

We have celebrated the power of many women, past and present. It is time now to celebrate ourselves. Within each of us is the same life and light and love. Within each of us lie the seeds of power and glory. Our hearts can heal, our minds can seek faith and truth and justice. Spirit of God, be with us in our quest.[10]

In one particular worship service for National Women's Day, we used the following intercessions, written by two South African women students:

We pray for our homes and families, and for all homes;
that they may be places of love and support and nurture.
On this day we pray especially for all women homemakers:
Lord, hear our prayer.

We pray for all those who are victims of violence, domestic violence,
and those caught up in the suffering of war and poverty.
On this day we pray especially for all women:
Lord, hear our prayer.

We pray for all those in academia,
who have the responsibility of seeking
and imparting knowledge.
On this day we pray especially for all women academics:
Lord, hear our prayer.

We pray for all professionals.
Grant that they may be strengthened in their desire to do
what is right for the good of our society.
On this day we pray especially for all women professionals:
Lord, hear our prayer.

We pray for all pioneers,
who by their courage and determination
seek to change our world for the better.
On this day we pray especially for all women:
Lord, hear our prayer.

We pray for all those in Your Church, who seek to serve You
through serving one another.
On this day we pray for all women who have made a difference in our lives, our mothers, our teachers, our helpers, our
friends. We pray that the good you have instilled in them
will shine through in us:
Lord, hear our prayer. [11]

These are some of our worship materials and our experiences with women-
identified liturgies in Cape Town. There have been other women's groups in
South Africa, albeit with a different focus than ours, that have met regularly
through the years. One women's group formed within the Peace and Justice
Network of the Anglican Church in Southern Africa. From time to time this
group conducted women-church worship services. There was also a Movement for the Ordination of Women in Durban in the early 1990s, which
focused mostly on the ordination of women priests in the Anglican Church.
There are groups of the International Grail Movement in Cape Town, Gaut-
eng, and Durban. In Cape Town, the Grail women have met regularly for
many years for discussion and worship, as well as for occasional seminars that
include worship services. More recently, the Grail women have acquired a
retreat center in a country area, where interfaith workshops and programs
with the local communities take place. There are other women's groups that
focus on spirituality and discuss books or poetry but do not worship together,

and small women's groups that have met for support and discussion and prayer. There is a chapter of the Circle of Concerned African Women Theologians in Cape Town and, more recently, in Durban. Again the focus is not on worship but on women doing and writing theology.[12] There is also the network of nongovernmental organizations and church-based groups focusing on violence against women or on women and HIV/AIDS. As violence against women has become a more public problem over the last decade, so the number of organizations dealing with counseling, caring, training, and advocacy has increased. There are also the political women's groups such as the Women's League of the African National Congress. All these groups are part of the larger context of South Africa and of women's lives in South Africa.

WOMEN CHURCH: WATER IN A DESERT

At the University of Cape Town, where I am chaplain, the women's movement was dormant for the past five years and has only very recently attempted to revive itself again. This may be a symptom of how women are feeling in general: tired of struggling in so many different ways and tired of having to organize their own support networks and to sponsor events in addition to all the other organizing that is part of their lives. Now that the intense years of political struggle are past and we face new struggles of socioeconomics and gender in our country, perhaps the energy to begin again will return.

It remains important for us to try to understand just why Women Church in South Africa continues to reflect the title of this essay, "like water in a desert." The title is taken from a Xhosa saying: *amanzi entlango*, which depicts water as a scarce and life-giving resource in the desert. Why is it that so many of us know that we need to worship together in ways that are feminist, creative, inclusive, and nurturing—yet there are so few women with energy to make such worship a reality? Why did it take us so long to begin again? Why does our group feel that we can meet three times a year but that monthly meetings would not be manageable, as we do not have the time? These questions deserve our thinking and analysis. I can offer only my limited personal reflections, as an English-speaking, white, South African, woman priest, trained theologically in the United States. Speaking with various women about these questions, answers remain elusive. Certainly, women struggle on many different fronts in South Africa, including struggles for sheer survival. Poverty, lack of access to health care, rape and domestic violence, HIV/AIDS—these are some of the issues women face in improving the quality of life for women in our country. The demands are so pressing, and the needs so relentless, that many women find it difficult to balance their work, family, and other commitments.

In this context, Women Church is but one need, and one that gives way to other commitments. The desire to create women-identified sacred space thus is pushed aside so that other needs can be met. It is also clear that Women Church fulfills particularly the need and desire of middle-class women, while thousands of women are dealing with the need for survival, for clean water, and for enough income to eke out a living for their families. This is the reality of our South African context: Women Church here will always be a middle-class experience. This does not make it less legitimate but rather reflects our complex realities as women who are bonded together as sisters yet at the same time divided by race and class. In our fledgling women-church group that is being reborn in Cape Town, we acknowledge that we are middle-class and mostly white, but we are not willing to let that stop us from meeting and exploring a feminist spirituality that is creative and nurturing. We dare not ignore our need to which Women Church responds.

Perhaps the words on a wall hanging in my office come close to this truth. The wall hanging was made for me by Anglican university students during the struggle to ordain women as priests. It says, "South Africa will never be free until the women are free." The students wanted to show that race and gender were intertwined as part of a deeper struggle and that gender issues were a legitimate "struggle" activity. I now keep that wall hanging visible to remind myself and others that gender issues in South Africa are always a challenge, that talking of freedom in South Africa is complex and complicated, and that in many ways freedom for women is a long way off despite all the rhetoric and advances that have actually been made. Conversations with many women who are still in churches or who have left their churches long ago continually remind me that many women long for a more women-friendly worship space in the church, a space that is less rigid, less masculine, and less traditional, yet has not lost the richness and rootedness of tradition. Our women-church experiences are like water in a desert—desirable, necessary, but scarce.

CONCLUSION

As a woman priest committed to the transformation of the church and to the nurture and care of women's spirits, I find myself continuing to reflect on the previous women-church initiative and why it did not last. I also continue to wonder how we women can honor our own limits and strength, saying "no" to carrying an overload of responsibilities, while also taking initiatives and working to organize our own support and creativity. As I currently explore with other women this new initiative at my church, we are faced once more with the realities of the struggle of gender issues in South Africa—a unique yet also universal struggle. In this essay I have attempted to reflect on the previous women-church group and its activities, within the larger South African context. I have described our current realities and the explorations of a new women-identified liturgical endeavor for women. I have highlighted some of the prayers and liturgies that have been most meaningful and inspiring. Of necessity, my perspective cannot be normative: the experience of a white, South African, English-speaking woman, church activist, and now Anglican priest surely has its own flavor. But I hope that these personal reflections shed light on the nature of gender issues and worship in and out of the church in South Africa. I believe with all my heart that the struggle for women's rites must continue. There must be a welcoming and nurturing space for women in the church. As women of faith we know we need such a space; we long for it and desire it and hope that there will come a time when this space is less like water in a desert and more like an overflowing fountain of life.

Postscript

Liturgy in Women's Hands: A New Site

TERESA BERGER

> *God may well operate . . . in a particular construct of textual tra-*
> *dition, but what about the rituals and feasts? What about the*
> *prayers and practices of women?*
>
> Rebecca Chopp

The narratives and the liturgies of *Dissident Daughters* stand by themselves as
eloquent testimonies to the faith-ful struggle for women's rites in the church.
In that sense, this book does not need a postscript. On the other hand, I very
much see these narratives as pointing beyond themselves. *Dissident Daughters*
not only reveals how women-identified liturgies and rituals have come to circulate globally but hints at how this global theological flow calls for a new and
deeper understanding of the life of the church in our time. By contesting traditional liturgical practices and yet using that site and its symbolic resources,
the knowledge inscribed in *Dissident Daughters* poses profound challenges: to
rethink the nature and boundaries of the church, to identify afresh the core of
its tradition, and to reassign the locus of interpretive authority. Taking up this
challenge, the postscript will argue that women-identified liturgies can be seen
as a new yet faithful way of traditioning in the life of the church.

As a theologian rooted, for better or for worse, in the North Atlantic world,
and as one engaged in the material-social practice of academic theology, I
encounter women-identified liturgical communities worldwide with the limits and the strengths of my own subject position. One such limit-strength is
my rootedness in the theological culture of my European upbringing and formation. To put it more concretely, I bring to the encounter with women-
identified liturgical communities across the globe a "fluency" in traditional

theological categories. One such traditional category this fluency foregrounds
in the encounter with women-identified faith communities and their liturgical practices is the question of tradition and traditioning. It is this question that
I have chosen as the focus for this postscript.

MRS. MURPHY IN THE PEW

One of the distinctive developments in theological work over the past twenty
years—coinciding with yet detached from the rise of feminist liturgical practices—has been the (re-)emergence of the liturgy as a source for theological
reflection.[1] Theologians from a broad spectrum of positions now claim liturgy
as a fundamental site for understanding, interpreting, and configuring the
Christian faith. These "liturgical" theologians often summarize their claim by
an oscillating shorthand version of a patristic axiom: *lex orandi, lex credendi*,
"the law of praying is the law of believing"; "worship shapes faith"; "as you
pray, so you believe." What is striking about this development is the way in
which these theologians occlude the distinct shape of the prayers and practices
of women, and especially the surge of women-identified liturgical practices
witnessed to in *Dissident Daughters*. While emphasizing that God operates not
only in textual traditions but also in "the rituals and feasts," these theologians
clearly do not attend to "the prayers and practices of women."[2]

The reasons for this inattentiveness are multiple, but three such reasons
stand out. First, the theological recourse to liturgical tradition is based on a
liturgical historiography that is inattentive to the profoundly gendered nature
of worship practices in the Christian community. That is, liturgical tradition
continues to be constructed as gender-blind or gender-neutral, and our understanding of liturgical history thus continues to be shaped by complex forms of
marginalization, of silencing, and of misnaming of women's prayers and practices. Theologians claiming this liturgical tradition for their work cannot but
reproduce the androcentrism of the liturgical master narrative. Second, this
androcentrism is exacerbated by the nature of the theological arguments made
through the recourse to liturgical tradition. As Rebecca Lyman notes, "Many
theologians have used liturgy or devotion as a conservative weight for theological work or development."[3] An example might be the favor that the axiom
lex orandi, lex credendi has enjoyed in arguments against the use of inclusive language in the liturgy.[4] Reference to liturgical tradition here and elsewhere is
tantamount to conservative theological moves. A theological recourse to liturgical tradition has thus apparently been capable only of engendering "liturgical erectitude."[5] Third, the claim to liturgy as a theological site has produced
its own forms of gendered discourse. Discussions of the distinction between
lex orandi as a form of "primary" theology, and *lex credendi* as a form of "sec-

ondary" theology, often point to a "Mrs. Murphy" as the one in the pews who engages in primary theology. The secondary theologian is tacitly coded as male.[6] It does not take a feminist theologian to notice that most Mrs. Murphy analogies are stereotypically gendered and a caricature of the diversity of (worshiping) women's lives.[7] Mrs. Murphy clearly is no dissident daughter. With the gendered metaphor of a Mrs. Murphy, however, a seemingly natural alliance comes to be established between, on the one hand, women, *lex orandi*, and nonscholarly liturgical "experience," and, on the other hand, men, *lex credendi*, and scholarly reflection on liturgy. As other forms of malestream epistemology,[8] the theological recourse to the liturgy, too, is gendered, with the privileged aspects of knowledge being coded as masculine while the nonreflective emotions and the body (Mrs. Murphy is always "in the pew"; the male secondary theologian is seemingly locationless) are gendered as feminine. Not surprisingly, it takes a dissident daughter to ask what would happen if Mrs. Murphy arose from her pew and took liturgical matters into her own hands.[9]

In light of the problematic constructions of gender in the theological turn to the liturgy, it is understandable that feminist theologians only recently have begun to give more sustained attention to themes of, broadly speaking, liturgical theology.[10] Two examples are Susan A. Ross's *Extravagant Affections: A Feminist Sacramental Theology* and Elizabeth A. Johnson's *Friends of God and Prophets: A Feminist Theological Reading of the Communion of Saints*. Ross rethinks fundamentals of sacramental theology in light of the liturgical practices of women and of feminist theory. She rightly asks, If the axiom *lex orandi, lex credendi* suggests that the primary context for theological reflection is worship, what or whose worship do we privilege?[11] For Ross, the answer is clear: Both the official worship of the church and women-identified liturgies count as *lex orandi* to which theology has to be attentive. Elizabeth Johnson's book points in a similar direction. She actually begins with an allusion to a feminist liturgical community and focuses her work on "the current resurgence of women's practices of memory."[12] These women's practices of memory are the crucial building block for Johnson's feminist reading of the communion of saints. Both Ross and Johnson, then, point to the need to reconfigure *lex orandi* while embracing a theological recourse to liturgical tradition.

Given the fact that theological work as a whole, however, has neither drawn on a gender-attentive narrative of liturgical tradition nor paid any attention to current liturgical traditioning in women's hands, I see reflection on a feminist reconfiguring of the liturgy and liturgical traditioning as a pressing task. The women-identified liturgical communities featured in *Dissident Daughters* attend to this task on the level of liturgical practice. My particular task as a theologian has been to lift up and to make available the rich array of women's liturgical traditioning from all over the globe. But my task as a theologian is not exhausted in the collection of narratives of *Dissident Daughters*. These very narratives raise questions of ongoing theological discernment: having engaged dissident daughters' voices where do we go from here theologically?[13]

In what follows, I want both to honor the theological turn to the liturgy and at the same time claim women's prayers and practices as a prominent, if largely hidden, part of the liturgical tradition of the church. While the historical reconstruction of a liturgical tradition that is gender-attentive will have to await another day,[14] my argument here focuses on the contemporary surge of women-identified liturgical practices, displayed so well in the narratives gathered in *Dissident Daughters*. I contend that these women-identified prayers and practices offer possibilities of challenging, broadening, and reconfiguring established claims to the liturgy as a theological site. I begin by highlighting four recent (and quite divergent) developments within the scholarly realm that substantiate my claim to women's liturgical practices as fundamentally important to theological work, and, indeed, to the life of the church. I then offer two small pointers to the material contours of women's *lex orandi*, past and present. I conclude with some thoughts on the nature of a feminist appeal to liturgical tradition.

"Seven for boys, and six for girls"?

My argument for women-identified liturgies as a theological site can draw substantially on well-established arguments for the importance of liturgical tradition for theological reflection. Since the publication of Geoffrey Wainwright's *Doxology: The Praise of God in Doctrine, Worship and Life* two decades ago,[15] a growing number of Protestant theologians have joined the many Orthodox and Catholic theologians who consciously draw on liturgical materials for their work.[16] As a result of this development, the liturgy is once again appreciated as a fundamental part of the Christian tradition and as a crucial source of theological reflection. Although there are distinct differences between theologians as to how *lex orandi* and *lex credendi* are to be related— from claims to the priority of doxology over theology, to the subordination of the liturgy to dogma, to an interpretation of worship as theology—all these proposals are part of the (re-)turn to the liturgy that so profoundly marked recent theological work.

Because women's faith practices are both an integral and a distinct part of Christian tradition, the fact that the peculiar shape of women's liturgical practices remains invisible constitutes a distinct problem in this theological return to the liturgy. Gender as a fundamental marker of liturgical life is occluded and thus written out of what comes to be constructed as "The Liturgical Tradition." For example, in most theological claims about the importance of the Eucharist for the life of the church, there is no acknowledgment of the peculiar ways in which women's gender has shaped, circumscribed, and, last but not least, restricted their engagement with this sacrament. More than half of the church, in its gendered particularity, remains invisible in these claims about the centrality of the Eucharist. To put it more humorously, the girl's response to the priest's question, "How many sacraments are there?" highlights what much liturgical theology has veiled: "Seven for boys, and six for girls."[17] Theologians claiming the liturgical tradition as a source for theological reflection have remained satisfied with the first half of the girl's insight. There is no surprise here, since, overwhelmingly, these theologians have belonged to the gender for whom the answer "seven" seems appropriate.

Women's Ways of Worship

Although women's faith practices continue to be written out of the recourse to liturgical tradition, there has been a burgeoning interest in women's ways of worship outside of theology proper. It is startling to realize how much we have learned of women's liturgical practices from authors other than theologians who profess the crucial importance of worship for theological reflection. I can highlight only a few of these works here, and, indeed, will have to limit myself to more recent studies within the Christian tradition.

In the 1980s, Elaine Lawless published two ethnographic studies of women in pentecostal worship services. *God's Peculiar People: Women's Voices and Folk Traditions in a Pentecostal Church* focuses on women's use of testimony as a way of creating space for women's voices to be heard in worship. In *Handmaidens of the Lord*, Lawless analyzes the preaching styles and strategies of white pentecostal women pastors. Lawless's studies reveal how women in very traditional liturgical contexts nevertheless create distinct space for themselves and their faith.[18] Mary McClintock Fulkerson sharpened this ethnographic analysis with feminist theological tools. In a chapter on Appalachian pentecostal women, McClintock Fulkerson reads these women's performances of Scripture, prayer, testimony, and preaching as peculiar regimes of resistance.[19] Gisela Muschiol's magisterial study *Famula Dei* examines the liturgical life of women's communities in Romano-Merovingian Gaul. Muschiol shows that the center of daily life for these women was a liturgy that the women themselves shaped and celebrated under the liturgical presidency of their abbess, including hearing confession and absolving.[20] These women thus had a considerable measure of control over their own liturgical lives. Robert Orsi, in his study *Thank You, St. Jude*, focuses on the prayers and practices of American Catholic women devoted to St. Jude Thaddeus, the patron saint of hopeless causes.[21] Orsi uses ethnographic research to read women's prayer practices as ways of negotiating particular cultural shifts in their lives.

Two studies of African-American slave women begin to map these women's extensive ritual practices (especially conjure) and healing work.[22] Marie Griffith's *God's Daughters: Evangelical Women and the Power of Submission* examines the lives and narratives of North American members of the Women's Aglow Fellowship, an international charismatic Christian women's group. Griffith, similarly to Orsi, weaves together in-depth ethnographic research, careful textual analysis, and insights from cultural studies in order to read practices of prayer as a lens through which to view women's strategic ways of negotiating their daily lives.[23] Lesley Northup's *Ritualizing Women* approaches its subject, namely, "what women do when they get together to worship," by drawing broadly on diverse methodological tools, for example, ritual studies, gender studies, anthropology, and sociology, as well as by attending to diverse faith communities, from Christian feminist groups to Korean women shamans.[24] Northup's study offers an analysis of patterns and emphases that emerge in women's ritualizing. If Northup ranges broadly indeed, Carol Ann Muller focuses on a very particular group of women: the author examines the ritual practices of women in the South African Church of the Nazarites, especially their sacred songs, dances, dreams, miracle narratives, and fertility rituals. Muller's interest lies in the feminized power these ritual performances provide for Nazarite women.[25] Kay Turner, who wrote her dissertation in folklore on Mexican American women's home altars, published a broader study of the tradition of women's altars in 1999. In her study, Kay highlights the long and widespread tradition of women's altars as a "site of subversion" in cultures that usually distance women from official altars in manifold ways.[26]

What these diverse studies show, whether they are concerned with Romano-Merovingian women's communities, women's devotion to a particular saint, charismatic women's prayer meetings, or feminist ritualizing, is the simple fact that gender shapes liturgy in manifold ways. However, given that none of these studies is explicitly theological, the impact of gender on *lex orandi*—and the consequences for any claim to liturgy as a theological site—remain unexplored. Women's faith practices are simply seen as exciting ethnographic, cultural, and historical material. In other words, these studies have not affected theological reflection in any sustained way.

The Turn to Ecclesial Practices

The recent theological attention to practices, particularly in postliberal narrative theologies with their emphasis on the traditional practices of the church, also coincides with my argument that women's liturgical practices are fundamentally important to theological reflection. Postliberal theologies understand the church and its canonical texts as a cultural-linguistic universe into which people are initiated and by which they are formed. These theologies consequently turn to traditional ecclesial practices, particularly baptism and the Eucharist, as shaping Christian identity and as constituting the most foundational source for theological reflection.

I take from this theological turn to the church and its texts and practices the poignant reminder of the importance of what the faith community has actually done through the ages. One of the distinct weaknesses of this approach, however, is the assumption that there is an easily discernible, pristine core of fundamental texts and practices in the tradition of the church, and that these texts and practices are gender-blind and not marred by the pervasive historic marginalization of women. Those texts and practices thus become sheltered from critique and reconfiguration. For most postliberal theologians, a hermeneutic of trust is assumed, and ecclesial practices continue to be drawn on normatively as if they are not also practices of domination and marginalization.

Privileging Ordinary Sites

I turn to a fourth development in theology in order to thread it into my claim for women's liturgical practices being of fundamental importance for theological reflection. This fourth development can be described as a turn to ordinary sites of the production of Christian meaning. There are many different forms this particular theological turn can take, such as attention to local theologies, attention to the marginalized in various liberation theologies (for example, the poor of the base ecclesial communities in liberation theology, black slaves and their African-American descendants in black theology, different groups of women in feminist theologies), and attention to popular religiosity, lived religion, or "theologies of ordinary people,"[27] to name only the most obvious. Rather than privileging official texts and doctrines of the church, these approaches focus on the symbolic and material productions of ordinary Christians. Their discourses and sites for the production of Christian meaning become fundamental sources for theological reflection. Clearly, this approach is congenial to reading women's liturgical practices as an important source for theological reflection. In actuality, however, little theological work has been done concretely on women's ways of worship as one of those ordinary sites that are to inform theological reflection.

Although the four strands highlighted above are rooted in quite different theological presuppositions, they each, in some of their argumentative moves, coincide with my claim that women's liturgical practices are of fundamental importance for theological work and for the life of the church. From the turn to liturgy as a theological site I derive the claim to women's ways of worship as a locus of insight to which theology has to attend. From recent research into a variety of women's devotional practices, I gain the insight of women's practices of prayer as distinct forms of ritual, forged in the crucible of women's lives. From the postliberal turn to the practices of the community of faith, I derive the insistence on women's ways of worship as an ecclesial practice, a fundamental part of the life of the church through the ages. With the turn to ordinary sites as sources for theological reflection, I lift up women's ritual practices, often found at the fringes of official worship, as an important site of the theologies of ordinary people. I thus claim women's *lex orandi* as an ancient and ever-new ecclesial practice and as an integral yet distinct part of "The Liturgical Tradition." A fundamental problem for this claim is that we have not yet recovered much of women's liturgical history and, therefore, can only wonder about the impact of gender on constructions of liturgy and about its consequences for any claim to liturgy as a theological site. In order to show that there is much to (re-)discover about the shape of women's ways of worship, past and present, I want to offer two brief pointers to women's practices of prayer in the Christian tradition. I will conclude with some thoughts on the nature of a feminist appeal to liturgical tradition.

WOMEN'S PRAYERS AND PRACTICES, PAST AND PRESENT

Women have been liturgical practitioners through the ages, even if often neither in their own right nor in their own rite. Unfortunately, no liturgical history is available to date that goes beyond the problematic add-women-and-stir approach. Liturgical "facts" continue to be constructed as gender-blind or gender-neutral, with little or no recognition that what comes to be counted as "fact" is always theory-specific.[28] As feminist research has shown again and again, a theory oblivious to gender as a fundamental marker of reality will, first, present seemingly ungendered facts; second, thereby occlude an important shaper of historical practices; and third, therefore offer few guidelines for shaping practices in a world where gender systems are in crisis. For a feminist reconfiguration of *lex orandi* the task is clear—namely, to begin to write gender back into the liturgical tradition. Such work is not about discarding the tradition but about uncentering malestream constructions by inscribing a gender-attentive narrative in their place.

Let me illustrate the above claims with a brief look at two distinct traditions of women's practices of prayer: the biblial accounts and the surge of women-identified liturgical practices embodied in *Dissident Daughters*. A look at the Scriptures offers a glimpse of the problems related to reconstructing women's ways of worship. As far back as the earlier parts of the Hebrew Scriptures, songs and prayers are put in the mouths of women—but only about ten of the nearly three hundred instances of recorded prayers or allusions to prayer in the Hebrew Scriptures even purport to be those of women.[29] If we would look for a biblical *lex orandi*, then, the asymmetrically gendered amount of the evidence is striking. The content of the prayer traditions also speaks to the power of gender in shaping *lex orandi*. The majority of prayers put in women's mouths in the Hebrew Scriptures are related to women's reproductive and maternal roles. There is Hagar's desperate plea in the face of her dying child (Gen. 21:16f), Leah's praise of God at the birth of her son (Gen. 29:35), the blessing over Naomi by her women friends on the occasion of Ruth's marriage to Boaz (Ruth 4:14), and Hannah's agonizing prayer for a son (1 Sam. 1:10) followed by her exuberant praise after the prayer is answered (1 Sam. 2:1–10). Disproportionally, then, women's *lex orandi* in the Hebrew Scriptures is shaped by women's reproductive and maternal roles (even if these are coded differently, namely, much more broadly, than today). That these roles exhaust neither women's lives nor women's prayers becomes visible in two powerfully prophetic voices of prayer and praise in the Hebrew Scriptures: Miriam's triumphant song after the crossing of the Red Sea (Exod. 15:21), which is part of a larger women-centered ritual under Miriam's leadership; and the mighty song of Deborah (Judg. 5:1–31) after Jael's killing of Sisera. In the Apocryphal/Deuterocanonical books, indeed, prayer "often undergirds female actions that are courageous, unconventional and subversive."[30]

Looking to the New Testament, we find two prayers put in the mouths of women that became part of the liturgical tradition of the church. Mary's song of praise at her encounter with Elizabeth (Luke 1:46–55), known by its Latin opening word *Magnificat*, has its place in the daily evening prayer of the church. Elizabeth's prophetic blessing of Mary, "Blessed are you among women, and blessed is the fruit of your womb" (Luke 1:42), is part of the prayer loved by many Catholics as the *Hail Mary*, a key part of the rosary. These two biblical songs of praise, as their counterparts from the Hebrew Scriptures, are situated within women's reproductive and maternal roles. Both Elizabeth and Mary are pregnant, miraculously so, and their praises emerge out of the two women encountering each other as bearers of distinctly God-sent children. Beyond the powerful voices of these two pregnant women, however, the other women described in the New Testament as praying and praising God remain speechless in the recorded testimony—from the prophet Anna (Luke 2:38), to "certain women" devoting themselves to prayer with the other disciples of Jesus after the ascension (Acts 1:14), to the four nameless daughters of Philip who prophecy (Acts 21:9). This uneven witness of the Scriptures to the prayers and practices of women continues within the Christian tradition. Two thousand years of women's prayers and ways of worship remain largely hidden; their painstaking reconstruction has only just begun. Where prayers and practices of women do surface, they are often related to women's bodily and reproductive functions.

Given this historical occlusion of women's prayers and practices, the surge of contemporary women-identified prayers and practices is a telling contrast to "The Tradition" (although if we reconfigured this tradition in gender-attentive ways, the contrast would be much less stark). These vibrant songs, prayers, and rituals, I suggest, already allow a glimpse at the shape of a theological recourse to the liturgy that is gender-attentive. What emerges as a women-identified form of liturgical traditioning? What might feminist ritual knowledge disclose?[31] Granted that it is too early to write a theology on the basis of women's ways of worship throughout history, it is worth anticipating what it might look like. How would one write a liturgical theology attentive to the distinct shape of women's *lex orandi?* Taking *Dissident Daughters* as an example, one might say that such a theology would attend to women as subjects of the liturgy who confront the Holy in the crucible of women's lives. In other words, this theology would begin with the presence of women and of women's bodies in worship rather than being predicated on their absence or on their presence as a problem. This theology, then, foregrounds women's liturgical practices as a primary site of experience and reflection on God.

A women-identified liturgical way of doing theology would also take clues from the careful interplay between liturgical tradition and a reconfiguring of the tradition through women's lives witnessed to in so many of the new liturgies (where a ritual of anointing will be offered to a survivor of rape, an exorcism might be directed at the evils of patriarchy, and a Good Friday liturgy can center on women's suffering). Such a theology would adopt the rich and intense pleasure of symbols readily apparent in women-identified liturgies. It would be a theology not dependent on binarist constructions of the ordinary and the sacred but one able to claim sacred space in all of life, especially in the ordinary of women's lives so often subject to trivialization and marginalization. With the poetic and imaginative language of women-identified liturgies, such a theology speaks the language of passion and compassion unafraid. From these liturgies' ability to bring women's diverse lives into the presence of the Holy One, this theology takes clues about presencing women in theological discourse all the while healing and hallowing that presence. And a theology nurtured by women-identified liturgical practices must of necessity embrace a vision of a church deeply aware of the ever-shifting boundaries and many ambiguities of the community of faith, all the while struggling to embody healing and justice. Last and most important, such a theology will attend to God-talk in ways revelatory of Her Who Is Worshiped in women-identified liturgies: the Root of Wisdom, the Weaver of the Web of Life, the Divine

Midwife and Passionate Sister, Sophia.[32] The wealth of these images in women-identified liturgies witnesses to the intensity of the search for new and authentic ways of naming and encountering God.

Theology does well to listen to these prayers and practices of women. Two reasons in particular lead me to stress this claim. First, a theological turn to liturgy, given its own interpretive commitments, can only be enriched by drawing on the centuries-old and ever-new wisdom of women liturgical practitioners. Why impoverish the Christian tradition by inattentiveness to the prayers and practices of more than half of the body of Christ? A second reason for my insistence on the importance of a theology attentive to women's lives is the work this tradition-friendly approach does in reconfiguring what counts as Christian tradition in the first place. I want to conclude with some thoughts on this subject in light of a challenge issued by Kathryn Tanner.

RECONFIGURING LITURGICAL TRADITION

In a wise challenge to feminist theologians, Kathryn Tanner has argued that feminist theologians do well to "remain traditional." She writes, "The influence of feminist theology is strengthened to the extent it wrestles constructively with the theological claims that have traditionally been important in Christian theology; the more traditional the material with which it works, the greater the influence of feminist theology."[33] Tanner's starting point for this challenge is a reconceptualization of the task of theology on the basis of Marxist and poststructuralist theories of culture. These theories enable her to read theology as a site of struggle over symbolic resources and as an always-selective, never-stable site of the production of meaning. For Tanner, this reading of theology through the lens of cultural theories means that feminist theology becomes most effective and convincing not in distancing itself as far as possible from the tradition but in claiming tradition as a site of struggle over meaning today. Thus, the more feminist theology uses and realigns elements that have been appropriated by patriarchal interests, the greater the feminist claim on theological credibility. Tradition, here, quite clearly is not understood as a fixed and unified block of material that is merely passed on and received. Rather, tradition is seen as constructed in the here and now in an ongoing struggle over a diversity of practices and interpretations. As such, what comes to be designated as tradition is first, highly selective, but second, rather unstable, open to redesignation.[34]

Tanner's argument resonates with my own effort to construct a feminist account of a liturgical way of doing theology. Like Tanner, I am convinced that feminist theology's appeal is strengthened by tradition-friendliness in the sense of claiming as many elements as possible from the tradition while at the same time reconfiguring what is authorized as "Tradition." The claim to liturgy as a site of theological reflection is a seemingly traditional move while the reconfiguration of *lex orandi* in light of women's ways of worship expands the very meaning of liturgical tradition. Tanner's reading of tradition as a struggle over meaning today is also helpful in interpreting the contemporary surge of women-identified liturgical practices. Rather than designating these practices as a decisive break with and the very undoing of "The Tradition," women-identified liturgical practices can instead be seen as part and parcel of the continuous construction and reconstruction of liturgy in the life of the church.

In reconfiguring liturgical tradition and traditioning in gender-attentive ways, we will undoubtedly discover what the women-identified liturgical practices embodied in *Dissident Daughters* make so very clear: that women engage the liturgy in the crucible of their own lives, including its manifold ways of marginalizing. But we will also discover what André Myre has emphasized with a view to the biblical witness: "There is a word of God to women, spoken millenniums ago [and continuing to be spoken!], a word which has not yet been heard, a word to which the men who wrote the Bible have not really given testimony."[35] Confronting and acknowledging this "word of God to women" forces us to rethink notions of revelation, liturgical tradition, and authority in the church, to name just a few. Confronting and acknowledging this word of God to women also forces a new listening to the word of God that women hear today and to which they witness amidst continuing ways of silencing. The prayers and practices of *Dissident Daughters* are indeed a crucial site of this word of God to women becoming flesh in our time.

Notes

Introduction

1. The sentence appeared on an OXFAM poster, now sadly out of print. The poster can be seen in a photograph in *The Challenge of Local Feminisms: Women's Movements in Global Perspective*, Social Change in Global Perspective, ed. Amrita Basu with the assistance of C. Elizabeth McGrory (Boulder, Colo.: Westview Press, 1995), 156.

2. An ongoing struggle over appropriate ways of naming the subject-matter of this book lies behind this (less than elegant) choice of wording. Several possibilities are at hand, each with specific strengths and weaknesses. The simplest description, "women's liturgies," is both the broadest and also the least appropriate. *Dissident Daughters*, after all, does not include any trace of women's liturgies as they have been celebrated over the past 1,500 years in religious and monastic communities of women. Neither does the book include the prayer practices of, say, pentecostal or evangelical women. Important ritual spaces of women in the Christian tradition are thus not covered. On the other side of the spectrum of possibilities for naming the book's subject matter is the term "feminist." It is clearly embraced and valued by the majority of the women writing here and claims a place at least in the subtitle to *Dissident Daughters*. But "feminism" does not enjoy universal popularity for women-identified struggles, particularly not in parts of the postcolonial world or within marginalized communities in the First World. African-American women coined the term "womanist" and Hispanic women named themselves "mujeristas" in attempts to distinguish their women-identified struggles from (white) feminism. African women also do not readily recognize themselves in the present book project when described as "feminist liturgies." Feminism for them can carry images of a "bourgeois" and "First-World" movement of white middle-class North Atlantic women, which is not applicable to their struggles. But the term "feminist" has also come under scrutiny from feminist scholars themselves, since feminism has not escaped essentialist and universalizing postures. In light of these complexities, I have chosen to write of women-identified liturgies or women's rites as a way of creating space between "women's liturgies" on the one hand and "feminist" liturgies on the other. The space created through this choice points to the emergence of a broad range of rituals—in different cultural contexts and amidst differing gender systems—all gendered specifically from and to the social location of women and with a view to enabling women's lives to flourish.

3. I will be using the terms "liturgy," "ritual," and "rite" interchangeably for the women-identified religious celebrations that are the subject matter of this book. My justification lies in the fact that dissident daughters use a variety of terms to

name their ritualizing. I attempt to stay true to this variety, although as a liturgical scholar I gravitate towards the term "liturgy."

4. This point is forcefully made by Lisa Lowe and David Lloyd in the introduction to their book *The Politics of Culture in the Shadow of Capital* (Durham, N.C.: Duke University Press, 1997), 1–32.

5. To name but one example, Denis R. Janz's book, *World Christianity and Marxism* (New York: Oxford University Press, 1998), simply presupposes the existence of two discrete entities that can meaningfully be described as "World Christianity" (or the "Christian world") and "Marxism."

6. Arjun Appadurai notes this point in his "Grassroots Globalization and the Research Imagination," *Public Culture* 12 (2000): 1–17, here 4.

7. WATER and *Con-spirando* are two groups that have intentionally sought to build something akin to a sustained transnational network.

8. I am indebted for this terminology to Robert J. Schreiter, *The New Catholicity: Theology Between the Global and the Local* (Maryknoll, N.Y.: Orbis Books, 1997), 15–21. Schreiter highlights feminist theologies as one of four new global theological "flows," which he defines as "theological discourses that, while not uniform or systemic, represent a series of linked, mutually intelligible discourses that address the contradictions or failures of global systems" (16).

9. Lata Mani, borrowing from Chandra Mohanty, develops this notion in her essay, "Multiple Mediations: Feminist Scholarship in the Age of Multinational Reception," in *Knowing Women: Feminism and Knowledge*, ed. Helen Crowley and Susan Himmelweit (Cambridge, Mass.: Polity Press, 1992), 306–322.

10. Some of the liturgies of the Women's Liturgy Group in New York City, U.S.A., have been documented in Janet R. Walton, *Feminist Liturgy: A Matter of Justice*, American Essays in Liturgy (Collegeville, Minn.: Liturgical Press, 2000), 48–80. There are two women-identified liturgical groups in Germany that have published their liturgical materials in book form; see Christine Hojenski et al., eds. *"Meine Seele sieht das Land der Freiheit." Feministische Liturgien—Modelle für die Praxis* (Münster: edition liberacíon, 1990) and Barbara Baumann et al., *Frauenliturgien. Ein Werkbuch* (München: Kösel, 1998). For the situation in the Netherlands, see Denise J. J. Dijk, "Developments in Feminist Liturgy in the Netherlands," *Studia Liturgica* 25 (1995): 120–128. For St. Hilda Community in England, see *Women Included: A Book of Services and Prayers* (London: SPCK, 1991; revised and updated ed. 1996, *The New Women Included*) and, recently, Elaine Graham, "A view from a room: feminist practical theology from academy, kitchen or sanctuary?" in *Liberating Faith Practices: Feminist Practical Theologies in Context*, ed. Denise M. Ackermann and Riet Bons-Storm (Leuven: Peeters, 1998), 129–152, esp. 141–148.

11. As far as I can see, Arlene Swidler's edited volume *Sistercelebrations: Nine Worship Experiences* (Philadelphia: Fortress Press, 1974) is the first volume of feminist liturgies to be published. Sharon and Thomas Neufer Emswiler's broader collection of "non-sexist" devotional materials, *Women and Worship: A Guide to Non-Sexist Hymns, Prayers, and Liturgies* (San Francisco: Harper & Row, 1974) was published in the same year.

12. See the subtitle of Marjorie Procter-Smith's book *In Her Own Rite: Constructing Feminist Liturgical Tradition* (Nashville: Abingdon Press, 1990; reprint: Akron, Ohio: OSL Publications, 2000).

13. Ronald L. Grimes, *Reading, Writing, and Ritualizing: Ritual in Fictive, Liturgical, and Public Places* (Washington, D.C.: Pastoral Press, 1993), 5.

14. *The Woman's Prayer Companion: Praying Life Events and Celebrating Women of Inspi-*

ration in Breviary Format, featuring all-inclusive Language, 3rd ed. (Indianapolis, Ind.: Carmelites of Indianapolis, 1995); *The Ladies' Pocket Prayer Book: A Manual of Prayers and Devotions for Catholic Women*, new ed. (New York: Catholic Book Publishing Company, 1950).

15. Anita Corrine Donihue, *When I'm on My Knees: Devotional Thoughts on Prayer for Women* (Uhrichsville, Ohio: Barbour & Co., 1997).

16. *Women of Prayer: Released to the Nations* (Lynwood, Wash.: Women's Aglow Fellowship International, 1993).

17. Hazel T. Wilson, ed., *Women at Prayer: Private and Universal Prayers for the Women of America* (Boston: Pilgrim Press, 1948), 12.

18. *Women of Prayer: An Anthology of Everyday Prayers from Women around the World*, compiled by Dorothy Stewart (Chicago: Loyola Press, 1999).

19. See the early article by the Italian Catholic Adriana Zarri, "Woman's Prayer and a Man's Liturgy," in *Prayer and Community*, Concilium 52, ed. Herman Schmidt (New York: Herder & Herder, 1970), 73–86.

20. Sharon and Thomas Neufer Emswiler, *Women and Worship: A Guide to Non-Sexist Hymns, Prayers, and Liturgies* (San Francisco: Harper & Row, 1974), 3, 34.

21. Miriam Therese Winter, *WomanWord: A Feminist Lectionary and Psalter. Women of the New Testament* (New York: Crossroad, 1991), 266, used with permission.

22. Rosemary Radford Ruether, *Women-Church: Theology and Practice of Feminist Liturgical Communities* (San Francisco: Harper & Row, 1985), 67.

23. Examples can be found in Beatrice Aebi et al., eds., *Sinfonia Oecumenica: Worship with the Churches in the World* (Gütersloh/Basle: Gütersloher Verlagshaus/Basileia Verlag, 1998), 74, 152, 186, 396, 400, 452, 620, 734.

24. This story has been told in a variety of ways, e.g., Susannah Herzel, *A Voice for Women: The Women's Department of the World Council of Churches* (Geneva: World Council of Churches Publications, 1981); Melanie A. May, *Bonds of Unity: Women, Theology, and the Worldwide Church* (Atlanta: Scholars Press, 1989), 15–58; Pauline Webb, *She Flies Beyond: Memories and Hopes of Women in the Ecumenical Movement* (Geneva: World Council of Churches Publications, 1993).

25. Cf. Patricia R. Hill, *The World Their Household: The American Woman's Foreign Mission Movement and Cultural Transformation, 1870–1920*, Women and Culture Series (Ann Arbor: University of Michigan Press, 1985), 63f.

26. For an example of a liturgy from the Women's World Day of Prayer, see the one prepared by Native American Women, "Mother Earth is in Pain," in *Sinfonia Oecumenica*, ed. Beatrice Aebi et al., 884–897.

27. Cf. *The Place of Women in the Church on the Mission Field* (New York: The International Missionary Council, 1927).

28. I borrow this distinction from Reinhild Traitler, "An Oikoumene of Women?," *The Ecumenical Review* 40 (1988): 178–184.

29. See, for example, Constance F. Parvey, "The Continuing Significance of the Community of Women and Men in the Church Study: its Mixed Meanings for the Church," in *Beyond Unity-in-Tension: Unity, Renewal and the Community of Women and Men*, ed. T. F. Best (Geneva: World Council of Churches Publications, 1988), 34–43.

30. See Michael Kinnamon and Brian E. Cope, eds., *The Ecumenical Movement: An Anthology of Key Texts and Voices* (Geneva/Grand Rapids: World Council of Churches Publications/Wm. B. Eerdmans Publishing Co., 1997), 231. Ibid., 231–237, reproduces the text of Chung's address.

31. See Irja Askola and Nicole Fischer-Duchable, *Living Letters: A Report of Visits to the*

Churches during the Ecumenical Decade—Churches in Solidarity with Women (Geneva: World Council of Churches Publications, 1997), and Lynda Katsuno-Ishii and Edna J. Orteza, eds., *Of Rolling Waters and Roaring Wind: A Celebration of the Woman Song* (Geneva: World Council of Churches Publications, 2000).

32. The ritual is documented in Nancy J. Berneking and Pamela Carter Joern, eds., *Re-Membering and Re-Imagining* (Cleveland: Pilgrim Press, 1995), 18–20.

33. Theologically, I take this further in my essay "The 'Separated Brethren' and the 'Separated Sisters': Feminist and/as Ecumenical Visions of the Church," in *Ecumenical Theology in Worship, Doctrine and Life*, ed. David S. Cunningham et al. (New York: Oxford University Press, 1999), 221–230.

34. This was the title of a "special issue on women" in *Ford Foundation Report* 31:1 (Winter 2000). See also the book edited by Amrita Basu with the assistance of C. Elizabeth McGrory, *The Challenge of Local Feminisms: Women's Movements in Global Perspective*, which grew out of the Ford Foundation's Women's Program Forum.

35. For more, see Dana L. Roberts, *American Women in Mission: A Social History of Their Thought and Practice*, The Modern Mission Era, 1792–1992 (Macon, Ga.: Mercer University Press, 1996).

36. Cf. Patricia R. Hill, *The World Their Household: The American Woman's Foreign Mission Movement and Cultural Transformation*, esp. 3, 8.

37. Cf. Patricia Ward D'Itri, *Cross-Currents in the International Women's Movement, 1848–1948* (Bowling Green, Ohio: Bowling Green State University Popular Press, 1999), 39.

38. Cf. Leila J. Rupp, *Worlds of Women: The Making of an International Women's Movement* (Princeton: Princeton University Press, 1997), and Deborah Stienstra, *Women's Movements and International Organizations* (New York: St. Martin's Press, 1994).

39. I am obviously indebted, in the shaping of this notion of a feminist Atlantic, to Paul Gilroy's *The Black Atlantic: Modernity and Double Consciousness* (Cambridge: Harvard University Press, 1993).

40. Flora Davis, *Moving the Mountain: The Women's Movement in America since 1960* (New York: Simon & Schuster, 1991), and Ruth Rosen, *The World Split Open: How the Modern Women's Movement Changed America* (New York: Viking Press, 2000) both provide detailed accounts of the movement in the United States.

41. See the ground-breaking book by Robin Morgan, ed., *Sisterhood is Global: The International Women's Movement Anthology* (Garden City, N.Y.: Anchor Press/Doubleday, 1984).

42. Susan Stanford Friedman, *Mappings: Feminism and the Cultural Geographies of Encounter* (Princeton: Princeton University Press, 1998), 4.

43. A case in point is the book edited by Bonnie G. Smith, *Global Feminisms since 1945*, Rewriting Histories (New York: Routledge & Kegan Paul, 2000).

44. As Haleh Afshar and Stephanie Barrientos succinctly state in the introduction to their book *Women, Globalization and Fragmentation in the Developing World*, Women's Studies at York Series (New York: St. Martin's Press, 1999), 1.

45. For more, see Alice Mastrangelo Gittler, "Mapping Women's Global Communications and Networking," in *Women@Internet: Creating New Cultures in Cyberspace*, ed. Wendy Harcourt (New York: Zen Books, 1999), 91–101.

46. Elizabeth A. Johnson, *Friends of God and Prophets: A Feminist Theological Reading of the Communion of Saints* (New York: Continuum, 1998), 27.

47. Lucy Tatman, "Thoughts and Hopes on the Future of Feminist Theology/ies," *Feminist Theology* 22 (1999): 93–100, esp. 97, has been helpful to me here. Tatman also rightly emphasizes the fact that white feminist theology itself is no homoge-

neous enterprise, but shaped in very distinct ways by region, confessional tradition, sexual preference, class, and theological methodology, to name just five.

48. For a feminist indictment of the latter, see also the book by Ellen T. Armour, *Deconstruction, Feminist Theology, and the Problem of Difference: Subverting the Race/Gender Divide* (Chicago: University of Chicago Press, 1999).

49. Cf., for example, Musimbi Kanyoro, "My Grandmother Would Approve: Engendering Gospel and Culture," *Feminist Theology* 20 (1999): 53–70 (with pointers to more of the literature by African women).

50. Elisabeth Schüssler Fiorenza, "The Will to Choose or to Reject: Continuing Our Critical Work," in *Feminist Interpretation of the Bible*, ed. Letty M. Russell (Philadelphia: Westminster Press, 1985), 125–136, here 126.

51. Schüssler Fiorenza, "The Will to Choose or to Reject," 135.

52. Catherine Bell, *Ritual: Perspectives and Dimensions* (New York: Oxford University Press, 1997), 238.

53. Cf. Lesley A. Northup, *Ritualizing Women: Patterns of Spirituality* (Cleveland: Pilgrim Press, 1997), 11, 22.

54. See the documentary film "Women of the Wall," directed and produced by Faye Lederman, 1993.

55. The book edited by my colleague Karen Westerfield Tucker, *The Sunday Service of the Methodists: Twentieth-Century Worship in Worldwide Methodism* (Nashville: Abingdon Press, 1996) is a notable exception.

56. For a critique of this assumption, see Grimes, *Reading, Writing, and Ritualizing,* 12–19.

57. Lieve Troch, "The Feminist Movement in and on the Edge of the Churches in the Netherlands: From Consciousness-raising to Womenchurch," *Journal of Feminist Studies in Religion* 5, no. 2 (1989): 113–128, here 114.

58. For this point about emancipatory struggles in general, see Lisa Lowe and David Lloyd, "Introduction," 3.

59. Reading Lawrence Venuti's *The Translator's Invisibility: A History of Translation,* Translation Studies (New York: Routledge & Kegan Paul, 1995) has encouraged me to claim translation as a "locus of difference" instead of homogeneity. The latter, after all, is predicated on the translator's invisibility and the illusory effect of transparency. Venuti emphasizes that Anglo-American culture "has long been dominated by domesticating theories that recommend fluent translating" (21).

60. Cf. Roland Robertson, "Glocalization: Time—Space and Homogeneity—Heterogeneity," in *Global Modernities*, Theory, Culture & Society, ed. Mike Featherstone et al. (London: Sage Publications, 1995), 25–44.

61. See, for example, Leo Ching, "Globalizing the Regional, Regionalizing the Global: Mass Culture and Asianism in the Age of Late Capital," *Public Culture* 12 (2000): 233–257, here 257.

62. Cf. Sharon Rose Joy Ruiz-Duremdes, ed., *From Darkness to Light*, Creative Studies for Women in the Churches 1 (Quezon City: National Council of Churches in the Philippines, Program Unit on Women of the Commission on Christian Education, 1991), 46.

63. See "Korean Woman Jesus: Drama Worship," *Journal of Women and Religion* 13 (1995): 45, and "Women Church of Korea," *In God's Image* (June 1990): 57.

64. See Yeta Ramírez, "El poder de los simbolos," *Con-spirando* 19 (March 1997): 36, and "Creation Story: Latin American Reflection," *In God's Image* (Summer 1991): 21.

65. *Reading, Writing, and Ritualizing,* 17 describes feminist ritualizing as a form of "countercultural ritualizing."

66. I borrow the expression from the title of Sue Monk Kidd's book, *The Dance of the Dissident Daughter: A Woman's Journey from Christian Tradition to the Sacred Feminine* (San Francisco: HarperCollins, 1996).

67. Troch uses this description in her insightful article, "The Feminist Movement in and on the Edge of the Churches in the Netherlands."

68. The Chicana poet Gloria Anzaldúa focused attention on the border as a shared space with her much-acclaimed book *Borderlands/La Frontera: The New Mestiza* (San Francisco: Spinsters/Aunt Lute, 1987). For the theological work the notion of "borderland" can do, see, for example, María Pilar Aquino and Roberto S. Goizueta, eds., *Theology: Expanding the Borders*, The Annual Publication of the College Theology Society 43 (Mystic, Conn.: Twenty-Third Publications, 1998), and, from a European perspective, Hedwig Meyer-Wilmes, *Rebellion on the Borders* (Kampen: Kok Pharos Publishing House, 1995). Not surprisingly, one of the dissident daughters has made use of Anzaldúa's work for her own: see Ute Seibert-Cuadra, "Leben en la frontera oder auf der Grenze oder en el límite," in *Zwischen-Räume. Deutsche feministische Theologinnen im Ausland*, Theologische Frauenforschung in Europa 1, ed. Katharina von Kellenbach and Susanne Scholz (Münster: LIT, 2000), 101–111.

69. I myself have previously identified ten clusters as distinctive features of liturgies shaped by women for women, cf. Teresa Berger, *Women's Ways of Worship: Gender Analysis and Liturgical History* (Collegeville, Minn.: Liturgical Press, 1999), 121–143. For other ways of describing the characteristics of feminist liturgies, see Diann L. Neu, "Women Revisioning Religious Rituals," in *Women and Religious Ritual*, ed. Lesley A. Northup (Washington, D.C.: The Pastoral Press, 1993), 158–167; Mary Collins, "Principles of Feminist Liturgy," in *Women at Worship: Interpretations of North American Diversity*, ed. Marjorie Procter-Smith and Janet Walton (Louisville, Ky.: Westminster John Knox Press, 1993), 11–15; and Marjorie Procter-Smith, "Marks of Feminist Liturgy," *Proceedings of the North American Academy of Liturgy* (1992): 69–75.

70. The term has been introduced into theological work by Kathryn Tanner, *Theories of Culture: A New Agenda for Theology*, Guides to Theological Inquiry (Minneapolis: Fortress Press, 1997), 144.

71. Cf. Kathryn Tanner, "Theology and Popular Culture," in *Changing Conversations: Religious Reflection and Cultural Analysis*, ed. Dwight N. Hopkins and Sheila Greeve Davaney (New York: Routledge & Kegan Paul, 1996), 101–120.

72. J. K. Gibson-Graham make this point forcefully in the preface to their book *The End of Capitalism (as we knew it): A Feminist Critique of Political Economy* (Cambridge, Mass.: Blackwell Publishers, 1996), VIIf.

73. Cf. Liz Stanley, "Is There Life in the Contact Zone? Auto/biographical Practices and the Field of Representation in Writing Past Lives," in *Representing Lives: Women and Auto/biography*, ed. Alison Donnell and Pauline Polkey (New York: St. Martin's Press, 2000), 3–30, here 27.

74. See Appadurai, "Grassroots Globalization and the Research Imagination," 7.

75. Cf. Ada María Isasi-Díaz, "On the Birthing Stool: Mujerista Liturgy," and Delores S. Williams, "Rituals of Resistance in Womanist Worship," in Proctor-Smith and Walton, eds., *Women at Worship: Interpretations of North American Diversity*, 191–210, 215–223.

76. Martin W. Lewis and Kären E. Wigen, *The Myth of Continents: A Critique of Metageography* (Berkeley: University of California Press, 1997).

77. See, for example, Dipesh Chakrabarty, "The Time of History and the Times of the

Gods," in Lowe and Lloyd, eds., *The Politics of Culture in the Shadow of Capital*, 35–59.

78. Miriam Therese Winter described dissident daughters in these terms in an e-mail to the author, January 25, 2000.

79. Mercy Amba Oduyoye, "Third World Women's Theologies: Africa," in *Dictionary of Third World Theologies*, ed. Virginia Fabella and R. S. Sugirtharajah (Maryknoll, N.Y.: Orbis Books, 2000), 219–221, here 219.

80. See, for example, the fascinating studies gathered in Jean and John Comaroff, eds., *Modernity and Its Malcontents: Ritual and Power in Postcolonial Africa* (Chicago: University of Chicago Press, 1993), and the issue on African rituals in *TDR: A Journal of Performance Studies* 32, no. 2 (1988).

81. See the study by Linda E. Thomas of healing rituals in an African-instituted church, *Under the Canopy: Ritual Process and Spiritual Resilience in South Africa*, Studies in Comparative Religion (Columbia: University of South Carolina Press, 1999).

82. See the articles by Mercy Amba Oduyoye, "Women and Ritual in Africa"; Rosemary N. Edet, "Christianity and African Women's Rituals"; and Anne Nasimiyu-Wasike, "Christianity and the African Rituals of Birth and Naming"; in *The Will to Arise: Women, Tradition, and the Church in Africa*, ed. Mercy Amba Oduyoye and Musimbi R. A. Kanyoro (Maryknoll, N.Y.: Orbis Books, 1992), 9–24, 25–39, 40–53.

83. See her recent publication *Postcolonial Feminist Interpretation of the Bible* (St. Louis: Chalice Press, 2000).

84. Musa Dube in an e-mail to the author, January 25, 2000.

85. Nyambura Njoroge in an e-mail to the author, January 26, 2000.

86. The closest one comes to African Christian women's groups that ritualize regularly, with a story of growth, struggle, and evolving liturgical patterns with a women-centered orientation, might well be found in religious communities of women. The Roman Catholic Church in Africa has been engaged in a vibrant process of liturgical inculturation; a striking example on the level of women's religious communities are the Poor Claires in Lilongwe, Malawi, whose liturgy is inculturated not only into African patterns, but more specifically into the lives of African women. Thus, in the entrance procession, the gospel book might be brought in inside a large earthenware pot that a woman carries on her head. The nuns also incorporate a variety of traditional Malawi women's dancing patterns into their liturgical celebrations and use ululation and hand claps as a sign of reverence. In a particularly striking example of inculturating the liturgy into African women's lives, a morning prayer service begins not with the ringing of bells but with the traditional sounds of the early morning for African women: sounds of pounding a mortar and pestle and sounds of sifting grain (the liturgical celebrations described here are documented on video; see Thomas A. Kane, *The Dancing Church*, VHS [Mahwah, N.J.: Paulist Press, 1991]). Striking as these are, the women-specific liturgical adaptations of the Poor Claires do not belong to a larger movement of women-identified dissidence within the church and thus remain outside the confines of this book.

87. It struck me only late in the process of editing this book that all the pieces had been written in one or the other European colonizers' language.

Chapter 1 Come, Sophia-Spirit

1. You can visit us on the Web at http://www.hers.com/water.

2. We authored liturgies for historic women-church conferences in the United States: 1983, Chicago, Ill., "Woman Church Speaks"; 1987, Cincinnati, Ohio,

"Women-Church: Claiming Our Power"; 1993, Albuquerque, N.M., "Women-Church: Weavers of Change"; 1995, Crystal City, Va., Women's Ordination Conference, "Breaking Bread and Doing Justice"; and for liturgies at the Call to Action Conferences: 1997, Detroit, Mich., "Thanks to Valiant Women"; and 1998, Milwaukee, Wisc., "We Are the Image of God."

3. Women-church is an international, ecumenical movement of local feminist spirituality communities that engage in liturgy and social change. See Diann L. Neu and Mary E. Hunt, *Women-Church Sourcebook* (Silver Spring, Md.: WATERworks Press, 1993); Rosemary Radford Ruether, *Women-Church: Theology and Practice of Feminist Liturgical Communities* (San Francisco: Harper & Row, 1985); Diann L. Neu, "Women-Church on the Road to Change," in *Defecting in Place: Women Claiming Responsibility for their own Spiritual Lives*, ed. Miriam Therese Winter et al. (New York: Crossroad, 1994), 241–247. For more on women's spirituality groups, see *Defecting in Place*.

4. These liturgies will be published in Diann L. Neu's forthcoming three volume series, *WATER Spirit*.

5. Diann Neu and Ronnie Levin, *A Seder of the Sisters of Sarah: A Holy Thursday and Passover Feminist Liturgy* (Silver Spring, Md.: WATER, 1986); Diann Neu et al., *Miriam's Sisters Rejoice: A Holy Thursday and Passover Feminist Seder* (Silver Spring, Md.: WATER, 1988); Diann Neu et al., *Together at Freedom's Table: A Feminist Seder* (Silver Spring, Md.: WATER, 1991).

6. Elisabeth Schüssler Fiorenza introduced the term *kyriarchy* in her book *But She Said: Feminist Practices of Biblical Interpretation* (Boston: Beacon Press, 1992). *Kyriarchy* (the rule/reign of the Lord/master/father/husband) explicates that patriarchy is not just a dualistic male dominance but an interstructured social system of multiplicative structures of oppression including sexism, heterosexism, racism, class exploitation, and colonialism.

7. "Come, O Holy Spirit, Come" ("Wa wa wa Emimimo"), Nigerian traditional chant, trans. I-to Loh, in *Bring the Feast: Songs from the Re-Imagining Community* (Cleveland: Pilgrim Press, 1998), 11, copyright World Council of Churches; used with permission. Words adapted by Diann Neu and Cindy Lapp.

8. "Sing Lo! Sing, O Sophia," African-American Spiritual, words adapted by Miriam Therese Winter, *Songlines: Hymns, Songs, Rounds, and Refrains for Prayer and Praise* (New York: Crossroad, 1996), 74; used with permission.

9. This feminist version of the Pentecost story was adapted by Diann Neu for this liturgy.

10. The verses for "Veni, Sancte Spiritus" were written by Diann Neu and Cindy Lapp for this liturgy.

11. "Guide Our Feet," based on an African-American Spiritual, arr. Jane Ramseyer-Miller, in *Bring the Feast: Songs from the Re-Imagining Community* (Cleveland: Pilgrim Press, 1998), 17. Diann Neu and Cindy Lapp adapted the words of this spiritual for our Pentecost liturgy.

12. This eucharistic prayer was written by Diann Neu for the feminist liturgy, "We Are the Image of God," first celebrated at the 1998 Call to Action Conference in Milwaukee, Wisc.

13. "In Your Presence," in Colleen Fulmer, *Dancing Sophia's Circle* (Albany, Calif.: The Loretto Spirituality Network, 1994), 22–24; used with permission.

14. "Spirit Movin' Where She Will," in Colleen Fulmer (music) and Martha Ann Kirk (ritual and dance), *Her Wings Unfurled* (Albany, Calif.: The Loretto Spirituality Network, 1994), 64; used with permission.

15. "Dancing Sophia's Circle," in Colleen Fulmer, *Dancing Sophia's Circle* (Albany, Calif.: The Loretto Spirituality Network, 1994), 16–17; used with permission.

Chapter 2 Women Rise Up, Close Ranks!

1. You can visit us on the Web: www.creapozo.com.
2. The final statement is published, in English, in *Second Latin American and Caribbean Feminist Meeting, Lima, Peru*, Isis International Women's Journal 1, ed. Maria Teresa Chadwick et al. (Rome: Isis International, 1983), 15.
3. Rivkah Unland Vaage, "Círculo de Feministas Cristianas—Talitha Cumi: A Latin American Christian Feminist Theology?" (Th.M. thesis, Toronto School of Theology, Victoria University, 1996), 13 (unpublished manuscript).
4. This liturgy was celebrated on January 25, 1986, and first documented, in a different form, in Vaage, "Círculo," 86–87. Vaage also mentions that a collection of other liturgies that had been celebrated and documented on paper was lost at some point in the early 1990s. There is, thus, no documentation of the early liturgies of *Talitha Cumi*.
5. The text, both in Spanish and in English, is available in *Twentieth-Century Latin American Poetry: A Bilingual Anthology*, ed. Stephen Tapscott (Austin: University of Texas Press, 1996), 266–268.

Chapter 3 Dissident Daughters Celebrate

1. Cf. Irena Sibley, *The Bilby and the Bunyip: An Easter Tale* (Port Melbourne: Thomas C. Lothian, 1998).
2. Cf. Shirley Murray, "Where God Enlightens," in *Every Day in Your Spirit: New Hymns Written Between 1992 and 1996* (Carol Stream Ill.: Hope Publishing Company, 1996), 30.
3. For a succinct overview of feminist theological voices in Australia, see Elaine Wainwright, "Weaving a Strong Web: Feminist Theo/alogizing in an Australian Context," in *Feminist Theology in Different Contexts*. Concilium, ed. Elisabeth Schüssler Fiorenza and M. Shawn Copeland (Maryknoll, N.Y.: Orbis Books, 1996), 17–25.
4. C.B.E. and O.B.E. stand for "Commander of the Order of the British Empire" and "Officer (of the Order) of the British Empire," respectively. These are awards by the British Government for outstanding community service.
5. Jeanne Cotter, "From My Mother's Womb," in *Bring the Feast: Songs From the Re-Imagining Community* (Cleveland: Pilgrim Press, 1998), 15, copyright Mythic Rain Productions; used with permission.
6. Author anonymous. The text is often used as a chant at women's protest marches.
7. "'No' Song," in Colleen Fulmer (music) and Martha Ann Kirk (ritual and dance), *Her Wings Unfurled* (Albany Calif.: The Loretto Spirituality Network, 1990), 44; used with permission.
8. Mary Daly and Jane Caputi, *Websters' First New Intergalactic Wickedary of the English Language* (Boston: Beacon Press, 1987), 70, 192–93.
9. This is a feminist song, reworded, but sung to the tune of the spiritual "Jacob's Ladder." The original feminist version, "We Are Dancing Sarah's Circle," was written by Carole A. Etzler in 1975.
10. Shirley Murray, "Come, Celebrate the Women," in *In Every Corner Sing: The Hymns of Shirley Erena Murray* (Carol Stream, Ill.: Hope Publishing Company, 1992), 11. This is our adaptation, for this particular worship service, of Carole A. Etzler's song "We Are Dancing Sarah's Circle," sung to the tune of the spiritual "Jacob's Ladder."

Chapter 4 Celebrating Women's Power

1. Catharina Halkes edited one of the early collections of feminist liturgies, *Op water en brood* (Baarn: Ten Have, 1981).
2. Cf. Riet Bons-Storm, *The Incredible Woman: Listening to Women's Silences in Pastoral Care and Counseling* (Nashville: Abingdon Press, 1996), 18–20.
3. Cf. Lieve Troch, "A Method of Conscientization: Feminist Bible Study in the Netherlands," in *Searching the Scriptures, Volume I: A Feminist Introduction*, ed. Elisabeth Schüssler Fiorenza (New York: Crossroad, 1993), 351–366.
4. For more, see Denise J.J. Dijk, "Developments in Feminist Liturgy in the Netherlands," *Studia Liturgica* (1995): 120–128, and "The Feminist Christian Liturgical Movement in the Netherlands," *Doxology* (1998): 28–32.
5. At the beginning of the 1980s, the majority of women in *Vrouw-en-Geloof Beweging* turned their back on the broader feminist spirituality movement and on the goddess movement in the United States and Germany. The work of spokeswomen of these movements was considered to contain anti-Jewish and apolitical elements.
6. My narrative of the *Oecumenische Vrouwensynoden* owes much to other women's writings on these developments, especially Wies Stael-Merkx, "De eerste Europese Vrouwensynode: een vooruitblik," *Mara* 9:4 (June 1996): 6–7; Ans Brandsma, "Vrouwensynode tussentijds: 1987-1992," *Konvooi* 4 (1997): 3; Annelies Knoppers, "Een conferentie voor en door vrouwen. De ideeën achter de tweede oecumenische vrouwensynode," *Mara* 5:3 (May 1992): 32–41.
7. Some of the women involved also participate in other working groups, such as "Wrong Connection," a Christian lesbian group. For more on the intersections between the two groups, see Denise J.J. Dijk, "Appropriation of Cultural Symbols in Christian Liturgy: A Lesbian and Gay Case from the Netherlands," *Yearbook of the European Society of Women in Theological Research* 6 (1998): 31–45. Note that all the participants are *white*.
8. Willemien Boot, "Kies het leven: een workshop voor zwarte vrouwen," in *Verslag van de 2e Oecumenische Vrouwensynode. 22-27 augustus 1992*, ed. Nelleke Allersma. This was a report published by the Foundation *Oecumenische Vrouwensynode* 1993, 6–61.
9. Ans Kits et al., eds., *Zij-sporen. Liturgie in het spoor van vrouwen* (Gorinchem: Narratio, 1997).
10. Juul Barten, Corrie Baggerman, Denise Dijk, Fokkelien van Dijk-Hemmes, Diewerke Folkertsma, Neely Kok, Suze Kroon, Aat Leker, Christien Koetsveld, Janneke Vons, Annemiek Way, Nel van de Wijk, Tannie van Zoest, and Corrie Vollenhoven.
11. Huub Oosterhuis, "Die mij droeg," in *Liturgische Gezangen voor de Viering van de Eucharistie* (Hilversum: Gooi en Sticht, 1979), 315.
12. By Martha Kosian. Published as "The Song of the Mothers of the Plaza de Mayo," in *Eva's Lied twee. 57 geloofsliederen door vrouwen*, ed. Josephine Boevé-van Doorn et al. (Kampen: Kok, 1988), 48–49.
13. Published in Diewerke Folkertsma, *Eva, poets je appel: tot ze glanst* (Gorinchem: Narratio, 1992), 27.
14. In *Liedboek voor de kerken* ('s-Gravenhage: Boekencentrum, 1973), 116.
15. Huub Oosterhuis, "De steppe zal bloeien," in *Liturgische Gezangen II* (Hilversum: Gooi en Sticht, 1985), 102–103.
16. Refrain in Huub Oosterhuis, "Gij die geroepen hebt: 'licht'," in *Liturgische Gezangen II*, 8.
17. *Pottenbakster* has a double meaning here: She (God) who is a potter, and She who has "baked pots," i.e., created lesbian women [the Dutch word *"pot"* also means "dyke"].

18. Gonny Luypers, "Lied om mee te gaan," in *Eva's Lied. 42 liederen door vrouwen*, ed. Wil van Hilten et al. (Kampen: Kok, 1984), 33.

19. Huub Oosterhuis, "Dat wij vol stromen," in *Liturgische Gezangen voor de Viering van de Eucharistie* (Hilversum: Gooi en Sticht, 1979), 279.

Chapter 5 We Are the Daughters of God

1. 여성교회 (*YeoSong KyoHoe*) can be translated as "Women Church," although its more literal translation is closer to "feminine church." For more, see Sook Ja Chung, "Partnership and the Women's Church," *In God's Image* 18 (1999): 36–39.

2. See, for example, Ahn Sang Nim, "Feminist Theology in the Korean Church," and Chung Hyun Kyung, "'Han-pu-ri:' Doing Theology from Korean Women's Perspective," in *We Dare to Dream: Doing Theology as Asian Women*, ed. Virginia Fabella and Sun Ai Lee Park (Maryknoll, N.Y.: Orbis Books, 1989), 127–134, 135–146; Oo Chung Lee, *In Search of Our Foremothers' Spirituality* (Seoul: Asian Women's Resource Center for Culture and Theology, 1994); Sook Ja Chung, "A Woman Leader of Minjung—Miriam," in *Affirming Difference, Celebrating Wholeness: A Partnership of Equals* (Hong Kong: Christian Conference of Asia: Women's Concerns Desk, 1995), 105–118.

3. *Women Church: Stories of the First Ten Years*, Women Church Resource No. 15 (Seoul: Women Church, 1999).

4. We also network broadly with other groups. 여성교회 is a full member of the Women's Committee of the Korean National Council of Churches and the Korean Council for the Women Drafted for Military Sexual Slavery by Japan. We are also affiliated with the Korean Association of Women Theologians and the Asian Christian Institute for Women and Culture.

5. *Our Hymns,* Women Church Resources No. 8 (Seoul: Women Church, 1995).

6. Since 1994, 여성교회 has published its own series, "Women Church Resources."

7. All these drama manuscripts are published (in Korean) by Women Church, in *Korean Woman Jesus*, Drama Resource Book No. 1 (Seoul: Women Church, 1994), 113–141.

8. This liturgy is available in English: "Korean Woman Jesus: Drama Worship," *Journal of Women and Religion* 13 (1995): 45–50.

9. This liturgy was published, in Korean, in our "Women Church Series" as Vol. 12. The texts were generated within 여성교회.

10. *Our Hymns*, No. 129, "Look at the Birds Flying the Sky" (words from Matthew 6:25–34). All the texts from *Our Hymns*, a publication of 여성교회, are used with permission. The translation is mine.

11. *Our Hymns*, No. 152, "New Meeting."

12. Song of Desperation: "Years and Months Flow" (words by Chang Soo Chul).

13. Words by Chang Soo Chul. 덩실덩실, *Dunhshil*, is a term for a Korean way of dancing.

14. Words by Lee Kun Yong. 아하라디아 산사디아, *Aharadia SanSadia*, is an expression of joy and excitement. 캥맥캥, *Kengmekkeng*, signifies the sound of a small gong.

15. Words by Sook Ja Chung; used with permission.

Chapter 6 Ritual That Transforms

1. For more, see I. P. (Trish) Wilson, "Reading the 'Montreal Massacre': Idiosyncratic Insanity or the Misreading of Cultural Cues," in *Ethnographic Feminisms: Essays in*

Anthropology, Women's Experience Series 7, ed. Sally Cole and Lynne Phillips (Ottawa: Carleton University Press, 1995), 259–277.

2. Charlotte Caron, *To Make and Make Again: Feminist Ritual Theology* (New York: Crossroad, 1993), 143.

3. Rosemary Radford Ruether, *Women-Church: Theology and Practice of Feminist Liturgical Communities* (San Francisco: Harper & Row, 1985), 3.

4. This was the title of an article by Patricia McLean and Theresa Topics, printed in *The London Free Press* (December 5, 1998): 16.

5. Audre Lorde, "Poetry Is Not A Luxury," in *Sister Outsider: Essays and Speeches* (Trumansburg, N.Y.: Crossing Press, 1984), 36.

6. Cf. Mary Daly's definition of this hyphenated word "Re-calling the Original intuition of integrity; healing the dismembered Self," in Mary Daly and Jane Caputi, *Websters' First New Intergalactic Wickedary of the English Language* (Boston: Beacon Press, 1987), 92.

7. Adrienne Rich, "Natural Resources," in *The Fact of a Doorframe: Poems Selected and New, 1950–1984* (New York: W. W. Norton, 1984), 261.

8. "Ancient Pines," by Loreena McKennitt, from her album *Parallel Dreams* (Stratford, Ontario: Quinlan Road, 1989).

9. "This Tough Spun Web," by Carolyn McDade, from her album *This Tough Spun Web: Songs of Global Struggle and Solidarity* (Orleans, Mass.: Surstey Publishing, 1984); used with permission.

10. Caron, *To Make and Make Again*, 227.

Chapter 7 Springtime: September in Chile

1. The text was translated from the Spanish by William Jarrod Brown.

2. Teresa Valdés and Marisa Weinstein, *Mujeres que sueñan. Las organizaciones de pobladoras en Chile 1973–1989* (Santiago: FLACSO, 1993) give a detailed account of the work done by women's organizations during that time.

3. Cf. Sandra Palestro, *Mujeres en movimiento, 1973–1989*, Serie de Estudios Sociales 14 (Santiago: FLACSO, 1991).

4. In the 1980s, various ecumenical organizations and training centers created women's programs, such as the *Programa Teología desde la Mujer del CEDM* and the *Programa Teología desde la Perspectiva de las mujeres* of the Evangelical Theological Faculty of Chile. In other organizations, religious issues surfaced within various women's programs, some of which included work on development (SEPADE, CEMURI).

5. Ute Seibert, *Mujeres configurando espacios: Programa Teología desde la Mujer del Centro Ecuménico Diego de Medellín 1983–1993* (Santiago, 1994), unpublished manuscript.

6. The Spanish term *con-spirando* contains a double meaning that in English cannot be rendered with one word: *con-spirando* can mean both "to breathe together" and "to conspire."

7. "'Con-spirando juntas': hacia una red latinoamericana de ecofeminismo, espiritualidad y teología," *Con-spirando* 1 (1992): 2–5. This text is a product of collective reflection; the redaction is Elena Aguila's; used with permission.

8. For more, see Josefina Hurtado and Ute Seibert, "Introducción: acerca de ritos y poderes," in *Cuaderno de ritos* (Santiago: Colectivo Con-spirando, 1995), VI–VIII. The book provides a collection of rituals created and celebrated by *Con-spirando*.

Chapter 8 Women Gather for Worship

1. When our twenty-eight-year-old son died, I and my family were able to create a funeral service that was helpful to us and to his friends and was true to him. None

of us attended church any longer for a variety of reasons, but we were allowed to hold our ritual in the Roman Catholic Church that we had attended for over twenty years and where we still had strong connections with the community. We sat in front of the altar, around the coffin, and led the service; the priest sat in the congregation.

2. Diann Neu, "Blessed Be the New Year," in *Celebrating Women*, new ed., ed. Hannah Ward et al. (Harrisburg, Pa.: Morehouse Publishing, 1995), 127–128; used with permission (the text was first sent to WATER donors in 1992/1993 as a new year blessing).

3. This prayer was written by Lala Winkley based on Matt. 11: 2–5, Luke 4:17–19, and Micah 6:8; used with permission.

4. "Millennium Resolution," copyright NewStart 2000; used with permission.

Chapter 9 God, Our Sister and Friend

1. Iben Gjerding and Katherine Kinnamon, eds., *No Longer Strangers: A Resource for Women and Worship* (Geneva: World Council of Churches Publications, 1983).

2. Constance F. Parvey, ed., *The Community of Women and Men in the Church: The Sheffield Report* (Geneva: World Council of Churches Publications, 1983).

3. Published in Gjerding and Kinnamon, *No Longer Strangers*, 54.

4. This is a song based on a text James Oppenheim wrote in 1912. The author suggested that girls supporting a strike in Lawrence, Massachusetts, carried a banner inscribed with "Bread and Roses." Oppenheim's text has been set to music and is a favorite song of the women's movement. The song is published in a variety of songbooks, both religious and secular. "Bread and Roses" was used at the European Women's Synod in 1996 and appears in its hymnbook.

5. "Sister, Carry On," by Carolyn McDade, in Carolyn McDade and Friends, *Sister, Carry On*, cassette and book (Orleans, Mass.: Surtsey Publishing, 1992); used with permission.

6. Rachel Conrad Wahlberg, "Woman's Creed," in *Jesus and the Freed Woman* (New York: Paulist Press, 1978), 155–157.

7. "Stay with Us through the Night," by Walter Farquharson, in *Voices United: The Hymn and Worship Book of The United Church of Canada* (Etobicoke, Ont.: The United Church Publishing House, 1996), 182; used with permission.

Chapter 10 Air Moves Us

1. The text was translated from the German by Carrie Maus.

2. The name translates into *Women's Study and Education Center of the Protestant Church of Germany*, with "Protestant" meaning not any and every community of Protestant Christians in Germany but the Lutheran, Reformed, and United (Lutheran-Reformed) Churches of Germany. You can visit the center on the Web at www.ekd.de/fsbz.

3. The text of this opening liturgy is published in Herta Leistner, ed., *Laß spüren Deine Kraft. Feministische Liturgie. Grundlagen, Argumente, Anregungen* (Gütersloh: Gütersloher Verlagshaus, 1997), 120–125.

4. For more, see Elisabeth Moltmann-Wendel's *Autobiography* (London: SCM Press, 1997).

5. For more, see, for example, the article by Hedwig Meyer-Wilmes, "Persecuting Witches in the Name of Reason," in *The Fascination of Evil*. Concilium, ed. David Tracy and Hermann Häring (Maryknoll, N.Y.: Orbis Books, 1998), 11–17. Hedwig Meyer-Wilmes has collaborated with our center on several occasions and currently serves as president of the European Society of Women in Theological Research.

6. Cf. Fanny Martin et al., eds., *Cymbals and Silences: Echoes from the First European Women's Synod* (London: Sophia Press, 1997).
7. Leistner, ed., *Laß spüren Deine Kraft*; Ute Knie and Herta Leistner, eds., *Laß hören deine Stimme. Werkstattbuch Feministische Liturgie* (Gütersloh: Gütersloher Verlagshaus, 1999).
8. See, for example, the collection *Ecumenical Decade 1988–1998: Churches in Solidarity with Women. Prayers and Poems, Songs and Stories* (Geneva: World Council of Churches Publications, 1988).
9. The texts are taken from Hildegard's treatise on natural philosophy and medicine. We used the German text, *Heilkunde* (Salzburg: Otto Müller Verlag, 1957), 100–101. An English translation of Hildegard's treatise is provided in *Holistic Healing* (Collegeville, Minn.: Liturgical Press, 1994), 39–40.
10. "Air Moves Us," by Cathleen Shell, Cybele, Moonsea, and Prune, recorded on *Chants: Ritual Music* from Reclaiming Community & Friends (Sebastopol, Calif.: Serpentine Music Productions, 1987); used with permission. To obtain a copy of the recorded chant, see Reclaiming's Web site: www.reclaiming.org.
11. Betty Wendelborn's song can be found in her collection, *Sing Green: Songs of the Mystics*, 2nd ed. (Auckland, N.Z.: Pyramid Press, 1999), 1. For more information, see Betty Wendelborn's Web site: www.muzique.infi.net.nz.

Chapter 11 Lady Wisdom as Hostess for the Lord's Supper

1. See footnote 11.
2. Cf. my article "Sophia: Symbol of Christian and Feminist Wisdom?" *Feminist Theology* 16 (1997): 32–54.
3. Cf. *Svenska Dagbladet*, April 10, 12, and 13 (1995).
4. A more detailed analysis of this movement in Sweden is found in my dissertation on feminism and liturgy in the Church of Sweden: *Feminism och liturgi—en ecklesiologisk studie* (Stockholm: Verbum, 2001). The dissertation examines about thirty examples of liturgies celebrated in Sweden during the Ecumenical Decade of Churches in Solidarity with Women.
5. The same free relationship to the biblical text is present in much of the worship material from the Ecumenical Decade of Churches in Solidarity with Women. I interpret this as a critique of the high status of the noninterpreted biblical texts in the dominant liturgical tradition.
6. Cf. Gordon W. Lathrop, *Holy People: A Liturgical Ecclesiology* (Minneapolis: Fortress Press, 1999), esp. 202–205.
7. The Chapter of the Diocese of Stockholm, May 21, 1996, Dnr 95/C97/22, p. 3, my translation.
8. See Brian Wren, *What Language Shall I Borrow? God-Talk in Worship: A Male Response to Feminist Theology* (New York: Crossroad, 1989) for more on this kingafap-language, as Wren calls it in short.
9. When there is no explicit reference to a text, the latter was created within the women's group responsible for the *Sofia-mässor* and is used with permission. Martha Middlemiss translated the liturgical texts used in this *Sofia-mässa* into English.
10. The song is an adaptation of a text from the Song of Songs. The author is anonymous, but the song has circulated quite widely in Nordic hymnbooks and worship manuals.
11. This prayer is a poem by Hans Granlid, from his *Gyllene Stunder* [Golden Moments] (Stockholm: R&S, 1974); used with permission.

12. Text by Helene Egnell. Printed only in the bulletin for the *Sofia-mässa* and used with permission.
13. Text by Christina Lövestam. Printed only in the bulletin for the *Sofia-mässa* and used with permission.
14. The text is taken from Hymn 835 by Christina Lövestam, in *Psalmer i 90-talet* [Hymns in the Nineties] (Stockholm: Verbum, 1994); used with permission.
15. See Janet Morley, *All Desires Known* (Harrisburg, Pa.: Morehouse Publishing Co., 1994), 87.
16. Hymn 803, text by Per Harling, in *Psalmer i 90-talet* [Hymns in the Nineties] (Stockholm: Verbum, 1994); used with permission.

Chapter 12 African Woman: Arise and Eat, for Your Journey Is Long

1. The two 1999 seminars are described in detail in Pauline Muchina and Jana Meyer, "African Women: The Spirit of God is Upon You!," *Ministerial Formation* 88 (2000): 35–46.
2. Cf. Daphne Madiba, "African Women and Culture; African Women and Religion," unpublished paper presented at the Kalahari Desert School of Theology, 1999.
3. Wendy Esau, in unpublished *Seminar Notes of the African Women's Theologies Seminar*, Kalahari Desert School of Theology, Kuruman, 1999; used with permission. The notes are also available on the Web site of the Kalahari Desert School of Theology: http://home.spg.co.za/kmmt/awtseminar.html.
4. Malebogo Mothibi, in unpublished *Seminar Notes* (note 3).
5. Cf. Nathan Isaacs, "Reflection on Scripture: Gospel of Matthew Chapter 1:1–17," in unpublished *Seminar Notes* (note 3).
6. Cf. Olga Maria Raimundo Choto, "Cultura Africana Como Fonte da Teologia de Mulheres Africanas" and "Mulher Africana e Religião," unpublished papers presented at the *Seminário Ecuménico de Teologia de Mulheres Africanas*, Maputo, Mozambique, 1999. Excerpts translated by Jana Meyer and included in Muchina and Meyer, "African Women" (note 1).
7. Eva das Dores Benedito Gomes, "Mulheres Africanas e a Igreja," unpublished paper presented at the *Seminário Ecuménico de Teologia de Mulheres Africanas*, Maputo, Mozambique, 1999. Excerpt translated by Jana Meyer and included in Muchina and Meyer, "African Women" (note 1).
8. Cf. Telma Armindo, in unpublished *Seminar Notes of the Seminário Ecuménico de Teologia de Mulheres Africanas*, Maputo, Mozambique, 1999.
9. In Pauline Muchina and Jana Meyer, unpublished "Final Report of the Ecumenical Seminars in African Women's Theologies," 1999. See Attachment A "Evaluation Results" and Attachment C "Message of the Seminar Participants, Mozambique."
10. Information on the 2000 seminar in Mozambique comes from the unpublished *Seminar Notes of the Seminário do Círculo Ecuménico de Teólogas Africanas, Maputo, 2000* and from a telephone interview with the Rev. Olga Maria Raimundo Choto, coorganizer of the seminar, on December 27, 2000. Translated by Jana Meyer.

Chapter 13 *Pista-Lakbayan:* Celebrating the Journey to Shalom in the Year of Jubilee

1. Literally, a "Festival-Journey." *Pista-Lakbayan* is always a communal act of sharing a common vision and journey. It is a creative and celebrative occasion.
2. AWIT's present national coordinator is Sharon Rose Joy Ruiz Duremdes, the first layperson and first woman to be General Secretary of the National Council of Churches in the Philippines. The other previous national coordinators were

Rebecca Asedillo, a United Methodist deaconess, and this writer. Benedictine sister Mary John Mananzan, the Executive Director of the Institute of Women's Studies in Manila, was one of the founding members of AWIT. Some of the best-known Christian feminist voices in Asia today are those of Filipinas, many of whom are members of AWIT and EATWOT, such as Sr. Virginia Fabella, Sr. Mary John Mananzan, Sr. Rosario Battung, Sharon Joy Ruiz Duremdes, the Rev. Lydia Niguidula, Elizabeth Dominguez, Arche Ligo, Agnes Miclat Cacayan, Lilith Usog, Sr. Nila Bermisa, the Rev. Elizabeth Tapia, Jane Montenegro, Emma Cantor-Orate, and Sophie Bodegon.

3. I am grateful for their permission to include our liturgy in this article.
4. From the story collection of Sr. Rosario Battung, RGS; used with permission.
5. Elizabeth S. Tapia, "An Open Letter to my Niece. A Filipino Woman's Vision of the Church of the Future," published in *Women Magazine* of the Lutheran World Federation, vol. 52 (March 2000).
6. Organized by the Women's Desk of the National Council of Churches' Program Unit on Ecumenical Education and Nurture, this *Pista-Lakbayan* was spearheaded by the Executive Director, Carmencita Karagdag. The March 2000 *Pista-Lakbayan* was a sequel to the November 1999 *Pista-Lakbayan* in Pagsanjan Laguna. The 1,500 women who participated came from rural and urban areas and from various church and sectoral groups. The Pagsanjan Covenant was later presented to and adopted by the National Convention of the Council of Churches in the Philippines and the various women's organizations celebrating International Women's Day 2000.
7. "If We Hold On Together" is a song from the 1988 Universal Studios' motion picture "Land Before Time." Diana Ross is the performing artist.
8. Jane Parker Huber, "Called as Partners in Christ's Service," in *A Singing Faith* (Philadelphia: Westminster Press, 1987), 68; used with permission.

Chapter 14 Like Water in a Desert

1. Carolyn McDade, "This Ancient Love," from her album *As We So Love* (Orleans, Mass.: Surtsey Publishing, 1996); used with permission.
2. The author of this prayer is Margaret Donaldson, Professor Emeritus of Church History in the Divinity Department of Rhodes University, Grahamstown, South Africa. She currently conducts a monthly Celtic meditative worship service and gives lectures and workshops on Celtic Christianity. Her prayer is used with permission.
3. Cf. Jim Cotter, *Love Re-membered: Resources for a House Eucharist* (Sheffield and Evesham: Cairns Publications in association with Arthur James LTD, 1996), 39-47.
4. Alla Renée Bozarth, "Bakerwoman God," in *Womanpriest: A Personal Odyssey* (New York: Paulist Press, 1978), 217–218.
5. Cf. Judith Plaskow Goldenberg, "Epilogue: The Coming of Lilith," in *Religion and Sexism: Images of Woman in the Jewish and Christian Traditions*, ed. Rosemary Radford Ruether (New York: Simon and Schuster, 1974), 341–343.
6. Janet Morley, *All Desires Known* (Harrisburg, Pa.: Morehouse Publishing Co., 1992), 15.
7. Cf. Morley, *All Desires Known*, 87–88; Hannah Ward et al., eds., *Celebrating Women*, new ed. (Harrisburg, Pa: Morehouse Publishing Co., 1995).
8. Rachel Conrad Wahlberg, "Woman's Creed," in *Jesus and the Freed Woman* (New York: Paulist Press, 1978), 155–157.
9. Jim Cotter, *Prayer at Night: A Book for the Darkness*, 4th ed. (Sheffield: Cairns Publications, 1991), 42.

10. Ann M. Heidkamp, "A Litany of Women's Power," in *Women's Prayer Services*, 3rd ed., ed. Iben Gjerding and Katherine Kinnamon (Mystic, Conn.: Twenty-Third Publications, 1991), 25; copyright World Council of Churches, Church Women United; used with permission.

11. Gillian Walters and Jacqui Mohlakoana, students at the University of Cape Town, authored this prayer; used with permission.

12. The Cape Town chapter recently published its first book: Denise Ackermann et al., eds., *Claiming Our Footprints: South African Women Reflect on Context, Identity, and Spirituality* (Stellenbosch: EFSA Institute for Theological and Interdisciplinary Research, 2000).

Postscript

1. I first developed the argument that follows in my article "Prayers and Practices of Women: *Lex Orandi* Reconfigured," *Yearbook of the European Society of Women in Theological Research* 9 (2001): 63–77.

2. Rebecca S. Chopp, *Saving Work: Feminist Practices of Theological Education* (Louisville, Ky.: Westminster John Knox Press, 1995), 80.

3. Rebecca Lyman, "*Lex orandi*: Heresy, Orthodoxy, and Popular Religion," in *The Making and Remaking of Christian Doctrine*, ed. Sarah Coakley and David A. Pailin (Oxford: Clarendon Press, 1993), 131–141, here 138–139.

4. To name just one example, Richard J. Schuler, "*Lex orandi, lex credendi*: The Outrage of Inclusive Language," *Sacred Music* 121, no. 2 (1994): 6–10.

5. I borrow the expression from Ronald L. Grimes's wonderfully witty and satirical piece "Liturgical Supinity, Liturgical Erectitude: On The Embodiment of Ritual Authority," *Studia Liturgica* 23 (1993): 51–69.

6. Cf. Aidan Kavanagh, *On Liturgical Theology* (New York: Pueblo, 1984), 146–147.

7. Cf. Paul V. Marshall, "Reconsidering 'Liturgical Theology': Is there a *Lex Orandi* for all Christians?," *Studia Liturgica* 25 (1995): 129–151, here 147. Colleen McDannell notes similarly how categories of gender are used to distinguish liturgical art, which is coded as "virile," from liturgical kitsch, which is depicted as "effeminate;" see her *Material Christianity: Religion and Popular Culture in America* (New Haven: Yale University Press, 1995), 163–197.

8. For more, see Rebecca Chopp, "Eve's Knowing: Feminist Theology's Resistance to Malestream Epistemological Frameworks," in *Feminist Theology in Different Contexts*, Concilium, ed. Elisabeth Schüssler Fiorenza and M. Shawn Copeland (London/Maryknoll, N.Y.: SCM Press/Orbis Books, 1996), 116–123.

9. See Ninna Edgardh Beckman, "Mrs. Murphy's Arising from the Pew: Ecclesiological Implications," *The Ecumenical Review* 53 (2001): 5–13.

10. An exception to this is the handful of feminist theologians in liturgical studies; see esp. Marjorie Procter-Smith, *In Her Own Rite: Constructing Feminist Liturgical Tradition* (Nashville: Abingdon Press, 1990; reprint: Akron, Ohio: OSL Publications, 2000), and *Praying with Our Eyes Open: Engendering Feminist Liturgical Prayer* (Nashville: Abingdon Press, 1995).

11. Susan A. Ross, *Extravagant Affections: A Feminist Sacramental Theology* (New York: Continuum, 1998), 30–31, see also 203–204.

12. Elizabeth A. Johnson, *Friends of God and Prophets: A Feminist Theological Reading of the Communion of Saints* (New York: Continuum, 1998), 26.

13. I find myself in full agreement with Kathryn Tanner on the relationship between academic theology and everyday Christian practices: "Academic theology is . . . about Christian social practices in the sense that it asks critical and evaluative

questions of them." Tanner goes on to argue that academic theology differs from the theological reflection of everyday life and forms a social practice in its own right, with is own distinct process of production. See Kathryn Tanner, *Theories of Culture: A New Agenda for Theology*, Guides to Theological Inquiry Series (Minneapolis: Fortress Press, 1997), 80.

14. For a beginning, see Teresa Berger, *Women's Ways of Worship: Gender Analysis and Liturgical History* (Collegeville, Minn.: Liturgical Press, 1999), and Teresa Berger, "Women's Rites: Liturgical History in Fragments," in *The Oxford History of Worship*, ed. Karen Westerfield Tucker and Geoffrey Wainwright (New York: Oxford University Press, 2003), forthcoming.

15. Geoffrey Wainwright, *Doxology: The Praise of God in Doctrine, Worship and Life* (New York: Oxford University Press, 1980).

16. For an overview over recent developments, see Teresa Berger, *Theology in Hymns? A Study of the Relationship of Doxology and Theology according to "A Collection of Hymns for the use of the People Called Methodist" (1780)* (Nashville: Abingdon Press, 1995), 31–57.

17. The story is told in Ross, *Extravagant Affections*, 21–22.

18. Elaine J. Lawless, *God's Peculiar People: Women's Voices and Folk Tradition in a Pentecostal Church* (Lexington, Ky.: University Press of Kentucky, 1988); *Handmaidens of the Lord: Pentecostal Women Preachers and Traditional Religion* (Philadelphia: University of Pennsylvania Press, 1988).

19. See Mary McClintock Fulkerson, "Joyful Speaking for God: Pentecostal Women's Performances," in *Changing the Subject: Women's Discourses and Feminist Theology* (Minneapolis: Fortress Press, 1994), 239–298.

20. See Gisela Muschiol, *Famula Dei. Zur Liturgie in merowingischen Frauenklöstern*, Beiträge zur Geschichte des alten Mönchtums und des Benediktinerordens 41 (Münster: Aschendorff, 1994).

21. See Robert A. Orsi, *Thank You, St. Jude: Women's Devotion to the Patron Saint of Hopeless Causes* (New Haven: Yale University Press, 1996).

22. See Yvonne Chireau, "The Uses of the Supernatural: Toward a History of Black Women's Magical Practices," and Sharla Fett, "'It's a Spirit in Me': Spiritual Power and the Healing Work of African American Women in Slavery," both in *A Mighty Baptism: Race, Gender, and the Creation of American Protestantism*, ed. Susan Juster and Lisa MacFarlane (Ithaca, N.Y.: Cornell University Press, 1996), 171–188, 189–209.

23. See R. Marie Griffith, *God's Daughters: Evangelical Women and the Power of Submission* (Berkeley, Calif.: University of California Press, 1997).

24. Lesley A. Northup, *Ritualizing Women: Patterns of Spirituality* (Cleveland: Pilgrim Press, 1997), 1.

25. See Carol Ann Muller, *Rituals of Fertility and the Sacrifice of Desire: Nazarite Women's Performance in South Africa*, Chicago Studies in Ethnomusicology (Chicago: University of Chicago Press, 1999).

26. Kay Turner, *Beautiful Necessity: The Art and Meaning of Women's Altars* (New York: Thames & Hudson, 1999), 19.

27. See Kathryn Tanner, "Theology and Popular Culture," in *Changing Conversations: Religious Reflection & Cultural Analysis*, ed. Dwight N. Hopkins and Sheila Greeve Davaney (New York: Routledge & Kegan Paul, 1996), 101–20.

28. I am indebted for this concise formulation to Linda McDowell, *Gender, Identity and Place: Understanding Feminist Geographies* (Minneapolis: University of Minnesota Press, 1999), 227.

29. Cf. Patrick D. Miller, "Things Too Wonderful: Prayers of Women in the Old Testament," in *Biblische Theologie und gesellschaftlicher Wandel*, ed. Georg Braulik et al. (Freiburg: Herder, 1993), 237–251, here 237.

30. Toni Craven, "'From Where Will My Help Come?': Women and Prayer in the Apocryphal/Deuterocanonical Books," in *Worship and the Hebrew Bible*, Journal for the Study of the Old Testament. Supplement Series 284, ed. M. Patrick Graham et al. (Sheffield: Sheffield Academic Press, 1999), 95–109, here 99.

31. I adopt the term "ritual knowledge" from Theodore W. Jennings influential article, "On Ritual Knowledge," which originally appeared in 1982 in the *Journal of Religion*. The article is reprinted in *Readings in Ritual Studies*, ed. Ronald L. Grimes (Upper Saddle River, N.J.: Prentice-Hall, 1996), 324–334.

32. For more on these new ways of naming the Holy One, see, for example, the three volumes of Mary Kathleen Speegle Schmitt, *Seasons of the Feminine Divine: Christian Feminist Prayers for the Liturgical Year, Cycles A–C* (New York: Crossroad, 1993–1995).

33. Kathryn Tanner, "Social Theory Concerning the 'New Social Movements' and the Practice of Feminist Theology," in *Horizons in Feminist Theology: Identity, Tradition, and Norms*, ed. Rebecca S. Chopp and Sheila Greeve Davaney (Minneapolis: Fortress Press, 1997), 179–197, here 192.

34. For a more detailed account, see Kathryn Tanner, *Theories of Culture*, 128–138.

35. André Myre, "The New Testament in the *Women's Bible Commentary*," in *Women Also Journeyed with Him: Feminist Perspectives on the Bible* (Collegeville, Minn.: Liturgical Press, 2000), 83–98, here 97.

List of Contributors

Ninna Edgardh Beckman was born in Sweden in 1955. She is a Lutheran theologian with a doctorate from the Theological Faculty of Uppsala University, Sweden. The subject of her thesis (published in Swedish in 2001) is feminism and liturgy from an ecclesiological perspective. She is also the author of books on Sophia/Wisdom in the Christian tradition and on the realization of the Ecumenical Decade of Churches in Solidarity with Women 1988–1998. She is a contributor both to *Feminist Theology* and to *The Ecumenical Review*. Her e-mail address is *Ninna.Edgardh@teol.uu.se*. Her postal address is Diakonivetenskapliga institutet, Samaritergränd 2, 753 19 Uppsala, Sweden.

Teresa Berger, the editor of *Dissident Daughters*, was born in Germany in 1956. She studied theology in England, Germany, and Switzerland, and holds doctorates in both Catholic Liturgical Studies and in Protestant Systematic Theology. She is a Roman Catholic theologian and has taught theology at the Divinity School of Duke University in Durham, North Carolina (U.S.A.), since 1985. Her e-mail address is *tberger@div.duke.edu*. Her postal address is Divinity School, Duke University, Durham, NC 27708, U.S.A.

Sook Ja Chung was born in Japan in 1936 as a second-generation Korean. She studied in Japan, Korea, and the United States. She holds a Doctor of Ministry degree in Feminist Theology, with a concentration in biblical studies. She is an ordained pastor in the Presbyterian Church in the Republic of Korea (PROK) and has served as a general secretary of the Korean Association of Women Theologians (KAWT) and as the pastor of 여성교회. She also works for the Women's Center for Migrant Workers. Since 1975, she has facilitated, for ecumenical groups all over Asia, workshops on reading the Bible from the perspective of the oppressed. Her e-mail address is *sjck@unitel.co.kr*. Her postal address is 102-1402, LG Apt., Kumgok-dong, Namyangjoo-shi, Kyunggi-do 472-010, South Korea.

Denise J. J. Dijk was born in the Netherlands in 1944. She studied theology in the Netherlands and in Lexington, Kentucky (U.S.A.) and holds a doctorate in Liturgical Studies. She served as a pastor in a nursing home and taught feminist theology at the Theological Faculty of the Free University in Amsterdam for several years. Since 1986, she has taught women's studies in religion and liturgy at Kampen Theological University in the Netherlands. In 1998, she was ordained as a minister in the Dutch Reformed Church. Her e-mail address is *DijkMeerburg@compuserve.com*. Her postal address is Van Goudoeverstraat 9, 3814 BD Amersfoort, The Netherlands.

Wilma Jakobsen was born in South Africa in 1959. Having taught in a local high school, she journeyed the route of theological studies in the United States and South Africa. She was one of the first women priests in the Anglican Church in Southern Africa. She has worked in diverse church situations and completed further studies at Union Theological Seminary in New York. She currently works as the Anglican chaplain at the University of Cape Town. Her e-mail address is *wilma@xsinet.co.za*. Her postal address is 6 St Paul's Crescent, Rondebosch, 7700 South Africa.

Herta Leistner was born in Germany in 1942. She is an ordained deacon in the Lutheran Church and worked for many years in Christian education for young girls. For nineteen years, she led a Lutheran Educational Center in Bad Boll, Germany, which under her leadership became a center of feminist activism within the church. She completed her doctorate in theology in 1993 with a thesis on identity formation of lesbian women in the church. Since 1993, she has led the Women's Study and Training Center of the Lutheran Church in Germany. Her e-mail address is *fsbz.leistner@ecos.net*. Her postal address is Frauenstudien- und -bildungszentrum der EKD, Herzbachweg 2, 63571 Gelnhausen, Germany.

Coralie Ling, an Australian with an Angloceltic heritage, was born in Melbourne in 1939. She first studied education and then later theology and obtained an International Feminist Doctorate of Ministry in 1999 through the program set up by Letty Russell and Shannon Clarkson in association with San Francisco Theological Seminary. She was ordained as a minister in the Methodist Church in 1969 and is now a minister in the Uniting Church in Australia. She has been pastor of Fitzroy Uniting Church in Melbourne since 1991. Her e-mail address is *fitzuca@netspace.net.au*. Her postal address is PO Box 94, Fitzroy 3065, Victoria, Australia.

Patricia McLean, osu, was born in 1935 and has been a member of the Ursulines of the Chatham Union in Canada since 1958. She is committed to the education of women. She holds Masters Degrees in Education (University of Toronto) and in Religion and Culture (Laurier). For the last twenty years her energies have been focused on the spiritual advancement of women. This she has accomplished through academic teaching in the Religious Studies Department at Brescia College (an affiliate of the University of Western Ontario in London), through the Women's Centre at Brescia, as a founding mother of the Finders Keepers Feminist Spirituality Conferences, and through her involvement in the active women's community in the London region. Her e-mail address is *pmclean@julian.uwo.ca*. Her postal address is 8 Thornton Avenue, London, ON N5Y 2Y2, Canada.

Jana Meyer was born in the United States in 1966. She holds a Masters of Divinity from Union Theological Seminary and a Masters of Social Work from Hunter College in New York City. She has also studied theology at the Universidad Biblica Latinoamericana in Costa Rica. She has served as a social worker in Mozambique with the United Methodist Church of Mozambique and the Mennonite Central Committee, in addition to urban social work in the United States. Currently she works in Louisville, Kentucky, with immigrant and refugee survivors of domestic violence. Her e-mail address is *meyerjana@hotmail.com*. Her postal address is P.O. Box 14451, Louisville, KY 40214, U.S.A.

Pauline Muchina was born in Kenya in 1966. She is an Anglican theologian with a Ph.D. from Union Theological Seminary in New York. Her dissertation focused on how faith can be an agent of political and social transformation, especially in the eradication of poverty in Africa. Pauline currently holds a consultancy position with the World Council of Churches and examines the impact of racism in the current trends of globalization. She is a member of the African Women's Network and the Circle of Concerned African Women Theologians and has participated in several international women's conferences, such as the 1995 Beijing World Conference on Women, the 1998 World Council of Churches Decade Festival in Harare, the United Nations 1998 Conference on Women and Economic Empowerment, and the United Nations 2000 preparatory meeting for the World Conference against Racism. Her e-mail address is *pmuchina@hotmail.com*. Her postal address is 3725 Blackstone Avenue Apt. 3F, Riverdale, NY 10463, U.S.A.

Diann L. Neu was born in the United States in 1948. She is a Catholic feminist who cofounded and codirects WATER, the Women's Alliance for Theology, Ethics and Ritual, in Silver Spring, Md. She holds a Masters of Sacred Theology and a Masters of Divinity from the Jesuit School of Theology at

Berkeley, Calif. She is a licensed psychotherapist who holds a Masters in Clinical Social Work from The Catholic University of America in Washington, D.C. She coordinates the Women-Church Convergence, is a member and past board member of the Women's Ordination Conference, and liturgizes with SAS, the Washington, D.C., area women-church community. She is currently writing an anthology of her liturgies and studying for her Doctor of Ministry with an International Feminist Emphasis at San Francisco Theological Seminary at San Anselmo, Calif. Her e-mail address is *dneu@hers.com*. Her postal address is WATER, 8035 13th Street, Silver Spring, MD 20910-4803, U.S.A.

Rosanna Panizo was born in Callao, Peru, in 1955. Originally trained as an engineer, she studied theology in Peru, Costa Rica, and the United States. She was the first woman ordained in the Methodist Church of Peru and served as rector of the Methodist seminary in Lima for several years. Since 1998, she has pastored churches in North Carolina and worked especially with Hispanic outreach ministries. Her e-mail address is *rospaniz@duke.edu*. Her postal address is 307 Hammond Street, Durham, NC 27704, U.S.A.

Veronica Seddon was born in England in 1937 and brought up within the Roman Catholic Church. She received a B.Sc. (Honors) and worked as a scientist for five years. Since 1975, she has been a painter. She has been married for almost forty years and has four children, the eldest of whom died at age twenty-eight of leukemia. In 1982, she started a local women's group after hearing Rosemary Radford Ruether speak in London and has been an active feminist ever since. Her e-mail address is *seddon@peter-veronica.co.uk*. Her postal address is 42 Priory Road, Hampton, Middlesex TW12 2PJ, United Kingdom.

Ute Seibert was born in Germany in 1955. She studied theology in Germany and is an ordained Lutheran pastor and a body therapist. From 1982–1988, she taught biblical theology in Nicaragua. Currently she lives and works in Santiago de Chile. She is a founding member of *Con-spirando*, an ecumenical, multidisciplinary women's collective working in ecofeminist theology and spirituality. Her e-mail address is *conspira@bellsouth.cl*. Her postal address is *Con-spirando*, Casilla 371-11, Correo Ñuñoa, Santiago, Chile.

Elizabeth S. Tapia was born in 1950 and grew up in the rural province of Bulacan in the Philippines. She is an ordained elder in the United Methodist Church in the Philippines and Academic Dean and Professor of Theology at Union Theological Seminary in Cavite, Philippines. She studied theology both in the Philippines and in the United States and holds a Ph.D. in theology from Claremont Graduate University in California. For many years, Elizabeth has been involved in ecumenical theological education, peace and human rights work, the women's movement, and women doing theology. She is a founding member of both the Association of Women in Theology and the Congress of Asian Theologians and a member of the Ecumenical Association of Third World Theologians. Her e-mail address is *eliztapia@yahoo.com*. Her postal address is Union Theological Seminary, Palapala, Dasmarinas, Cavite 4114, Philippines.

Auður Eir Vilhjálmsdóttir was born in Iceland in 1937. She studied theology in Iceland, France, and Norway. Through her work with the Lutheran World Federation, she came in contact with feminist theology. She is an ordained pastor in the National Evangelical Lutheran Church of Iceland and one of the founders and current pastor of *Kvennakirkjan*. She received an honorary doctorate of theology from the University of Iceland. Her e-mail address is *audureir@ismennt.is*. Her postal address is Kastalagerði 11, 200 Kópavogur, Iceland.